Homer: The Resonance of Epic

Classical Literature and Society

Series Editor: Michael Gunningham

Homer: The Resonance of Epic
Barbara Graziosi & Johannes Haubold

Ovid and His Love Poetry
Rebecca Armstrong

CLASSICAL LITERATURE AND SOCIETY

Homer: The Resonance of Epic

Barbara Graziosi
& Johannes Haubold

Duckworth

First published in 2005 by
Gerald Duckworth & Co. Ltd.
90-93 Cowcross Street, London EC1M 6BF
Tel: 020 7490 7300
Fax: 020 7490 0080
inquiries@duckworth-publishers.co.uk
www.ducknet.co.uk

A catalogue record for this book is available
from the British Library

ISBN 0 7156 3282 5

Typeset by e-type, Liverpool
Printed in Great Britain by
CPI Bath

Contents

Preface   7

Part I. Resonance   11
1. The Poet   15
2. The Poems   35

Part II. Resonant Patterns   63
3. Gods, Animals and Fate   65
4. Men, Women and Society   95
5. Death, Fame and Poetry   121

Notes   151
Bibliography   165
Index   173

Preface

This book is the result of many conversations about the Homeric poems, both among ourselves and with students, friends and colleagues. Students, in particular, relentlessly demanded that we face the question of how scholarly insights into Homeric poetry affect our appreciation of the *Iliad* and the *Odyssey*. The twentieth century was a very interesting period for the study of Homer: the sustained comparison between Homeric epic and a vast range of ancient and modern epic traditions, an ever more sophisticated understanding of oral poetry, the decipherment of Linear B, the sensational discovery of Akkadian epic – all have had a profound impact on Homeric scholarship. If one were to single out the most important contribution to the study of Homer in the last century, the work of Milman Parry would be a strong contender. Parry's comparison between South Slavic epic and the Homeric poems has had a major impact on our understanding of composition, but has left us with many questions about the implications of his insights for the interpretation of Homeric epic. It is to these questions that this book is devoted.

Students, especially those who first approach the poems in translation and cannot be drawn into discussions of hexameter lines at close range, insist on asking how an awareness of compositional techniques affects the overall interpretation of the poems. Often, scholars tend to answer this question in rather negative terms: for example, countless publications warn readers that they should not expect traditional adjectives to fit the context in which they are found; epithets, as well as longer 'formulas', are simply there to help the bard fill the line with the right number of long and short syllables. This kind of approach does not bode well for an exciting interpretation of the poems, especially not in translation, since the beauty and precision of the formulaic system is largely lost in languages other than Homeric Greek. Scholars sometimes go on to emphasise that Homer rose above the tradition to which he belonged and offered us the first truly literary and literate works of western civilisation. This view can be summarised as follows. The tradition to which the Homeric poems belong is invoked in order to explain their less attractive aspects, such as their formulaic language, their repetitiveness, or the ill-fitting adjectives, while Homer's 'greatness' emerges from comparisons with other towering figures from later times: Virgil, Dante, Tasso, Milton, James Joyce.

One wonders, then, what the ancient Greeks, who did not have the benefit of hindsight, made of the Homeric poems. Our book begins with the question how the Greeks of the archaic period understood the poems. One reason why we focus on early audiences is that they suggest an approach to Homeric epic which is challenging and rewarding for the modern reader. They were not interested in the mechanics of oral composition: they did not invoke 'formulas', 'type scenes', 'traditional narratives' or any of the technical terms which have become the stock-in-trade of modern Homerists. Neither, however, did they seek to identify and elevate the precise contribution of 'Homer' above the wider tradition to which the *Iliad* and the *Odyssey* belong. In fact, Homer was considered the author not just of those two epics, but also of many other early hexameter poems, some of which are extant (the *Homeric Hymns*), while others survive in fragments and summaries (the poems of the Epic Cycle, which tell the earlier and later stages of the Trojan War and the events of the Theban War, *The Sack of Oechalia*, and a comic poem called *Margites*).

We begin by asking what Homer and his poems meant in an archaic Greek context. We look at the way in which our earliest sources talk about Homer, how they depict him, what they say about his oeuvre, and how they characterise his relationship to Hesiod, the other major figure of the early Greek hexameter tradition. We argue that these two poets together represented the major authorities on the gods, the heroic past, and the overall history of the cosmos, from the time when Earth first emerged from Void, to the world as it is now. Homer and Hesiod do not just share the 'tools' of early hexameter epic, a common stock of epithets, formulas, type scenes, which are there to help them in the process of composition. They share a vision of the cosmos and how it developed through time. The traditional language of early hexameter reflects a precise understanding of the overall shape and history of the cosmos: Zeus is 'the son of Cronus', the heroes are 'godlike', two men 'as they are now' cannot lift stones that a single hero could throw with ease. Each early hexameter poem places itself very precisely within this overall history of the cosmos, a history which is embedded in the very language of epic. The Homeric poems, we argue, derive much of their meaning from the interaction between the particular story they tell and its resonance within the overall development of the cosmos.

In a sense, it could be said that this book examines the place of the *Iliad* and the *Odyssey* within the wider epic tradition not by looking at the formal characteristics of traditional epic such as, for example, metrical shape or formulaic economy, but by focusing on the meaning of traditional expressions. The formula 'Zeus the son of Cronus', for example, is not just a way of getting to the end of a line without taking too long over it: it tells us something important about this god, and hints at the significance of the succession myth in early Greek epic. The fact that Zeus succeeds his father Cronus yet should not in turn be replaced by his own son is crucial to the *Theogony*, and reverberates also through other poems, not least the *Iliad* itself. A shared 'formula', then, is also a shared insight into the epic cosmos. We hope that this book, with its overall focus on the meaning of traditional epic, will be of interest to the general reader who is familiar with the *Iliad* and the *Odyssey* in translation; but we also hope that it contains something that will appeal to professional scholars.

The first part of the book, 'Resonance' (Chapters 1 and 2), introduces the reader to ancient and modern approaches to Homer, and develops an approach to Homeric epic which focuses on its resonance, that is, its ability to evoke a web of associations and implications by referring to the wider epic tradition. We hope to show that the traditional character of Homeric epic, far from being an impediment to originality, makes the poems resonant with meaning. The second part of the book, 'Resonant Patterns' (Chapters 3 to 5), offers some examples of how the approach outlined in Part I can be used to interpret the poems. Because the book is conceived as an introduction, the examples chosen focus on central themes in the *Iliad* and the *Odyssey*: the gods, nature and fate (Chapter 3), Homeric society (Chapter 4), and the quest for fame on the part of individuals (Chapter 5). Taken together, Parts I and II provide the general reader with an up-to-date introduction to ancient and modern approaches to Homer and an overall interpretation of the poems. We hope that the more expert reader will find new insights concerning both the overall approach proposed and the light it sheds on particular aspects of the poems.

To cater for a diverse readership, all Greek texts are quoted in English. Where possible, we have printed Lattimore's translations of the *Iliad* and the *Odyssey*, which seem to be the most widely used by students. In some places, however, we have produced our own, in order to ensure that the translations we offer highlight the aspects of the texts that are under discussion. We are grateful to HarperCollins Publishers and to the University of Chicago Press for permission to print Lattimore's translations. We also wish to thank Faber & Faber Ltd for permission to quote the opening of Christopher Logue's *War Music* on p. 39.

The Homeric poems have enjoyed an extraordinary and long-lasting success. Each generation of listeners and readers contribute their own perspective on the poems: it is not possible, in the course of a short book, to do justice to all, or even most, aspects of Homeric interpretation. We privilege the views of archaic audiences, who heard the poems when their reputation was still in the making, as well as discussing modern approaches to Homeric epic. Readers may miss discussions of many important topics: for example, the role of the Homeric poems in ancient, medieval and modern education, their use as moral instruction, their place in the history of literary criticism. Endnotes also tend to be brief: we mostly refer to recent publications, rather than trace the long and tortuous history of particular debates. We hope, however, that the references we provide are sufficient to direct the reader to fuller discussions.

In preparing this book, we have been greatly helped not only by our students, but also by colleagues at the University of Durham, who made it possible for us to take an early term of research leave which we used to write the bulk of the book. We are also very grateful to Andrea Capra who suggested we spend our period of leave in Pisa, and to the colleagues and students at the Scuola Normale Superiore, who contributed much to making our stay pleasant and interesting. For a month in summer we also benefited from the generous hospitality of the Center for Hellenic Studies in Washington; Gregory Nagy, in particular, made time to discuss ideas and perspectives. Several friends have read and commented on drafts of the whole book: Elton Barker, Felix Budelmann, Andrea Capra, Pat Easterling, Rachel Foxley, Simon Goldhill, Maria Serena Mirto, and Robin Osborne. We are very grateful for their perceptive, detailed and challenging comments, and for their support especially during the final stages of writing and revision. We would also like to thank the series editor, Michael Gunningham, who welcomed the volume in Duckworth's new Classical Literature and Society series, and Deborah Blake for her unfailing support in the production of the book: we hope that our discussion, with its emphasis on the early audiences of Homeric epic, may be a fitting contribution to the overall themes of the series.

Our children, Laura and Roberto, kept us busy and happy while writing the book: it is dedicated to them.

Durham, 2004

Part I

Resonance

Brief introductions to the *Iliad* and the *Odyssey* usually start with a grand statement about the poems, their elusive author, and their place of honour in the history of literature. For example: 'The two great epics which go under the name of Homer bring European literature into existence with a bang.'[1] There are problems, however, with this kind of statement: it tells us something about the history of literature and quite a lot about European identity, but remains uninformative about the place and meaning of Homeric epic in early Greece. To archaic audiences of Homer, our concept of 'literature' would have been quite alien, as indeed the tags 'European' or 'western' which are routinely attached to the Homeric epics.[2] Moreover, the idea that the *Iliad* and the *Odyssey* sprang into existence out of nothing, 'with a bang', would have made no sense to the early audiences of Homer: they were perfectly aware that the poems developed out of a long and distinguished tradition of epic poetry.[3]

All these points emerge very clearly from an observation made by Herodotus, the fifth-century thinker, traveller and historian (a title some have denied him, because of his interest in, or propensity for, fiction and lies). About the river Oceanus, which is described in epic as the water that surrounds the earth,[4] he made the following claim: 'I do not know of the existence of a river Oceanus: I think that Homer, or one of the poets who lived before him, invented the name and introduced it into poetry.'[5] For Herodotus, then, Homer is not necessarily the earliest poet: it is possible that he took over the name 'Oceanus' from a predecessor.[6] So much, then, for the notion of Homer as the fountainhead of all literature. More challenging, perhaps, is Herodotus' insistence that no river named 'Oceanus' actually exists. The implication of the passage is that Herodotus has checked the claims made in Homeric epic against what is really the case, and found them wanting. Many readers will find Herodotus' approach to epic intolerably naïve: it seems strange to us that anyone could read Homeric epic as an account of how the world really is; surely, the Homeric poems are, and were always meant to be, literary fiction. Anyone who takes them as an authoritative account of the cosmos, or

11

feels compelled to argue against their authority as cosmic history (as Herodotus does), is a fool.

We are confronted here with a familiar problem which plagues not only the study of Homer and classics more generally, but human interaction *tout court*: 'either you think like me or you are a fool.'[7] Statements which reveal that the early Greeks had an attitude to the Homeric poems different to that which prevails among modern readers represent a challenge. One way to deal with the problem is to assume, against all evidence, that the Greeks understood the Homeric poems much as we do: Herodotus might have argued against some very silly people who took the poems as factual accounts, but intelligent Greeks surely took them as literary fiction rather than reliable accounts of how the world is, or was in the heroic age. This kind of attitude is anachronistic: many recent studies have emphasised the differences between ancient and modern concepts of truth, fiction, lies and poetry.[8] It is also clear that ancient readers tended to treat Homeric poetry as a reliable account of how things are.[9]

Another response is to posit a history of development and progress: in the work of Herodotus we see how the modern concept of fiction starts to emerge. He is just about able to conceive that poets make things up: before him the concept of fiction was hazier still, whereas in later Greek culture it was well understood; someone like Aristotle is a profound reader of Homer and an impressive literary critic whose insights approximate our own. This developmental approach has been very influential in the field of classics, but it has at least one serious drawback. It fails to acknowledge that we may have something to learn from the views of the early, supposedly more primitive Greeks: maybe they can in fact help us in the reading of Homer.

This book seeks to take seriously the challenge of understanding Homeric epic in its early Greek context.[10] We suggest an approach which respects the experiences of the early audiences of the poems, but we also take full advantage of recent scholarship on traditional epic. We start by analysing some fundamental concepts currently used in the study of Homer. In Chapter 1, 'The Poet', we compare ancient and modern views about the poet Homer and his relationship to Hesiod. In the second chapter, 'The Poems', we investigate how epic was understood in the archaic period and explore the connections between ancient views of Homeric poetry and modern insights into oral, or more generally traditional, epic. In the course of this analysis, we develop an approach to Homeric poetry which focuses on its 'resonance', that is, its ability to evoke a wider epic tradition and place itself in relation to that tradition. This approach, we argue, makes good sense of modern research into traditional poetry but above all respects ancient views about Homer and his art. A focus on resonance also helps to explain the extraordinary authority of the Homeric poems in early Greece: rather than being thought of as the first works of literature, they belonged to a vast and remarkably coherent tradition which encompassed the history of the cosmos from its origins to the present day.

1

The Poet

If there is one thing that people tend to know about the *Iliad* and the *Odyssey* it is that there is a 'question' concerning their author. Quite what the problem might be often remains unclear: formulations of 'The Homeric Question' range from the sophisticated to the abstruse. According to a famous anecdote, a schoolboy once remarked: 'Homer was not written by Homer, but by another man of his name.'[1] This might seem like a hopeless muddle, but some up-to-date scholarship reaches alarmingly similar conclusions. For example, a recent editor of the Homeric poems believes that one thing we certainly know about the poet of the *Iliad* is that he was not called Homer.[2] Paradox and contradiction are not limited to modern scholarship; quarrels and jokes about the identity of the poet and the composition of the *Iliad* and the *Odyssey* were common in antiquity too. Lucian, in the second century AD, famously ridiculed his contemporaries' obsession with the identity of Homer and the meaning of his work. In *A True Story* 2.20 (a text which is in fact a collection of lies), he claims that he has met Homer on the Island of the Blessed and has finally discovered the truth about him:

> I asked him, among other things, where he came from, pointing out that this was still being investigated among us to this day. He said: 'I am aware that some think I am from Chios, others from Smyrna and many from Colophon, but in fact I am Babylonian, and among my fellow-citizens I am not called Homer, but Tigranes. Afterwards, when I became a hostage (*homêreuô*) to the Greeks, I changed my name.' I also enquired about the lines that scholars consider spurious, and asked if he had written them. He said that they were all composed by himself. As a result, I rejected the work of Zenodotus, Aristarchus and their followers as utter nonsense. When he had given satisfactory answers to these questions, I asked why he started with the wrath of Achilles, and he said that it had occurred to him just like that, without any preparation. I also wanted to know whether he wrote the *Odyssey* before the *Iliad*, as most people claim, and he said he did not. That he was not blind – because they say that too about him – I found out at once: I could see it for myself, so I did not have to ask.

Lucian's Homer jokingly proposes an entirely new identity for himself: contrary to common opinion, he is in fact a Babylonian man known as Tigranes by his fellow citizens. This less than serious attempt to discover the 'real' Homer behind the many legends and suppositions captures well a common assumption that still drives modern approaches to the author of the *Iliad* and *Odyssey*: there must be a simple answer to the question of Homer's identity, and, given the right methods, it can be discovered. A recent example of this view can be found in Latacz's approach to Homer: he claims that the stories which circulated about the poet in the sixth century BC represent a 'false track' and that only modern scholarship has developed 'the means and method' to interpret the poems correctly, thereby enabling us to discover the real Homer behind the ancient legends.[3]

Unlike Lucian, Latacz is not joking. According to him, there really is an answer to the question of Homer's identity; and that answer, paradoxically, can be found only if we discount our earliest sources. His degree of optimism is astonishing, given the lack of consensus that has characterised debates over the last two or three millennia. That lack of consensus has a reason: there is no hard evidence on which to base theories about the identity of Homer. The Homeric epics are famously silent about their author: the name 'Homer' is not even mentioned in the poems, nor are we told much else about the bard who sings the epics. The ancient sources which do mention Homer represent him in ways that defy common notions of what is humanly possible: he is supposed to have been born in many different cities, to have been totally destitute and yet have performed for kings, to have composed an inordinately vast number of poems (poems which modern scholars tend to date to several different centuries), and to have died by slipping on dung after having failed to solve a children's riddle. As many scholars have pointed out, we are confronted with legends rather than factual accounts.[4] We are going to argue later in this chapter that these legends are nevertheless important for the interpretation of Homeric epic, but for now we need to make a more basic point. The Homeric Question cannot simply 'be solved'. We should rather aim to bear in mind a range of possibilities about how the Homeric poems might have been composed as well as an awareness of the parameters of the debate over the Homeric Question.

Perhaps the most striking feature of the debate, apart from its sheer extension through time, is the complex network of connections between arguments and positions across different centuries or even millennia. These connections range from the fundamental – we learn the name

'Homer' from our ancient sources, so there is at least one obvious continuity there – to the quirky and coincidental. Among the latter, we may count Lucian's presentation of Homer as a Babylonian, in view of the modern interest in the connections between Greek and Babylonian epic.[5] Now, it is easy to see that Lucian's reasons for presenting Homer as a Babylonian are not the same as those that inspire modern research into Greek and Near Eastern epic.[6] Yet in other cases, it is far less easy to disentangle ancient and modern speculations in order to construct a simple narrative of progress. An irreverent little couplet composed by Goethe neatly makes this point.

In the late eighteenth century, Friedrich August Wolf argued that the Homeric epics were a collection of orally composed poems. His arguments had a major impact on the history of classical scholarship: today, he is standardly presented as the first modern classicist in that he addressed the Homeric Question with philological rigour. However, Goethe was quick to undermine his claims to progress with a biting couplet:[7]

> *Wolf's Homer*
> Seven cities squabbled over which one gave birth to him;
> now that the Wolf tore him apart, let each of them have a piece.

Apart from the pun on Wolf's name and the general irreverence of the poem, Goethe casts doubt on Wolf's achievement by suggesting that there have always been arguments over the identity of Homer, and that a plurality of authors has always threatened to emerge from such arguments. Again, there are important differences between ancient quarrels over the birthplace of Homer and Wolf's analysis of the process of composition and texual fixation which lies behind the *Iliad* and the *Odyssey*. But the point is that there are also undeniable continuities between ancient and modern speculations about Homer. We have learned from our earliest sources not only the name Homer, but also the habit of disagreeing about him. For this reason, it is always possible to use the name Homer in order to equivocate, make fun and thereby challenge any claim to progress.

The problem is that equivocations over the name 'Homer' are not always as deliberate as Goethe's, and often cause genuine confusion. Students often ask what scholars mean by the name 'Homer', and whether there is any consensus beyond the many disagreements. These are important questions to which we now turn, also because they help us to place the argument of this book in the wider context of Homeric scholarship.

Part I. Resonance

The Homeric Question

Despite the many views about the identity of Homer and the process of composition which lies behind the Homeric poems, there are some points on which most scholars agree. There is a general consensus that the Homeric poems belong to a vast and ancient tradition of epic performance. The language and compositional techniques employed in the *Iliad* and the *Odyssey* are shared by several other early Greek hexameter texts. To be sure, some scholars have drawn attention to thematic variations and differences of diction between, say, the *Iliad*, the *Odyssey*, the *Homeric Hymns*, the poems of the Epic Cycle, the *Theogony* and the *Works and Days*,[8] but these variations should not distract us from the much more fundamental and striking consistency of language and compositional technique displayed in these poems.

All early Greek hexameter epic is composed in an artificial mixture of Ionic and Aeolic which was never spoken by a real-life community: it developed precisely for the purpose of singing the deeds of gods and men.[9] All early epic draws on a common pool of stock epithets, type scenes, traditional themes. The earth is 'black', women 'trim-ankled', the sea 'wine-coloured' not just in the *Iliad* and the *Odyssey*, but in other early hexameter poems too. Similarities do not end with these small-scale descriptions: speeches are introduced according to a standard set of formulas; heroes and gods bathe and get dressed according to a standard procedure which is described in several different early epics; strangers are greeted according to a precise pattern. Different hexameter poems share many other techniques of composition: for example, the catalogue, ring composition, and ekphrasis are important for our understanding of many early epic poems.[10]

It is generally agreed that the traditional language and modes of expression deployed in early hexameter epic evolved over a long period of time. Generations of bards sang of gods and men and, in the course of their performances, developed standard ways of referring to characters and of describing particular actions. Later bards could rely on earlier formulations in their own performances. They could also manipulate or explore tensions between standard expressions and the particular song they were singing: at the beginning of *Iliad* 22, for example, Apollo points out that 'swift-footed' Achilles cannot hope to run as fast as a god.[11] By drawing attention to the limitations of the standard description of Achilles, Apollo simultaneously defines his limitations as a mortal.

But if most scholars accept that the *Iliad* and the *Odyssey*, as indeed all early hexameter epic, belong to an age-old tradition of epic performance, the dispute continues over the role of a single poet generally thought of as 'Homer' within this wider tradition. Some scholars are struck by the drama, monumentality or coherence of the *Iliad* and the *Odyssey*, and define Homer as the bard responsible for the exceptional qualities they see in these two poems.[12] Others are struck by the differences between the *Iliad* and the *Odyssey* and accordingly argue that Homer composed only one of the two.[13] Some interpreters think of Homer as the first bard who chose to focus on the wrath of Achilles and the one responsible for the core of the *Iliad*, which was then developed into a monumental work by other bards.[14] Other critics think of Homer as the person responsible for a final written version of both poems.[15] There are also those who do not think of Homer as a person at all, but rather argue that the name is a conventional label for a particular type of poetry which developed over many centuries.[16]

Given the variety of views about Homer, it is understandable that students often feel confused. It is tempting to assume that the name Homer has a stable meaning across different scholarly publications, but this is in fact seldom the case. Disagreements about the date of Homer, for example, are linked to more fundamental differences over what Homer represents in the first place. Some scholars think of the poet as describing the world in which he lives. They consequently date the poems by looking at the kind of social structures and material objects described in the poems.[17] Others start from the premise that Homer was responsible for the overall coherence and unity of the *Iliad*, they then ask themselves which is the most recent historical event reflected in the poem, and proceed to date the *Iliad* on that basis.[18] Others think of Homer primarily as the person responsible for writing down the epics: they focus on the advent of the Phoenician alphabet and the moment in which the texts could, for the first time, become stable and fixed in writing.[19] Those who tend to think of the name 'Homer' as a label for a multiform and fluid tradition, date the poems to the time in which their recitation was institutionalised at the great Panhellenic festivals, arguing that this is when the texts became stable.[20]

It seems to us that in order to keep one's bearings it is important to hold on to some basic considerations. The first and most important is that the *Iliad* and the *Odyssey* stem from a rich and ancient epic tradition to which other poems, such as the Epic Cycle, the *Homeric Hymns*, the *Theogony*, the *Works and Days*, the *Catalogue of Women* also belong. Some obvious questions follow from this: what is the relationship between the *Iliad*, the *Odyssey* and this wider tradition? In what ways does an awareness of this tradition, of the themes, concerns, and modes of expression shared across different poems, affect the interpretation of the *Iliad* and the *Odyssey*? It is to these questions that the bulk of this book is devoted.

The second point to bear in mind when trying to assess the modern debate over the Homeric poems is that theories about the composition of the *Iliad* and the *Odyssey* are based on modern interpretations of the texts. Scholars agree that the ancient legends about Homer do not give us reliable information about the composition of the *Iliad* and the *Odyssey* (though, we would add, they offer some precious insights into the early reception of the poems). The question how the Homeric poems were composed is therefore addressed by reading the poems and trying to assess what process of composition best accounts for their nature. Since the poems tell us nothing explicit about their author, valid criteria are hard to come by. Many scholars feel that the sheer beauty and coherence of the poems are proof that a single, exceptionally gifted poet played a determining role in their composition.[21] They agree that there are many traditional elements shared with other epics, but claim that what makes these two poems stand out is the contribution of an individual bard of exceptional talent. This may be so, but it is important to sound a note of caution.

We, as modern readers of Homer, should be aware of our own preconceptions and limitations. The romantic notion of the literary genius has had such a hold on the western imagination that many modern readers find it impossible to see the Homeric poems as anything other than the works of a single creative genius. Alternative models of composition are quickly discarded as a slight to the quality and beauty of the Homeric poems. A recent collection of Homeric scholarship, for example, divides scholars between those who can appreciate the qualities of the *Iliad*, and 'primitivists' who insist on oral composition and thus demean the poem.[22] Here we stumble upon a problem that we have already encountered: either the Homeric poems conform to our already established notions of great literature, or they are no good. There seems to be little room for extending our views about what constitutes beautiful poetry.[23]

It may seem to some readers of this book that we are less than eloquent about the qualities of the *Iliad* and the *Odyssey* which make them unique: we do not begin by discussing these qualities, partly because other books do so admirably well,[24] and partly because we are taken by the beauty not just of the *Iliad* and the *Odyssey* but also of the wider epic tradition to which they belong. It seems to us that, if we develop an understanding and appreciation of the overall tradition, we will also be in a good position to appreciate the quintessential aspects of the two poems, such as the *Iliad*'s preoccupation with mortality, or Odysseus' determination to return to his wife. Insisting on the ways in

which the *Iliad* and the *Odyssey* are different from other early hexameter poems is not the only means through which one can draw
attention to their beauty: the fact that these poems rely on a vision of
the cosmos shared by the wider tradition provides an equally rewarding
key to their interpretation.

Homer in the archaic period

We have seen in the last section that the Homeric poems are reticent
about their author: in fact, they appear to go out of their way to conceal
any traces of his identity. At the same time, scholars have rejected the
archaic sources that do mention Homer as factually unreliable, with the
result that the identity of Homer becomes anybody's guess: there are
today as many views about the author of the *Iliad* and the *Odyssey* as
there are interpretations of the poems. It may be said that this is true
of all authors: different readers of Shakespeare's plays, for example, are
likely to form different impressions of the playwright. Yet, in the case of
Homer, differences of opinion are extreme. Virginia Woolf wrote of the
'man-womanly' mind of Shakespeare, but did not argue that he might
have actually been a woman.[25] In the case of Homer, even that has been
suggested: Samuel Butler famously claimed that the author of the
Odyssey was in fact an authoress.[26] Victorian obsessions with gender
and sexuality demanded that this possibility too be considered.[27]

An important point follows from this: theories about the identity of
Homer reveal something about those who describe him, precisely
because there is no hard evidence concerning the person or persons who
composed the Homeric poems. Samuel Butler's assumptions about
gender are manifest in his theory about the authoress of the *Odyssey*.
Likewise, the value placed on genius and originality affects many
discussions of the Homeric poems and their author. It seems that if we
want to gain a broader perspective on the poems, we could do worse
than start from what the Greeks of the archaic period thought about
the poet Homer: they shaped the later reception of Homeric epic.[28]
Ancient legends about Homer tell us little about how the poems were
actually composed, but they are a precious source of evidence if we want
to discover how the early Greeks approached the *Iliad* and *Odyssey*.
Like us, they based their notions of Homer on their experience of the
poems, but they reached very different conclusions from those that
prevail among modern readers. The story of Homer's blindness can be
used to illustrate this point.

In antiquity, Homer was widely thought to be blind. Stories about his
blindness pervade ancient portrayals of the poet and go back, in all

probability, to the sixth century BC.[29] Most modern scholars have been interested in Homer's blindness in order to assess whether the author of the *Iliad* and the *Odyssey* might conceivably really have been blind. Some scholars go as far as complaining that the ancient sources do not seem interested in this question. Mary Lefkowitz, for example, writes that the author of an ancient biography of Homer, the *Vita Herodotea*, 'does not try to explain in any serious way how the blind poet was able to compose so great an oeuvre'.[30] In this short statement, many of the problems with modern approaches to Homer become apparent: for a start, Lefkowitz does not question her own assumption that a blind man is unlikely to compose a great oeuvre – even a superficial look at the achievements of blind poets throughout history would have re-assured her. But that is hardly the main problem: at the heart of Lefkowitz's irritation with the account of Homer offered in the *Vita Herodotea* is the realisation that it fails to yield what she might call 'sensible' or 'realistic' answers concerning the identity of Homer. It is not just that the *Vita* depicts him as blind: he inhabits a very different world from the one described in the Homeric epics, and he composes a vast number of poems, poems which are today dated anywhere from the eighth century (*Iliad*) to Hellenistic or even Roman times (*Batrachomyomachia*). The picture of Homer we find in the *Vita Herodotea* does not conform to our expectations about credibility and historical accuracy.

Rather than dismissing ancient portrayals of Homer for not fulfilling our expectations, we should consider whether we have been asking the right questions of the ancient sources we have. Any anthropologist knows that the success of his or her fieldwork depends at least as much on the quality of the questions asked as on the reliability of the infor-mants.[31] The case of Homer, where thousands of years stand between us and the object of our study, is not so different. If we are interested in the meaning of Homeric poetry as conceived by its earliest audiences, it is up to us, as outside observers, to ask meaningful questions of our ancient sources. This seems particularly important in view of the fact that modern reconstructions of Homer's identity are themselves based on extrapolations from the *Iliad* and the *Odyssey*. Many modern discus-sions of Homer and his work fall into circular arguments: first scholars read the poems with a view to finding something out about their author, then they use their conclusions about authorship in order to interpret the poems.[32]

Altogether we may make more progress by asking why Homer was thought to be blind, rather than worrying about whether we think he really was. Similarly, we may ask ourselves why Homer was thought to live in a world so different from that depicted in the epics and why so many different epics were attributed to him. If we start with these questions, a picture of how early Greek audiences thought about Homer and his work quickly begins to emerge.

The *Odyssey* depicts one blind bard, Demodocus, who sings the most beautiful songs about heroes and gods.[33] We are told that the Muse loved him exceedingly, but that she counterbalanced the gift of song with the curse of blindness: he could describe far away events 'as if he had been there', but he was in important ways cut off from his immediate circumstances because he could not see what was going on around him.[34] Ancient readers thought of Demodocus as an autobiographical character, and with good reason: the kind of songs he performs resemble the Homeric poems in content and sheer virtuoso brilliance.[35] It is interesting, moreover, that in the *Odyssey* the figure of Demodocus mirrors that of the blind prophet Teiresias: while the bard tells Odysseus his past, the prophet tells him his future. This parallel between bard and prophet is not confined to the *Odyssey*: the figure of the blind seer is important in ancient Greek culture and clearly represents a model for ancient portrayals of Homer. The poet, like the prophet, has a special closeness to the gods and a special insight into their world: blindness becomes a physical marker of that insight. In the *Theogony*, the Muses grant the bard the ability to sing all that was and shall be, while in the *Iliad* the same ability is attributed to the prophet Calchas.[36] In the ancient sources Homer is represented in the guise of a prophet because he has a divine gift of insight. As we shall see, the concept of Homer as a figure inspired by the gods, and with a special insight into the divine world, is important for the interpretation of the poems; but for now we must turn to another aspect of the ancient portrayals of Homer which has troubled modern readers.

Latacz complains that, according to the ancient biographies of Homer, the poet inhabited a much humbler and more recent world than that described in the *Iliad* and the *Odyssey*: 'The image of the poet sketched in the *Lives* has hardly anything in common with the one that confronts us in the epics. The Homer of this legend is a blind, begging singer who hangs around with little people: shoemakers, fishermen, potters, sailors, elderly men in the gathering places of harbor towns. [...] The Homer legend anachronistically depicts the greatest poet of an earlier time.'[37] The early Greeks assumed that Homer lived long after the heroic world depicted in his poems: this assumption, far from being yet another reason for discarding ancient views about Homer, stems from an intelligent reading of Homeric epic. At various places, in the *Iliad* and the *Odyssey*, we find hints that the world 'as it is today' – that is, in the time of performance – is not the same as that depicted in the poems.[38] The bard, for example, tells us of heroes who threw stones so big that 'two men could not lift them these days'.[39] More generally, the world depicted in the similes seems more recent (and often less grand) than that of the main narrative: in order to illustrate a point, the bard sometimes makes a comparison with aspects of life as it is 'now'.[40] In another case, *Iliad* 12.10-35, the bard describes the death of Hector and the fall of Troy from the point of view of someone who does not belong to the age of the heroes. Clearly, there is a gulf between the world of the heroes and that of Homer and his audience: this gap is reflected in the way in which Homer was imagined by the ancient Greeks.

As will become obvious in the next chapter, the fact that, from the point of view of the audience, Homeric epic depicts an earlier time in the history of the cosmos is of crucial importance for its interpretation. However, before we explore the place of the Homeric poems within the overall history of the world, we must briefly consider what is perhaps the thorniest issue concerning the reception of Homer in the archaic period.

Modern readers think of Homer as the author of the *Iliad* and the *Odyssey* – or, in some cases, only the *Iliad* or parts of that poem. However, in the archaic period a vast number of poems were attributed to Homer. Many scholars have remarked on this fact,[41] though few have worked out its implications for the interpretation of Homeric epic. Homer's oeuvre was not defined by aesthetic criteria so much as by themes, such as the heroic past, or, more specifically, the Theban and Trojan Wars. When Aeschylus calls his tragedies 'slices from the banquets of Homer' he must have had the whole of the Trojan War cycle in mind (and possibly more), not just the relatively narrow compass of the *Iliad* and *Odyssey*.[42] Similarly, Pindar appears to have regarded the *Cypria* as a Homeric poem and draws no clear distinction between the themes and characters of the *Iliad* and *Odyssey* and those of other Trojan War epics. Once again, this implies that for him Homer composed all epic texts relating to that topic, including those that later Greek and modern readers think of as 'un-Homeric'.[43]

It is this Homer, the man who composed just about everything that was heroic epic in archaic Greece, who is praised or denigrated in our earliest sources. This has fundamental implications for our reading of the *Iliad* and the *Odyssey*. Rather than singling them out from other poetry of a similar kind, and marking the difference by thinking of Homer as the author only of the texts that meet our standards of literary excellence, ancient audiences invite us to see them as part of a much larger repertoire of epic song, all of which was considered Homeric. Quite how large this repertoire would have been it is difficult to say: some texts survive but many are lost. Homer was closely connected both to the Trojan and the Theban Sagas. Herodotus appears to attribute to him the whole of the Theban cycle, the *Epigoni* explicitly, though he expresses doubt as to whether that poem should properly be considered Homeric.[44] He also argues that the *Cypria*, which describes the first nine years of the Trojan War, is not by Homer because some of it contradicts what we find in the *Iliad*.[45] Here we catch a glimpse of the process of narrowing-down which in time led to Homer losing his claim to most heroic poetry.[46] Note, however, that Herodotus has to argue his case, which suggests that as late as the fifth century BC some readers did not share his views. There are other snippets of evidence which betray a preoccupation with the question of which poems should be called Homeric. In the biographical tradition we are told, for example, that Homer was very poor and that he gave away the *Cypria* to his son-in-law, Stasinus, as a dowry for his daughter. We are also told that he gave away the *Sack of Oechalia* (*Oechaliae Halosis*) to a certain Creophylus of Samos, as a gift in return for hospitality.[47] These stories suggest that some poems were regarded as less Homeric than others, in that they could be linked to the names of other poets. At the same time, Homer is presented as the ultimate source even for the poems that he chooses to 'give away'.

Not every text by Homer concerned the heroic era. The *Homeric Hymns* describe how the Olympian gods acquired their permanent place in the order of the universe.[48] Modern scholars routinely treat the *Hymns* as not being by Homer. They follow the example of later Greek readers, but early Greeks thought differently: Thucydides, for example, attributes the *Hymn to Apollo* to Homer.[49] Another poem which is often overlooked today is the *Margites*, which Aristotle still quotes as a work of Homer.[50] The *Margites* and the *Hymns* remind us that heroic themes were not the only ones that could be attributed to Homer in archaic times. At the same time, they suggest that the heroic poems defined the core of his oeuvre. The *Margites* appears to have been a parody of heroic epic. It was light-hearted in tone and probably not very long. The *Homeric Hymns*, on the other hand, appear to have served as preludes (*prooimia*) to the more substantial heroic songs.[51]

Within the wider Homeric oeuvre, then, some texts seem to have been considered more characteristic than others from an early time. The poems of the so-called Trojan cycle in particular remained closely linked to the name of Homer throughout antiquity, despite the fact that alternative authors were sometimes mentioned. Other texts, such as the *Hymns*, fell victim to later readers' determination to filter out what they regarded as unworthy of Homer. That process seems to have been under way by the fifth century and gathered pace in Hellenistic times. Before the fifth century, however, the name Homer, while suggesting exceptional authority, could not yet be used to play off one text against another on aesthetic grounds. In fact, its primary function seems to have been precisely to *elide* the boundaries between single texts and encourage audiences to place what they heard at any given performance in a much wider context of epic poetry. For ancient audiences, the name 'Homer' did not stand for a lone genius who single-handedly transformed the tradition he inherited from his predecessors. Rather, that name was a bond that tied the *Iliad* and *Odyssey* to a much larger tradition of epic narrative. We shall see in the next chapter that that bond finds its counterpart in the thematic, linguistic and stylistic resonances that pervade Homeric poetry at every level.

Ancient Greek audiences did not formulate their intuition that the *Iliad* and *Odyssey* were parts of a larger whole in the technical language of modern scholarship. They did not suggest that these texts were 'traditional', or that they derived much of their meaning from the resonant patterns which they shared with other texts. However, by thinking of them as Homeric texts, and by thinking of the Homeric oeuvre as a vast number of poems that were linked in theme and tone, they suggest something similar. Just as the tragedies of Aeschylus were 'slices from the banquets of Homer', so the *Iliad* and the *Odyssey* were slices from a wider tradition of Homeric epic.

It is tempting to speculate further about the reasons why the name Homer was linked to so many different epics in the archaic period. For example, it is possible that travelling performers of these epics found it useful to claim that 'Homer' had composed whatever they were performing, in that the name had great authority in the sixth century BC and would have helped to ensure an interest in the performance. This theory would fit many other aspects of the ancient legends about Homer: it would explain why Homer was thought to have travelled so much, and why there was so much controversy over his place of birth. Rhapsodes who travelled from city to city performing Homeric epic might have claimed that Homer had already been to the city they were visiting, or that they were the best performers because they came from the same city as he did. Certainly the Homer of archaic legend is modelled on the figure of the rhapsode.

If we wanted to speculate even further, we could ask ourselves why the name 'Homer' had so much authority in the first place: it is possible that a real, historical bard called Homer produced poems that were much admired, and that other poems were then attached to his name in order to ensure that they too received good publicity. It is equally possible, however, that the name 'Homer' is fictitious: some scholars have argued that it simply meant 'the man who fits together the song' or that it indicated the mythical ancestor of a group of historical epic performers, the Homeridae.[52] These are fascinating possibilities which cannot be settled beyond doubt: the name 'Homer' is not obviously fictional, although it is not obviously a 'real' name either. Whether Homer was associated with a more restricted set of works and gradually acquired other poems, before his oeuvre was narrowed down to the *Iliad* and the *Odyssey* in the course of the classical period, must remain a matter of speculation: we simply have no evidence to settle the question. What is clear is that our earliest sources present Homer as the author of a very vast number of epics.

This is, in fact, the main point. By evoking the absent author of the poems, audiences and performers actively postulated a connection between a specific text and its wider context. In a culture like that of archaic Greece, where written texts were rare and poems circulated through performance, the poems of wandering rhapsodes could easily appear alien, preposterous or just simply disconnected from the knowledge and experiences of particular audiences. To establish a situation of trust and understanding between the performer and his audience was of crucial importance under such circumstances. Demodocus, the bard of the *Odyssey*, needed no introduction to the Phaeacians, his regular audience at the court of king Alcinous. But a travelling rhapsode in the sixth century BC who for the first time arrived in a village or city did need one. More importantly, his songs needed to be in tune with what the audience already knew about the world, they needed to be credible, and resonant within a wider context of epic performance.

We shall see in the next chapter that a concern with resonance lies at the very heart of Homeric epic. Resonant patterns, which established shared meaning between performer and audience, pervade all aspects of the poems. The issue of Homeric authorship appears to have fulfilled a similar function. For archaic Greeks the most pressing question was not, as it tends to be for modern readers, what makes a text stand out as special. An authentic experience, for them, was not guaranteed by the original achievement of an individual author. Rather, they needed to know that the performer in front of them had something meaningful to say, that his song fitted in with a shared understanding of the world and its history.[53]

Homer and Hesiod

We have argued in the previous section that, in the archaic period, Homer was thought to be the author of most of the major epics known

27

to us: the *Iliad*, the *Odyssey*, the other epics dealing with the Trojan and Theban wars (Epic Cycle), the *Hymns*, the *Margites*, the *Sack of Oechalia*. Homer was thought to have given away some of these poems to minor poets, but it is clear that he was considered to be the ultimate source of all these epics. There is one poet, however, who stood on an equal footing with Homer. Hesiod is never presented as a beneficiary of Homer, he never accepts poems that Homer gives away. In fact, the Hesiodic poems were never attributed to Homer, or *vice versa*. These two poets had mutually exclusive oeuvres, and were often mentioned together as the two most authoritative poets of ancient Greece. If we want to understand the place of Homer in archaic Greek thought it is thus necessary to explore how his relationship with Hesiod was conceived, since it is above all in relation to this other, equally authoritative poet that his work was defined.

Unlike the Homeric poems, the *Theogony* and the *Works and Days* give us some information about their author. The name Hesiod is mentioned in the *Theogony* (line 22), while in the *Works and Days* we are told that he had a brother called Perses, in need of much advice, and that his father originally came from Cyme but resettled in Ascra in Boeotia 'bad in winter, foul in summer, and good at no time'.[54] In the *Works and Days* Hesiod claims that, unlike his father, he never travelled by sea, except once when he crossed the strait from Aulis to Euboea, in order to compete, and win, in the poetic contest which took place at the funeral of king Amphidamas.[55]

There has been much debate over whether the biographical information contained in the Hesiodic poems should be taken at face value, or whether it projects a particular poetic persona which fits the character and purpose of the poetry.[56] We need not enter this argument here. For our purposes, the most important point is that ancient audiences thought of Hesiod in ways that closely resemble their views of Homer. They accepted the biographical information contained in the poems: in fact, they took it as a basis for further speculation. As we shall see, the claims about winning a poetic competition at the funeral games of Amphidamas sparked a legend according to which on that occasion Hesiod won against Homer, no less. As in the case of Homer, archaic audiences attributed to Hesiod many poems whose 'authenticity' is now doubted, such as, for example, the *Catalogue of Women*. There was a tendency to accumulate poems, as well as biographical legends, under the name of Hesiod as well as that of Homer.

It will come as no surprise that modern scholars have tried to establish the 'true' relationship between Homer and Hesiod by ignoring what the ancients said about them and focusing, instead, on an analysis of the small selection of poems that they consider 'genuine', the *Iliad* and the *Odyssey*, the *Theogony* and the *Works and Days*. There has been a long and complex attempt to establish whether the Homeric poems are older than the Hesiodic ones, or *vice versa*.[57] The question, however, is difficult to settle: while there are some differences of diction between the Homeric and Hesiodic poems (narrowly defined), it is hard to decide how best to account for them. Moreover, the similarities between Homeric and Hesiodic Greek are overwhelming, as are the overlaps in content and techniques of composition, thus suggesting a close connection between the poems, rather than providing evidence for distinguishing them in terms of date of composition. No real progress has been made: *The Bluffer's Guide to the Classics* gives the following advice to the budding classicist: 'If someone claims that Homer is the earliest Greek poet, you will claim that Hesiod was, and vice-versa.'[58] It is hard to resist the suspicion that, once again, we have failed to ask the right questions of our ancient material.

The debate whether Homer is earlier than Hesiod or *vice versa* goes all the way back to antiquity. Accius, the Roman critic of the second/first century BC, claimed that Hesiod was older than Homer on the following grounds: Homer, he observes, never says that the Cyclops only has one eye, he simply assumes that everyone has already learned that from Hesiod.[59] This is a perceptive observation, though it only shows that Homer relied on knowledge of a wider epic tradition, and not necessarily on Hesiod's *Theogony* as we know it. If we look at discussions of the relationship between Homer and Hesiod before Accius, in the archaic and classical period, there is less of a preoccupation with establishing whether the Homeric poems depended on the Hesiodic ones or *vice versa*. In fact, the vast majority of sources mention Homer and Hesiod together, and often explicitly present them as contemporaries and rivals.[60] The story of the contest in which Hesiod defeats Homer of course assumes that they lived at the same time, but there are other contexts in which the two poets are mentioned together.

It is crucial for the overall argument of this book that Homer and Hesiod are regularly mentioned together as authorities on the gods, whether in order to undermine their portrayal of the divine or in order to draw attention to their authority as religious experts. Xenophanes complains about them (fr. 11 DK):

> Homer and Hesiod ascribe to the gods everything that is shameful and blameworthy among human beings: stealing, committing adultery and cheating one another.

We shall go back to Xenophanes' views in Chapter 3, but for now it is important to note that he is not alone in mentioning Homer and Hesiod in the same breath when discussing the gods. This is what Herodotus tells us about the origins of Greek religion (2.53.2-3):

> I believe that Hesiod and Homer lived 400 years before my time and not more. It is they who established the theogony for the Greeks. They gave epithets to the gods, defined their due honours and spheres of expertise and described their appearance.

When Homer is quoted as an authority on the gods, his name is mentioned together with that of Hesiod. Together, Homeric and Hesiodic poetry offer an authoritative and broadly coherent account of the Greek gods – which can then be either endorsed or challenged.[61] This is a crucial point to bear in mind when we come to discuss the Homeric gods in Chapter 3.

In order to understand how the Greeks of the archaic and classical period understood the relationship between Hesiod and Homer, there is no better place to turn than the story of their contest for poetic excellence, a version of which is preserved in the *Contest of Homer and Hesiod*. [62] In its present form, this text dates to the Antonine period (second century AD), but it contains material from the fifth and even the sixth century BC.[63] The *Contest* elaborates the hint contained in the *Works and Days* that Hesiod won an important poetic competition at the funeral games of Amphidamas, and suggests that Hesiod's rival was Homer. The story tells us in detail how the two poets competed against one another, as well as which one was declared the winner and why. This close comparison of Homer and Hesiod through a story of competition serves to define the fundamental characteristics of these two poets and, up to a point, tells us how the poetic traditions which went under their names were defined against one another in archaic and classical Greece.

The competition undergoes two main phases: in the first instance, Hesiod confronts Homer with impossible opening gambits, which he is asked to develop into a coherent and sensible rejoinder. Here is an example of the kind of challenge posed by Hesiod (*Contest* 8 West):

> 'Muse, come, of the things that are, shall be and were
> tell me nothing, rather bring to mind another song;'

Homer, who wants to solve the impasse fittingly, says:

> 'Never around the tomb of Zeus shall the pounding horses
> wear down the chariots, competing for victory.'

1. The Poet

Now 'Hesiod', as he is depicted in the *Contest*, echoes the opening of the *Theogony*: we have already seen that at lines 31-2 the Muses are said to grant Hesiod the ability to sing what was and shall be, and that at line 38 they tell of 'past, present and future'. Given that Hesiod claims the entirety of knowledge for himself, past, present and future, Homer is forced to remember 'another song'. This is not an easy task, but Homer answers brilliantly by pointing out that there will never be any funeral games in honour of Zeus: he is immortal forever. It is tempting to see this exchange between the two poets as a shrewd interpretation of their work: it is certainly true that the Hesiodic corpus, as conceived in antiquity, traces the development of the cosmos from the beginning, when Earth first gave birth to Heaven (*Theogony*) through to the birth of the heroes (*Catalogue of Women*), through to the world as it is today (*Works and Days*) and even to predictions of the future (*Ornithomanteia*). Homer, by contrast, focuses on particular problems or on crucial aspects of the overall story: the problem of mortality, the difference between gods and human beings. In the next chapter, we are going to look in further detail at Hesiod as the systematic poet of cosmic history and Homer as the singer of crucial moments within it. For now, however, we must continue with the story of the contest.

We are presented with a series of impossible opening lines uttered by Hesiod which are brilliantly developed into a sensible couplet by Homer. For example, Hesiod begins (*Contest* 9 West):

> As she had surrendered to marriage, Artemis the arrow-shooter ...

This is preposterous, since Artemis is a virgin goddess by definition. Homer, however, uses enjambment and what we would call 'a different punctuation' to solve the problem (*Contest* 9 West):

> As she had surrendered to marriage, Artemis the arrow-shooter
> killed Callisto with a shot from her silver bow.[64]

The goddess Artemis is restored to her proper role: the arrow-shooter kills a young girl at the threshold of marriage. Other challenges of this kind follow: they concern the diet and banqueting of the heroes, the battle of the Giants, the magnitude of the Achaean expedition. Together, Homer and Hesiod depict a well known and familiar world, which is only temporarily disrupted by Hesiod's opening lines. Together, the two poets display an unrivalled mastery of the hexameter verse.[65]

Since Homer is always able to compose an appropriate rejoinder, and

Hesiod shows no sign of running out of challenges, eventually king Panedes attempts to draw the competition to a close by proposing a different kind of challenge. He asks the two poets to recite the best passages from their poems. Hesiod chooses the so-called 'farmer's calendar', lines 383-92 of the *Works and Days*; whereas Homer recites two excerpts from *Iliad* 13, lines 126-33 and 339-44, which describe fighting in mass formation. At this point, the Greeks are ready to give Homer the prize, but Panedes points out that it is better to celebrate peace rather than war, and declares Hesiod the winner.

Many readers have observed that Homer seems to be the favourite right up until the end, when we are faced with this surprising conclusion. Yet, while the final outcome may not settle the question of who is the best poet, it certainly helps to define the core of Homer's poetry in relation to that of Hesiod. Aristophanes presents Homer as the poet of war and Hesiod as the poet of peace at *Frogs* 1033-6, thus showing that this perception of the two poets was widespread. Plato likewise presents Homer as the one poet of war, whereas he claims that both Homer and Hesiod treat the following topics: 'how the gods deal with one another and with human beings, what happens in heaven and in Hades, and how gods and heroes are born' (*Ion* 531c). In a sense, Plato's portrayal mirrors the *Contest* quite precisely: while in the first part of the competition Homer and Hesiod compose together and explore what can and cannot be said about gods and heroes, in the second section they find their own individual areas of expertise: war and peace.

Two conclusions follow from this. What is considered 'quintessentially Homeric' emerges from a contrast with what is thought to be Hesiodic, and *vice versa*. The qualities of the two poets, as well as their most characteristic themes, emerge most clearly when they are compared to one another. At the same time, it is important to note that the two poets are closely associated in the story of the contest, and indeed more generally. Homer completes the lines that Hesiod utters: not only do they share the techniques of hexameter versification, but they join forces in describing the world of gods and heroes. Their roles are complementary: Hesiod sings what was, is, and shall be; Homer focuses on what is and is not possible in this overall history. If Homer is the poet of war and Hesiod of peace, together they describe two fundamental aspects of the human experience. While the story of the contest between Homer and Hesiod reflects, to an extent, some typically ancient concerns with competition, wisdom, and the function of poetry, it also contains some clues which are useful for the modern interpreter of Homer. Above all, it teaches us that Homer and

Hesiod were closely associated in antiquity: their characteristic features emerged most clearly from a direct comparison, while together they were thought to give a coherent picture of the gods, and of human life. It is crucial to bear in mind these two general points when considering the place of the *Iliad* and the *Odyssey* in the wider early Greek epic tradition.

Conclusion

In this chapter we have looked in some detail at the way in which early Greek audiences thought about Homer. It is perfectly obvious that their interests and preoccupations are not the same as those of modern readers, or even those of later Greeks. Eventually, the Homeric poems became the foundation of literate education and the perception of Homer changed accordingly: for example, in the Hellenistic period, Homer was often depicted as a school teacher or a scribe, with a stylus and papyrus rolls in hand.[66] The image of the blind bard was not the only possible one. Yet it seems to us that early perspectives deserve particular attention in that they yield some important insights for the interpretation of epic. Whereas modern readers tend to think of Homer either as the author of one or two exceptional texts or as a label for a poetic tradition, early Greek sources, in a sense, combine these two approaches. For them, the name Homer evoked the image of a single, exceptionally authoritative bard, to whom a vast number of poems was attributed. The term 'Homeric' did not primarily convey an aesthetic judgement, but an interest in the content of the poems. Homer's name was associated in particular with heroic epic, but he could also be seen as an authoritative voice on the gods.

As well as the name 'Homer', early audiences also knew the names of other poets – some were seen as ancestors of Homer (Orpheus, Musaeus and, of course, Apollo himself), some were thought of as minor figures who inherited poems from Homer, or were linked to particular traditions which are now lost – but, above all, Hesiod.[67] Together, Homer and Hesiod formed a pair in the mind of archaic audiences. Some sources describe them as relatives, some as rivals, but above all they are mentioned together as authorities on the gods, as the singers of war and peace; in short, as the two most important, and complementary, epic poets.

The *Iliad* and the *Odyssey*, then, were not approached in isolation, but as slices from a larger banquet of song. This wider tradition provided a context within which early audiences approached the two poems. Unlike many modern readers, archaic audiences were not interested in towering, isolated texts, but in texts that could resonate with what they already knew about the cosmos. Exactly how the epics achieved that effect is the subject of the next chapter.

2

The Poems

In the first chapter, we argued that early audiences thought of Homer as the author of many hexameter poems: it seems that, from an archaic Greek perspective, the *Iliad* and the *Odyssey* belonged to a much wider range of Homeric epic. We have also suggested that Homer was closely associated with Hesiod, the only other poet who could compete with him in terms of authority and sheer breadth of oeuvre. Our ancient sources leave no doubt that the two poets were compared, contrasted and assessed in relation to one another. Together, they were mentioned as experts on the gods but, as we see most clearly in the story of the *Contest*, their work was also contrasted, with a view to defining the most characteristic themes of each poet. There is no doubt then that early Greek audiences did not approach the *Iliad* and the *Odyssey* in isolation but rather read them in relation to other poems attributed to Homer, and against the works of Hesiod. The crucial question to which we now need to turn is this: is there any indication within the Homeric and Hesiodic poems, as opposed to the early sources that discuss them, which encourages us to see them in relation to one another or, more generally, as belonging to a wider tradition of epic? In our overall approach to Homeric epic, this question provides the main starting point.

Epic and the history of the cosmos

Many scholars have studied the connections between different early hexameter poems by focusing on their language, themes and techniques of composition.[1] We have already seen in Chapter 1 that, although there are some differences of diction between different poems, the similarities are overwhelming. Projects like the *Lexikon des frühgriechischen Epos*, a multi-volume dictionary that examines in detail the language of all early hexameter poetry, have had a major impact on the way scholars look at the shared phrases and expressions between different poems and authors.[2] For the purposes of this book, however, we would like to start from the content of the poems attributed to Homer and Hesiod, rather than from the similarities in their language and form. We argue that the Homeric and the Hesiodic epics describe the same world, albeit from different perspectives and at different stages of development. This shared vision of the cosmos lies at the heart of the early epic tradition.

Let us start by looking at the main subjects of the Hesiodic corpus. The *Theogony* describes the origins of the cosmos: it tells us how Earth first came from Void, how she generated Heaven and how from these two primordial deities came a genealogy of gods to which Zeus and the other Olympians ultimately belong. The *Theogony* tells of two main revolutions of power: Heaven is succeeded by Cronus who is in turn replaced by Zeus. In order to avoid being replaced by a son, Heaven tries to prevent his offspring from being born: he presses his children inside the body of Earth. Eventually, however, Cronus castrates him, frees his siblings, and becomes the ruler of the gods. At that point, he is confronted with the same problem faced by his father, and decides to swallow his own children as soon as they emerge from the womb of their mother. Zeus, however, is hidden and saved: he eventually vanquishes his father and gains supreme power for ever. We are told that Zeus swallows his own wife Metis before she can give birth to a son destined to be stronger than the father: this represents a culmination of the strategies employed in the previous generations.[3] At the same time, the *Theogony* also insists that Zeus uses justice as well as might in order to secure and retain his power.[4] The poem goes on to recount the birth of the younger and less powerful Olympians, and finishes by discussing some borderline cases: gods born of mortal mothers, mortals with divine parentage.

This genealogical phase is then taken up by the *Catalogue of Women*, a poem which survives in fragments and was attributed to Hesiod in antiquity.[5] It tells us about mortal women who had sex with gods and gave birth to the demigods or heroes.[6] The poem ends with a catalogue of Helen's suitors, a brief account of the Trojan War and a description of the end of the heroic age. The end of the *Catalogue* (fr. 204) is difficult to interpret, not least because many words and even lines are missing, but it appears to describe the advent of the seasons, an event which marks the end of the race of heroes and the beginning of the world as it is now.[7] The *Works and Days* focuses precisely on the seasons, on how to cultivate the land and, more generally, on how to live in the present day.

There is no doubt, then, that these three poems are closely linked. This is most obvious, perhaps, in the case of the *Catalogue of Women*, which follows seamlessly from the *Theogony* both in terms of form and of content.[8] The relationship between the *Catalogue* and the *Works and Days* is harder to establish, not least because of the poor state of our evidence, but scholars have remarked on the similarities between the end of the *Catalogue* (fr. 204) and the tone and subject matter of the *Works and Days*.[9] Beyond the details of how exactly the beginning and ending of the poems fit together, we must, however, take a more general view of their relationship.

Together, the *Theogony,* the *Catalogue of Women* and the *Works and Days* give an overall account of the world, from its origins to what it is now. The account focuses on development and change through time, but it is more ambitious than a conventional 'history' in the modern sense: it tells us about the overall origins of the cosmos (a topic which today would probably belong to the field of physics), the birth of the gods and the development of the Olympian hierarchy (theology), the role of justice on Olympus and on earth (ethics), the genealogies of the heroes and the wars that brought them to their end (what we would probably call mythology), as well as practical advice on how best to behave today, in everyday life (agriculture, law, seafaring, etc.). It has been said that Hesiodic epic is not 'history' in the sense that it lacks 'dates and a coherent dating scheme'.[10] Still, as we shall see, the term 'universal history' or 'history of the cosmos' is not a bad way of describing the overall subject matter of the Hesiodic poems: it has the advantage of stressing the importance of development through time within the tradition, as well as its perceived reliability.[11] Before we look in more detail at the implications of epic as cosmic history we must, however, face an objection to our argument which will be on the tip of the tongue of our more expert readers.

There is great uncertainty about the dating of the *Catalogue of Women*. Some scholars think that it is earlier than the *Theogony*, others that it is considerably later.[12] Here we must, however, remember the perspective of our early audiences: they thought of the *Catalogue of Women* as Hesiodic, perhaps because they saw how well it fitted with the rest of the Hesiodic corpus. In other words, they were more interested in the internal coherence of the Hesiodic tradition, a coherence based on content, than on the time when each individual text reached a stage of fixation. The *Catalogue of Women*, as we have it, may well have been composed later than our versions of the *Theogony* and the *Works and Days*, but it is clear that the outline of its contents, the birth of the heroes, the wedding of Helen, the Trojan War, the end of the heroes, were well known to those who listened to the *Theogony*, the *Works and Days* or, for that matter, the *Iliad*. Tsagarakis, for example, has shown that *Iliad* 3 relies on an account of Helen's suitors very similar to the one we find in the *Catalogue of Women*.[13] What we are arguing, then, is not that our texts of the *Theogony*, the *Catalogue of Women* and the

Works and Days were composed in that order, but rather that they describe a well-established sequence of events which was known and respected by early bards and their audiences. It is this internal chronology that mattered to them. Early audiences would not necessarily have known or cared about the dates of composition of individual poems, still less about when they were first written down, but they would certainly have known that the *Theogony* gave an account of the beginning of the cosmos, that the age of the heroes came later, and that from the perspective of the present, the heroes themselves were long dead. What we argue is that this overall historical perspective is crucial for the interpretation of individual poems.

If Hesiodic poetry gives a general account of the history of the cosmos from its origins to the present day, the poems attributed to Homer 'zoom in' and explore in detail crucial moments within that history. Many *Homeric Hymns* recount the birth of an Olympian god, and how he or she came to be integrated within the divine hierarchy on Olympus: Zeus is already in power, but the divine hierarchy still needs to be worked out in detail. This is how Strauss Clay places the *Hymns* within the overall history of the cosmos: 'The Homeric poems show us the fully perfected and stable Olympian pantheon [...]: the *Theogony* reveals the genesis of the Olympian order and ends with the triumphal accession to power of Zeus. Between theogonic poetry and epic there remains a gap, one that is sealed by the Olympian narrative of the longer hymns.'[14] Our understanding of the relationship between the *Homeric Hymns* and the *Theogony* is slightly different from Strauss Clay's, although we agree on the overall lines of interpretation: the birth of the younger Olympians is told in the *Theogony*, but very briefly and without much exploration of detail. The *Homeric Hymns* work out episodes which are treated in passing within the Hesiodic corpus.[15] The same could be said about the heroic epics attributed to Homer. The Trojan War is described very briefly in the *Catalogue of Women*.[16] In the *Works and Days*, moreover, the end of the heroes is specifically linked to the Theban and the Trojan Wars. These wars, which are dismissed quickly in the broad-brush accounts of Hesiod, are painted in detail in the *Iliad*, the *Odyssey*, and other poems attributed to Homer.

There is another reason for believing that internal chronology was of the utmost importance for early bards and audiences. We know that at some point the *Iliad* and the *Odyssey* were arranged within a larger sequence of poems that treated the earlier and later stages of the Trojan War and the return of the heroes after the conflict. The last poem in this sequence, or 'cycle' to use the ancient term, dealt with the son of Odysseus and Circe, Telegonus. Quite when this overall cycle was put together is not certain, though it clearly reflects archaic notions about the overall sequence of events in the heroic age.[17] We know of an alternative opening for the *Iliad* which may have served to link it directly to a poem that told of the earlier stages of the Trojan War: the lines in question were already known to Aristoxenus in the fourth century BC.[18] Similarly, another attested line links the end of the *Iliad* to the beginning of its sequel, the *Aethiopis*.[19] The poems of the Cycle were meant to cover, together, the whole of the Trojan War, from its origins to the last born of the heroes, Telegonus. The poems dealing with the Theban War were similarly arranged in a cycle.[20]

Aristotle, in his discussion of Homer in the *Poetics*, stresses the fact that whereas poems like the *Cypria* cover a long sequence of events and provide raw material for many tragedies, the *Iliad* and *Odyssey* are tightly structured, and look at a very narrow span of time: their subject could be treated in one or two tragedies each.[21] This is an important observation, but it should not distract us from the fact that the *Iliad* and *Odyssey*, like the *Cypria*, were seen as part of a larger context.[22] What remains to be seen is whether there are any signs within these poems which encourage us to look at them as part of a wider tradition. This is a question to which most of the present book is devoted, but for now we can start with some preliminary considerations.

In his *Ars Poetica*, Horace observed that Homer did not start 'from the egg', *ab ovo*, that is, from the beginning of the story of the Trojan War, but rather plunged his readers into the thick of things, *in medias res*, and assumed they could work out where they were.[23] The first lines of the *Iliad* are a good example of this approach. After the proem this is what we hear (*Iliad* 1.8-10):

> What god then set them together in bitter collision?
> Zeus' son and Leto's, Apollo, who in anger at the king drove
> the foul pestilence along the host, and the people perished.

There is no summary of what went on before the pestilence, not even an indication of when, in the course of the war, the episode took place: we are left to work this out for ourselves. The contemporary poet Christopher Logue, in his adaptation of the *Iliad*, well captures this aspect of the poem. He starts with an image:[24]

> Picture the east Aegean sea by night,
> And on a beach aslant its shimmering
> Upwards of 50,000 men
> Asleep like spoons beside their lethal Fleet.

That is it: no summary, no introduction, no explanation, just the Achaean camp and, soon to come, Apollo's devastation of it. We are left to work out the rest for ourselves. The question then is how we are supposed to fill in the overall context. Logue, of course, relies on know-ledge of Homer's *Iliad* for his own poem; but what did audiences of the Homeric poems rely on? How did they know how to place the *Iliad* and the *Odyssey* within the wider history of the world? Did everyone have a detailed knowledge of other epic poems that circulated in archaic Greece, or could audiences infer the wider story from the *Iliad* and the *Odyssey* themselves? This is a crucial question that has been hotly debated in recent years.

Neo-analytic scholars of Homer have shown that the *Iliad* and *Odyssey* in fact contain, embedded in various episodes, asides, digres-sions and additions, a wider picture of what went on before and after what is told in the main narrative.[25] This is an important point because it explains, among other things, why the *Iliad* and the *Odyssey* can appeal to modern readers, who are not necessarily familiar with the wider epic tradition within which the poems were composed and performed. It also helps to explain the experiences of early audiences. We must assume that in the archaic period, just as today, different listeners had different levels of familiarity with the wider epic tradition. Some members of the audience will have known many different epics by Homer, Hesiod and other poets. Other listeners will have been less knowledgeable and yet will have enjoyed listening to the poems. In the course of the performance, they will have started to work out an overall picture of what went on before and after the main story. The point, then, is not that one needs to have full command of a whole poetic tradi-tion in order to appreciate the *Iliad* and the *Odyssey*; but rather that these two poems deliberately and carefully present themselves as part of a larger narrative. They display what Ruth Scodel has recently described as a 'rhetoric of traditionality'.[26]

The Homeric narrator, far from silently assuming 'background knowledge' on the part of his audience, actively challenges his listeners to situate the story within a wider history of the cosmos. At a basic level, the Homeric poems brim with allusions, flashbacks, and cases of foreshadowing to the immediate and distant future. If one wanted to explain all of them, one would end up writing a very long commentary, and Homeric commentaries do tend to be long. Our point, however, is not that one needs to know a great deal in order to enjoy the Homeric texts: experience shows that Homer speaks very directly to the uniniti-ated. Rather, we suggest that, by virtue of their peculiar tone and scope, the Homeric texts actively foster a sense of context and resonance, within a wider narrative of cosmic change through time. Later in this chapter, and indeed in Part II of the book, we are going to look in greater detail at the ways in which the *Iliad* and the *Odyssey* conjure up the whole history of the cosmos and place themselves within it. For now, however, the main point to bear in mind is that early hexameter poems share an understanding of the overall shape of history: first Earth and Heaven, then the birth of the gods, then the Olympian order, the birth of the heroes, the Theban and the Trojan Wars, the traumatic end of the heroic age, and ultimately the world as it is today.

This overall vision of history is conceived in genealogical terms. Much of Hesiodic poetry consists of family trees, seemingly endless lists of who descended from whom, when and how: we start with the gods, and eventually move on to the heroes, and the families to which they give rise. It is important to remember that real members of archaic audiences will have been able to trace the genealogy of their own families, or those of their more prominent fellow-citizens, all the way back to a hero, and ultimately a god. Genealogies are thus a powerful way of linking the past to the present. Like Hesiod, Homer relies on this conception of history as a divine family tree; but, unlike Hesiod, he focuses on significant conflicts between particular generations: Zeus and the younger Olympian gods in the *Homeric Hymns*; the gods and their mortal offspring in the heroic epics.

This difference of focus and scope between the Hesiodic and the Homeric poems has some implications at the level of narrative technique. In terms of tone, the Homeric texts are essentially dramatic, exploring an event from a multitude of viewpoints, while the Hesiodic poems tend to take the form of lists that introduce the forces which govern the universe.[27] In terms of narrative pace, the Homeric texts take hundreds, even thousands of lines to elaborate on a select number of critical events, whereas Hesiod covers huge sweeps of time and space in relatively few lines. For example, the *Homeric Hymn to Apollo*, which describes the crisis precipitated by the birth of Zeus' most powerful son, takes more than 500 lines to relate what the *Theogony* covers in a mere three lines. Similarly, the *Catalogue of Women* deals with the Trojan War in a few hundred lines, whereas the *Iliad* takes over 15,000 lines to tell us what happened during a small portion of the whole war, when Achilles demanded recognition for being the best of the Achaeans and the son of a goddess.

It is interesting that our early sources are aware of these differences between Homer and Hesiod. We have already seen that in the *Contest* Hesiod claims for himself 'what was, is and shall be' and asks Homer to remember 'another song'.[28] Homer solves the challenge by pointing out that Zeus, unlike the heroes, will never be celebrated by funeral games: the implication seems to be that whereas Hesiod gives us the overall picture of the history of the cosmos, Homer focuses on the crucial difference between gods and mortals. Other early thinkers seem to distinguish between the two poets in a similar way. Heraclitus, for example, presents Hesiod as a polymath, someone who knows many things, whereas, from Homer, he expects the quality of superior insight.[29] Even the characterisation of Hesiod as the poet of peace and Homer as the poet of war seems to reflect, in a sense, the overall characteristics of their work: Hesiod gives us a stable picture of how things are, Homer focuses on moments of upheaval. Yet beyond these differences, ancient audiences were also aware that Homer and Hesiod shared an overall vision of the cosmos and, in particular, the gods. We have already seen that, according to Herodotus, the two poets first revealed to the Greeks 'the births of the gods, their epithets, honours, spheres of expertise, and appearance'.[30] Plato, in the *Ion*, makes a similar point.[31] The emphasis is clearly on the gods and on their birth, but the implications of these genealogical narratives are far wider, and include the relationship between gods and mortals. Since heroes descend from gods, and are in turn succeeded by 'men as they are now', genealogy provides an overall account of the world from when the first goddess, Earth, mated with Heaven, to our own lives in the present day.

Early epic, then, is crucially concerned with the gods and with history as a divine family tree, which eventually branches out to the generations of mortals. As will soon become clear, the role of the gods in fact helps us to deal with a problem which we have carefully avoided until now: the status of epic as an account of the past. We originally introduced the term 'history of the cosmos' as a convenient way of emphasising that the universe depicted in early epic is subject to change through time, and that each poem carefully situates itself at a particular point in the overall history of the cosmos. There is, however, another reason why the term 'history' is an appropriate way of describing early Greek epic. Unlike our concepts of 'poetry', 'narrative', 'fiction', 'mythology' or, indeed, 'epic' itself, the term 'history' suggests to us a reliable and authoritative account of the past; and this is, we claim, precisely how early audiences thought of the Homeric poems. We have already seen that Herodotus has to make a case for his view that the name 'Oceanus' is simply the invention of Homer or some other poet before him. If we were interested in the origins of the concept of fiction, Herodotus would probably deserve more credit than he is usually given, but for the purposes of reading Homer it is much more important to realise that Homeric epic was not thought to be fiction by archaic Greeks. Even centuries after Herodotus, the epics were usually approached as an authoritative account of the distant past. It was generally accepted that, in broad outline at least, the events they reported were historical. Aristotle, for example, takes it for granted that the Trojan War actually happened. In the *Nicomachean Ethics*, he argues that it would be absurd to deliberate about the Trojan War: the conflict simply happened, and no amount of thinking, debating or doubting could ever change that.[32]

Aristotle's argument may well strike modern readers as strange, and for more than one reason. For a start, we usually think of Aristotle as a fine literary critic, well able to judge the artistic qualities of the *Iliad*: its unity, the selection and presentation of the material, its tragic qualities are at the heart of his discussion in the *Poetics*.[33] It may thus seem surprising that the Sack of Troy is taken as a paradigmatic example of 'something that happened in the past'. Modern scholars have relentlessly debated the historicity of the Trojan War: a recent and controversial exhibition, for example, attempted to enlighten the public about the differences between the mythical Troy depicted in Homer and the remains of the Bronze Age city excavated on the hill of Hisarlik.[34] One wonders, then, why Aristotle used the Trojan War as his example of a historical event that cannot be doubted. In more general terms, the question can be put like this: it is undeniable that the epics of Homer, and indeed Hesiod, were taken as authoritative accounts of world history. What we need to explore is the relationship between what we would call the 'poetic' qualities of the poems and their claim to historical accuracy.

Form and content

Today, poets tend to be associated with creativity, originality, the ability to make up a world in a poem: while poetry may contain a deeper truth, we do not read it as a reliable historical account. In archaic Greece, however, epic as a genre was approached as a history of the cosmos in its different phases: the birth of the gods, the age of the heroes, our own time. This may well seem strange to us when we come to read the Homeric poems: they do not strike us as historical narrative; on the contrary, they seem quintessentially poetic: they are full of vivid imagery, similes, evocative turns of phrase, supernatural events. They strike us, in short, as a product of the creative imagination, not as a source of accurate information about world history. This is no doubt partly because we do not share the Greeks' world-view. For example, we do not believe in the gods, do not sacrifice or pray to them at the most significant and dangerous stages of our life, such as childbirth, war, illness, death. For us, the gods are figures of speech, dazzling literary creations with no religious significance or truth about them. Other aspects of the Homeric world are usually thought to reflect some sort of historical reality, though scholars are concerned that literary embellishments distort the overall picture.

Generally, modern readers draw a sharp distinction between using the Homeric poems as historical evidence, and approaching them as works of literature. The contents of the poems tend to be split along this divide: for example, the Homeric gods belong to literary studies, whereas Homeric society, warfare, weaponry are the proper objects of historical enquiry.[35] This distinction between history and literature did not exist in the archaic period and, as we shall see in the second part of this book, can be counterproductive for the interpretation of the poems. In Chapter 4 we hope to show, for example, that Homeric society is best understood by considering the divine ancestry of the heroes. More generally, if we look at Homeric descriptions of the bard and his art, we find that beauty and truth go hand in hand; in fact, it seems that what is most poetic is, at the same time, most reliable. This is perhaps most obvious when we consider the figure of the Muse: many passages tell us that the Muses sing beautifully, but they are also presented as sources of accurate information. This is how the bard addresses the Muses at the beginning of the *Catalogue of Ships* (*Iliad* 2.484-92):

> Tell me now, you Muses who have your homes on Olympus.
> For you, who are goddesses, are there, and know all things,
> and we have heard only the rumour of it and know nothing.
> Who then of those were the chief men and lords of the Danaans?
> I could not tell over the multitude of them nor name them,
> not if I had ten tongues and ten mouths, not if I had
> a voice never to be broken, and a heart of bronze within me,
> not unless the Muses of Olympus, daughters
> of Zeus of the aegis, remembered all those who came beneath Ilion.

The Muses are the perfect source of knowledge because they are goddesses and know everything. The bard's own knowledge is ultimately divine, and the perspective he adopts is that of the daughters of Zeus 'who have their homes on Olympus'. This divine outlook on the world is an important aspect of early epic: we have seen that Homer and Hesiod were considered experts on the gods; now we are in a position to understand better why this was the case. It is not simply because the gods feature prominently in many of their poems, but also because the poets themselves explicitly rely on the insider knowledge of the Muses. The narrative of the bard is thus anchored in the very story he recounts: the history of the divine universe.

As we move down in the history of the cosmos, the gods become less central to the narrative: in the *Theogony* they dominate the entire poem, in the *Iliad* they are more prominent than in the *Odyssey*, which depicts the aftermath of the Trojan War, in the *Works and Days* the gods are distant powers to whom ordinary mortals appeal, for example, in their quest for justice. Yet all these poems recount a stage in the making of the divine universe, and accordingly they all begin with the Muses. Now, the Homeric gods do not know everything. For example, they can be oblivious to what is happening on earth, and can even be tricked by their fellow gods.[36] Similarly, the Muses as daughters of Zeus are 'all-knowing' only in the specific sense that they know everything there is to know about the history of the Olympian order. They 'please the mind of Zeus', as Hesiod puts it, by recounting how the gods came into being, Zeus came to rule forever, and the universe took shape.[37] Homer and Hesiod are experts on the gods because they derive their knowledge from them.

Modern readers have been puzzled by invocations to the Muses.[38] It is difficult to establish the exact tone and significance of these openings: should we think of them as a kind of literary convention or as a very genuine call for help and information? Are the poems that follow the literary creation of the bard or some sort of divinely revealed truth? And, finally, is the bard himself free to fashion his song, or should we think of him as some kind of shaman, divinely possessed by the Muse? These questions interested ancient readers too: Plato, in the *Ion*, famously tried to depict bards and rhapsodes as divinely inspired, and therefore hardly in control of their own words, or able to understand their meaning. However, if we look at the way bards are depicted within the Homeric poems themselves, a more nuanced picture emerges.

A passage at the beginning of the *Odyssey*, 1.337-9, discusses what responsibility the bard has for what he sings. In the first book, we catch a glimpse of life on Ithaca in the absence of Odysseus. The suitors sit and drink while they listen to the bard Phemius, who performs for them a song about the terrible suffering of the Achaeans on their way home from the Trojan War. Penelope, who is listening from her own rooms upstairs, finds this topic distressing and comes down in order to ask Phemius to sing something else:

'Phemius, since you know many other actions of mortals
and gods, which can charm men's hearts and which the singers celebrate,
sit beside them and sing one of these ...'

Telemachus, however, finds his mother's request unacceptable and asks
her not to interfere with the bard's choice of song (*Odyssey* 1.346-52):

'Why, my mother, do you begrudge this excellent singer
to give pleasure as his mind drives him? It is not the singers
who are to blame, it must be Zeus who is to blame, who gives out
to men who eat bread, to each and all, the way he wills it.
There is nothing wrong in his singing the sad return of the Danaans.
People, surely, always give more applause to that song
which is the latest to circulate among the listeners.'

Both Telemachus and Penelope assume that the bard can choose what he
sings, but Telemachus insists that he should not be pressurised by the
needs of his audience: this is an important point, because there is a
suggestion that Phemius is in fact pandering to the interests of the
suitors: they would certainly enjoy hearing that the Achaeans encountered difficulties on their way home.[39] The bard should be allowed to give
pleasure 'as his mind drives him'; yet it is clear that he is not actually free
to make up any story he pleases. Penelope does not ask him to sing the
'happy return of the Achaeans' and Telemachus points out that he should
not be blamed if they suffered on their way home: the responsibility for
that lies with Zeus. The song of the bard, then, corresponds to the reality
that is apportioned by Zeus. So, while Phemius is not presented as a
possessed visionary or a passive instrument of the Muse, his song reflects
what actually happened and what the gods decreed. Telemachus acknowledges pleasure, the delights of novelty, the input of the bard's mind (all
important aspects in modern notions of poetry) but also implies that
Phemius offers a reliable account of what Zeus metes out to each mortal.

It would seem, then, that the Muses guarantee the truthfulness and
accuracy of the bard's song in a historical sense: through his connection
with the divine, the bard can access what happened long ago and far
away: the Muses are always present, whereas ordinary mortals must
rely on 'hearsay', *kleos*. Yet, it seems that the relationship between the
bard and the Muses is not as simple as we have suggested so far. Hesiod,
in particular, warns us that the Muses can tell lies, if they choose to do
so, at *Theogony* 24-8:

This is what the goddesses said to me first, the Olympian Muses, daughters of Zeus the aegis-bearer: 'Shepherds that camp in the wild, disgraces,

merest bellies: we know to tell many lies that sound like truth, but we know to sing reality, when we will.'[40]

Hesiod seems to warn us that an invocation to the Muse is not, by itself, a guarantee of truthfulness, because the Muses can choose to lie in a convincing way. The bard tells us what he is told by the Muses, but they do not represent an absolute guarantee of truth and accuracy. Hesiod may imply that, in his case, the Muses decided to tell the truth,[41] but more interesting perhaps is the implication of his statement for his audience. Hesiod invites us to judge the accuracy of epic, without taking all invocations to Muses at face value. And there is another implication, which is important for our understanding of epic as an account of world history: the idea of 'lies that sound like truth' makes sense only if we know what the truth ought to sound like. In other words, there is an outward appearance to truthfulness which the Muses can imitate if they so choose. Thus, we may not expect every song that *seems* true to be so in fact. However, we would certainly expect a reliable account to bear signs of its truthfulness which can be appreciated by the audience.

The same intimate connection between poetic form and what we might call 'reliability' emerges from a passage in the *Odyssey*. When Odysseus arrives at the land of the Phaeacians, he is asked to tell his story and reveal his identity. It is a matter of some importance, for the Phaeacians, to establish whether Odysseus is lying or telling the truth, but they have no way of double-checking what he says: he has arrived alone and naked on their shore, without any evidence or witnesses that might corroborate his account. In book 11, he interrupts his story after performing a formal catalogue of women and claims, somewhat disingenuously, that it is late, and that they should all go to bed. King Alcinous, however, encourages him to continue and reassures him that his account is trusted because it sounds like a bardic performance (11.363-8):

> Odysseus, we as we look upon you do not imagine
> that you are a deceptive or thievish man, the sort that the black earth
> breeds in great numbers, people who wander widely, making up
> lying stories, out of no-where and beyond control. You have
> beauty upon your words, and there is sound sense within them,
> and expertly, as a singer would do, you have told the story.

Alcinous knows that lonesome travellers, like Odysseus, are especially prone to telling lies both because they may need to do so in order to survive and because they can get away with it. However, he points out that Odysseus' own words have *morphê*, 'shape', 'beauty', and that he can arrange the story expertly, as a bard would do. Odysseus, we are told, knows how to perform a catalogue (cf. *katelexas* in line 368) and this suggests that he is not just cobbling together a random lie. He follows a pattern and what he says tallies with what Alcinous expects of bards: an account from which one can learn something, a source of reliable information.

There is no straightforward relationship between epic poetry and truth: the Muses can lie, and Odysseus is certainly capable of lying, in fact he is the liar *par excellence*.[42] It is not easy for Alcinous to assess the reliability of his account, and it is not entirely easy for us either: many readers have observed that some of the most extravagant stories in the *Odyssey* are told by Odysseus rather than the bard himself.[43] Similarly, Hesiod warns us that not all bards who invoke the Muses should be taken as reliable sources of information: his own account may be true, but other bards should not necessarily be trusted. While the relationship between poetry and truth is not simple and could be studied in greater detail, there is one main point which emerges from the present discussion and needs to be borne in mind when reading the Homeric poems. Knowledge and the ability to articulate that knowledge go hand in hand. Bards who can perform a catalogue are more reliable than ordinary travellers who cobble together any old story. In short, the form of epic to some extent guarantees its content. In the next section, we look at how exactly the formal features of early epic help to create a reliable account of the world.

Resonance

Anyone reading the Homeric poems for the first time will be astonished by how repetitive they are. Achilles is called 'swift-footed' again and again and again (even when he is sitting in his tent). Apollo is frequently 'the archer'. Whenever Homeric characters have a meal, 'they put their hands to the good things that lay ready before them'.[44] At daybreak 'young Dawn shows again with her rosy fingers': a modern reader might complain that, although this is a nice image the first time round, the effect wears off after we hear it some twenty times in the course of the poems. Catalogues, which, as we have seen, take pride of place in the Homeric poems as displays of the bard's skill, are repetitive by definition and are generally spurned by modern readers. For a long time, scholars have tried to make excuses for the repetitiveness of Homeric epic; and yet it is precisely in the highly formalised features of the poems that we find a key to their status as reliable accounts of the past.

In the early twentieth century, Milman Parry offered a sophisticated analysis of Homeric language which aimed to show that each set phrase, or formula, used in the poems served a well defined metrical function.[45] Each line of epic is made up of a sequence of six 'feet', each comprising of one long syllable (represented by a dash: '–') followed by two short syllables (represented by the symbol '∪∪'), which can be replaced by a single long one. Parry showed that if the bard wanted to say, for example, 'Achilles' he could choose between different expressions, each of which was designed to take up a different number of syllables in the line. Depending on how many syllables he needed to fill in order to reach the end of the line, he could either say 'Achilles' or 'noble Achilles' or 'swift-footed Achilles' or 'swift-footed noble Achilles':

Foot 1	Foot 2	Foot 3	Foot 4	Foot 5	Foot 6
—∪∪	—∪∪	—∪∪	—∪∪	*dios A-* —∪∪	*chilleus* — —
—∪∪	—∪∪	—∪∪	*— podas* ∪∪	*ôkus A-* —∪∪	*chilleus* — —
—∪∪	—∪∪	*— ∪ po-* ∪	*darkês* — —	*dios A-* —∪∪	*chilleus* — —

Parry emphasised the principle of economy: he argued that there was only one formula for each metrical combination: if the bard had two feet left, he would have to say 'noble Achilles': no other formulas of that length were available to him. Parry offered detailed analyses of many formulaic systems, showing how different formulas developed in different grammatical cases and covered varying numbers of syllables. According to Parry, these systems were designed to provide the bard with a quick and sure way of filling the line without having to take too long thinking about options. The idea was, quite simply, that during an early stage in the development of epic poetry, bards improvised their stories on the spot and therefore needed ready-made blocks of language in order not to get stuck during performance. They developed a set of traditional phrases, or formulas, which fitted into the hexameter line and were later carried over into our written texts.

If we accept Parry's analysis – and, no matter how critical we may be, he does have a point when he talks about formulaic economy – then we are confronted with a difficult question. We may know something about the function of formulas, but what is their meaning? How should we interpret them? If they are simply there to fill the line and are developed for 'metrical convenience', then we might conclude that their meaning is of secondary importance. Depending on the space to be filled, the bard might say 'Achilles' or 'noble Achilles' or 'swift-footed Achilles': we should consider all these expressions as equivalent and refuse to see traditional adjectives, or 'epithets', as significant in any way. Parry's work has in fact given rise to an approach of this kind: 'metrical convenience' has become a common explanation for words or phrases which do not seem to fit the context in which they are found.

There are, however, some very serious problems with this kind of approach. For example, one might challenge Parry's view of Homeric language by pointing out that there are other ways of helping a bard under the pressures of performance. We now know of many different traditions of oral poetry, none of them 'formulaic' in quite the same way as early Greek epic.[46] More importantly, perhaps, Parry's approach seems deficient because it focuses exclusively on composition rather than reception. It may be true that formulaic systems were an aid to composition, but how did they strike early audiences? It is to this question that we need to devote our attention.

To appreciate the dangers inherent in Parry's approach, one might consider a hypothetical parallel from music. Mozart's music is perfectly formulaic at the level of harmonic structure, that is to say, it can be reduced to a relatively limited set of repeated sequences.[47] If one day in the distant future – at a time when classical music was no longer performed – someone discovered the scores of some Mozart sonatas he or she would probably be struck by their repetitiveness. Perhaps, if that person had scholarly ambitions, (s)he might speculate that Mozart emerged from a long line of improvisation, and that he used musical formulas in order to stay afloat during his performances. This theory could be bolstered by statistics and presented in a way that might strike readers as sophisticated and intriguing. Yet, the result of all that labour would be a disastrous misunderstanding. What the hypothetical scholar is lacking, above all, is any awareness of what Mozart's music 'does', i.e. what it communicates to its audiences. The same can be said for much early work on Homeric language.

More recently, scholars have come to realise that Homeric language, far from providing mechanical tools for the improvising bard, is an exceptionally expressive medium. To use an idea introduced by John Foley, it functions 'like a language, only more so'.[48] Foley suggests that traditional phrases evoke a much larger context of traditional story-telling: for example, Achilles is 'swift-footed' because running is his defining activity. All the most important stories about him are connected with swiftness of foot: he chases Hector to his death, and he is in turn shot in his heel by Apollo. Sometimes, the description 'swift-footed' fits the context in which it is used, for example, when Achilles chases somebody it makes sense to draw attention to his speed. In other cases, there is a dissonance between the way he is described and what he happens to be doing at the time: for example, for much of the *Iliad* Achilles refuses to move, although he is repeatedly called swift-footed. In these instances, we should not, however, dismiss the adjective as meaningless: rather, it reminds us of Achilles' most characteristic activity, and emphasises that something has gone wrong. Achilles' immobility is particularly alarming in view of his traditional epithets. Let us consider some examples.

The *Catalogue of Ships*, as we have seen, makes a great claim to completeness. Yet, ironically, its most remarkable entry speaks of an absence, a missing leader. Achilles the swift-footed is not taking part in the war, but resting in his tent (*Iliad* 2.681-8):

> Now all those who dwelt about Pelasgian Argos,
> those who lived by Alos and Alope and Trachis,
> those who held Phthia and Hellas the land of fair women,
> who were called Myrmidons and Hellenes and Achaeans,
> of all these and their fifty ships the lord was Achilles.
> But these took no thought now for the grim clamour of battle
> since there was no one who could guide them into close order,
> since he, swift-footed noble Achilles, was lying where the ships were.

A conventional approach will make little sense of the adjective 'swift-footed' in line 688. Achilles is currently refusing to stand on his feet (*keito* = 'he was lying'), let alone use them. To a reader coming to Homer for the first time it may not be obvious what the epithet 'swift-footed' is doing here. Parry would have argued that its use is determined by the metrical sequence required in the line, not the meaning of the expression. However, more recent scholars appreciate the dissonance between the situation that is being described and the overall tradition of story-telling about Achilles. It may seem paradoxical at first but one of the reasons why the adjective 'swift-footed' makes such good sense in the present context is precisely that it is at odds with it, thus drawing our attention to a disjunction between what is expected of Achilles in traditional story-telling and the crisis that is being described.

Once Achilles resumes fighting, his exceptional swiftness explains how he can wreak such havoc among the Trojans (*Iliad* 19-21). However, it also becomes the object of more subtle reflection in a scene where Apollo tricks him into a pointless pursuit. Towards the end of *Iliad* book 21, the god takes the shape of Agenor in a bid to relieve the Trojan side. Trusting in the swiftness of his feet, Achilles tries in vain to catch up with the god. He is lured away from the defeated Trojans, who use the brief moment of respite to reach the security of the Trojan walls. Once he has accomplished his task, Apollo teasingly addresses the hero (*Iliad* 22.8-13):

> 'Why, son of Peleus, do you keep after me in the speed of your feet,
> being mortal while I am an immortal god? Even yet you have not
> seen that I am a god, but strain after me in your fury.
> Now hard fighting with the Trojans whom you stampeded means
>   nothing to you.
> They are crowded in the city, but you bent away here.
> You will never kill me. I am not one who is fated.'

Apollo's speech starts from a variation on Achilles' traditional epithet. The irony is palpable: thanks to his famous swiftness Achilles has been achieving the exact opposite of what he intended. What is more, the god uses the episode to reflect on the limitations of the human condition. Achilles challenges the boundaries between gods and humans by being exceptional in almost every respect. He is the 'best of the Achaeans', and one indicator of his superiority is precisely his almost super-human swiftness. Yet, in the present passage, Achilles' exceptional qualities lead him astray. He is prevented from conquering Troy and escaping death at this decisive moment in his career precisely because he alone can almost keep up with a god. Apollo's lesson for Achilles is to stop exerting himself and accept the limitations of his existence. In this context the formula 'swift-footed Achilles' recurs with cutting poignancy (*Iliad* 22.14):

> Deeply vexed swift-footed Achilles spoke to him

This line is entirely traditional. Speech-introducing verses in Homer tend to be highly standardised and this one is no exception.[49] However, the traditional use of language in this circumstance is jarring. Achilles remains trapped in the parameters of his existence. However much he rages he cannot escape his fate. Apollo's earlier remark that he is not fated to die at the hands of Achilles reminds us that Achilles is indeed fated to die at the hands of Apollo. When he answers the god, furious and frustrated, the inevitability of formulaic language corresponds closely to the inevitability of his death. The story has a certain pattern, it is as it should be, and Homeric language embodies that pattern, and reminds us of it.[50]

The figure of Achilles, then, and the plot of the *Iliad* more generally are made more meaningful by the astonishing ability of Homeric language to evoke character traits and whole narratives with economy and precision. Repeated words or phrases such as 'swift-footed Achilles' trigger a chain of associations which, we suggest, work like acoustic resonance. They suggest connections in the mind of audiences and readers that are crucial to the story, yet do not appear to be consciously manipulated at the moment of performance. Epithets are very rarely invented on the spot. And even if they are, their main function is not to capture the moment that is being described in a unique way, but to tie that moment to the larger tradition and thus endow it with resonance. Sometimes, traditional language and immediate context resonate in harmony, for example, when Achilles after his long absence from the battlefield finally gets up and runs. At other times there is an unsettling dissonance between the immediate situation and the language used to describe it: swift-footed Achilles lies in his tent. In either case, however, the traditional description of Achilles is not meaningless, a matter of 'metrical convenience': formulas do not develop randomly; rather, they encapsulate the most deep-seated truths, the essence of particular characters, actions and stories.

We have illustrated the concept of resonance by looking at the formula 'swift-footed Achilles', but there are of course many other ways in which traditional formulations create a sense of richness and meaning within the poems. When the bard describes the death of Hector in *Iliad* 22, for example, virtually all the traditional motifs used to describe death on the battlefield are conjured up to depict this last duel in the poem. As a result, Hector's death functions as a kind of culmination for all the previous mortal encounters we witnessed earlier in the poem.[51] When we are confronted with traditional descriptions of daybreak, or of feasting, bathing, killing, we are invited to compare the particular instance with a larger set of resonant episodes, each of them expressive of the unfolding order of the universe. Of course different readers or members of an audience will weave slightly different associations, depending on their own memory and knowledge of epic, but resonance works well for the inexperienced, as well as for the professional bard, or Homeric scholar.

For example, even the most superficial reader of the *Iliad* will know that warriors are often compared to lions, and will be able to appreciate how battle narratives shape the encounter between Odysseus and Nausicaa in *Odyssey* 6.127-47:

> So speaking, noble Odysseus came from under his thicket,
> and from the dense foliage with his heavy hand he broke off
> a leafy branch to cover his body and hide the male parts,
> and went trusting in his strength, like some hill-kept lion,
> who advances, though he is rained on and blown by the wind, and both eyes
> kindle; he goes out after cattle or sheep, or it may be
> deer in the wilderness, and his belly is urgent upon him
> to get inside of a close steading and go for the sheepflocks.
> So Odysseus was ready to face young girls with well-ordered
> hair, naked though he was, for the need was on him; and yet
> he appeared terrifying to them, all crusted with dry spray,
> and they scattered one way and another down the jutting beaches.
> Only the daughter of Alcinous stood fast, for Athene
> put courage into her heart, and took the fear from her body,
> and she stood her ground and faced him, and now Odysseus debated
> whether to supplicate the well-favoured girl by clasping
> her knees, or stand off where he was and in words of blandishment
> ask if she should show him the city, and lend him clothing.
> Then in the division of his heart this way seemed best to him,
> to stand well off and supplicate in words of blandishment,
> for fear that, if he clasped her knees, the girl might be angry.

In many ways, the situation on the shore of Scherie falls outside the parameters of what is normal in Homeric epic and the world it describes. There is no obvious place in the structure of things for the encounter between a naked hero and a marriageable young girl. Accordingly, there is no type scene that could unproblematically capture the situation. What we find, instead, is an adaptation of familiar patterns for the purpose of describing an unconventional scene in all its danger and absurdity. The encounter between Nausicaa and Odysseus is cast in the form of a typical battle scene: Odysseus approaches like a lion, 'trusting in his strength', a typical image of the Iliadic warrior. He is 'ready to face the girls', just as his counterpart Nausicaa is ready to 'face' him, thanks to the 'courage' inspired by Athena. These elements of a traditional battle scene capture well some aspects of the situation: like an Iliadic warrior, Odysseus is in mortal danger; he *must* turn the encounter to his advantage or else perish miserably on a foreign shore. Yet, there are other ways in which the traditional register is jarring, even comical: Odysseus, the great warrior, is 'ready to face the girls'!

2. The Poems

It goes without saying that it is not in Odysseus' interests to kill Nausicaa; on the contrary, he must persuade her that she has nothing to fear: this is hard to do when you look like a ravenous lion. The dramatic flight of her maids raises the spectacle of Odysseus' failure and leads the hero to consider supplication as a last resort. In Homer, the defeated warrior typically supplicates his opponent in a desperate (and usually unsuccessful) bid to escape death.[52] The ironies of supplication in this different context are obvious: Odysseus thinks about it because he appears too strong, not because he is about to be killed. Yet, in a less direct sense, his life does depend on Nausicaa's good will. The problem, for him, is that supplication may not be appropriate in the circumstances: he realises, for example, that the girl may not like it if he touches her knees. In the end, Odysseus decides to adapt the traditional supplication scene: he speaks as a suppliant, but talks to her from a distance.

There could be no more telling reminder that the shape of words in Homeric epic corresponds directly to a shape of things. It should be emphasised that Odysseus, and with him the narrator, do not simply depart from the patterns of epic story-telling. This would be just as impossible as it would be to abandon all understanding of how the world works. Instead, resonant patterns combine in a new way to help us understand and situate a specific scene in the larger scheme of things. The process is not just illuminating but enjoyable too. As well as departing from the traditional grammar of the type scene, the encounter between the hero and the girl thus also affirms the adaptability and effectiveness of that grammar.

The resonance of Homer, then, lies in a precise understanding of how things are and, simultaneously, in the ability to capture that essence in hexameter lines. Form and content go together, the Muse helps with knowledge and articulation. It follows that bards are not free to make up their story as they please by changing, say, the character of their heroes. Achilles is swift-footed, even when he is angry with Agamemnon and refuses to move. Odysseus is not 'swift-footed', even when he wins the footrace in *Iliad* 23. Sometimes, a particular story is at odds with the unfolding order of the universe. Such disjunctions can be indicative of larger historical shifts: in an Iliadic world, Odysseus would not find himself naked on a shore, begging an unmarried princess for his life. Yet, that is precisely what he has to reckon with in the aftermath of the Trojan War. Odysseus has become a displaced hero, and the language and imagery used to describe him are as displaced as he is.

We started by asking what the meaning of traditional formulas and larger type scenes might be. Parry taught us that these features helped the bard in composition, but we wanted to know what they did for their audiences. The poet Anne Carson well describes the overall effect of Homeric language on audiences and readers. She writes:

> Of course there are several different ways to be. In the world of the Homeric epic, for example, being is stable and particularity is set fast in tradition. When Homer mentions blood, blood is *black*. When women appear, women are *neat-ankled* or *glancing*. Poseidon always has *the blue eyebrows of Poseidon*. Gods' laughter is *unquenchable*. Human knees are *quick*. The sea is *unwearying*. Death is *bad*. Cowards' livers are *white*. Homer's epithets are a fixed diction with which Homer fastens every substance in the world to its aptest attribute and holds them in place for epic consumption.[53]

This 'holding in place' is crucial for our understanding of epic. Alcinous is inclined to trust Odysseus because he speaks like a bard, his words 'have shape', he tells the audience how things are, and they can trust his account because it resonates with what bards say and what we know about the universe. The effect of Homeric epic on its early audiences must have been similar: they judged the performance of a particular bard or travelling rhapsode on its resonance within the wider tradition.

There is one further point to add to this overall picture as it is conveyed, among others, by Anne Carson. The Homeric world is not fixed and unbending; it is subject to change through time. Homeric formulas and type scenes, as well as all other traditional aspects of epic which we have not discussed in detail, are perfectly shaped to capture the development of the cosmos, from its origins to the present day. In fact, as we hope to show in the next section, the resonance of epic helps to situate a particular story or episode within the wider history of the cosmos.

Resonance and the history of the cosmos

Paolo Vivante once shrewdly observed that, when discussing traditional features of Homeric epic, scholars love to talk about exceptions, but spend very little time discussing the rule.[54] To an extent, we have been guilty of that tendency: in the last section, we discussed at some length instances in which traditional formulas and type scenes are at odds with the situation that is being described. We have suggested that when there is a tension between traditional formulations ('swift-footed Achilles', 'like a mountain lion …') and immediate narrative context, that tension points to a problem in the story. Achilles should not be lying in his tent; Odysseus has been driven off course in more than one sense when he meets Nausicaa. In order to illustrate the power of epic resonance we have, in short, focused on remarkable cases of dissonance between the expectations embedded in traditional epic language and the immediate narrative context. In order to counterbalance this taste for exceptions, we now look at an entirely standard aspect of early epic: the use of patronymics.

We argued at the beginning of this chapter that the overall history of the cosmos is conceived as a giant family tree beginning with Earth and Heaven, growing into the family of the Olympians, the heroes, and finally branching out into the present. One standard way of describing Zeus is 'father of gods and men':[55] this description makes sense, in that it emphasises the genealogical continuities between gods and men. Women, as we shall see, are more difficult to place: Pandora, the first woman, has no divine or human parents, she is fashioned by the gods out of earth and water.[56] With her, the continuity between gods and mortals is broken; but, as far as men are concerned, there is an unbroken connection, through genealogy, all the way back to the beginnings of cosmic history. One way in which epic reminds us of this overall genealogical structure is by the use of patronymics, adjectives which give us the name of a character's father. Zeus, for example, is *Kroniôn* or *Kronidês*, 'the son of Cronus'.[57] In the *Iliad* and the *Odyssey*, there is no explicit reference to the way in which Zeus came to replace his father as the ruler of all the gods; yet the epithet reminds us of the origins of Zeus' rule. Implied in the recurrent formula is a view of the universe not as a static system but as subject to change through time: first came Cronus, then his son Zeus. More generally, the Olympians are called *Ouraniônes* and *Ouranidae*, 'children of Heaven', reminding us that Heaven ultimately fathered them.[58] Embedded in these epithets is the early history of the gods, as it is told, for example, in Hesiod's *Theogony*: there is no need to recount that history in detail, it is part of the very language of epic.

Human beings are also standardly described by their patronymics: Achilles is 'the son of Peleus', Agamemnon and Menelaus are 'the sons of Atreus', Diomedes is 'the son of Tydeus', Odysseus 'the son of Laertes'. These phrases may well strike the modern reader as odd: surely, we do not need to be told countless times that Achilles is the son of Peleus, one reference might suffice. Christopher Logue, in his adaptation of the *Iliad*, standardly leaves epithets out.[59] There are in fact cases in which patronymics are particularly significant, and we shall turn to some examples shortly; but before we consider those special cases, we might make a more general point. Patronymics constantly remind us of the genealogical structure that underlies the epic world.

They assign to each person or god their place in the larger scheme of things and help to frame the narrative by lending it a temporal dimension. Diomedes, for example, is 'the son of Tydeus', and Tydeus fought in the Theban War, an important precedent for the Trojan conflict.

Sometimes, the temporal coordinates embedded in patronymics are explored in depth. For example, Tydeus was known for his excessive behaviour especially towards the gods, whereas his son Diomedes, in the *Iliad*, learns to respect the boundaries between gods and men.[60] The proper relationship between gods and men is an important theme in the *Iliad*, setting the action at a specific point in the history of the universe.[61] For Diomedes, the example of his father is problematic. Many characters expound on his patronymic and urge 'the son of Tydeus' to behave as Tydeus would.[62] At some point, Diomedes bluntly states that he 'does not remember his father' (*Iliad* 6.222), a desperate measure to break away from the problematic paradigm set by his father. The attempt, however, is immediately undermined in line 235 where he is again called *Tydeidês*, 'the son of Tydeus'. His traditional patronymic defines him in relation to his father, whether he likes it or not; just as the *Iliad* defines itself against the Theban saga. Both occupy a place in the order of things which cannot simply be changed or ignored.

Similar tensions are apparent in the epithet 'son of Peleus'. At the beginning of the *Iliad*, Achilles thinks of himself very much as his mother's son. It is Thetis who comes to his aid in book 1, and who initiates the plan of honouring him.[63] As an immortal goddess, she can appreciate the full extent of Achilles' grievance. Having given birth to a son who, unlike her, is *ôkymoros*, 'fated to die soon', she feels responsible for making amends. Peleus has a very different perspective: he is destined to age and die and would like the company and comfort of his own son as he grows old. Only towards the end of the poem does Achilles recognise his responsibilities as the mortal 'son of Peleus'.[64] The recurrent patronymics (Achilles is called 'the son of Peleus' already in the first line of the poem), remind us that Achilles is not the son of Thetis only: his mortal legacy is of crucial importance for the development of his character in the course of the *Iliad*.

We should say straight away that not all traditional adjectives evoke a sense of history. Whereas patronymics draw attention to the origins of individual characters and place them within an evolving family tree, other adjectives speak of stability through time.[65] For example, night is 'black' ever since the beginning of the world and mountains are 'great'.[66] For the ancient Greeks, as for modern readers, some aspects of the universe remain relatively stable,

whereas others are subject to development. Our point is that the resonant language of epic captures both aspects – the timeless and the
historical – with equal precision.

If we look at larger traditional patterns, such as typical scenes, we
see that they too help to place a particular poem or episode within the
wider history of the cosmos.[67] To be sure, there are some activities,
and traditional ways of describing those activities, which do not
change significantly through time: giving birth, for example, is
described in much the same language from the beginning of time, in
the *Theogony*, through to the world as it is now. The *Theogony*
describes some aberrant births, but generation, and the language of
generation, is largely stable throughout the development of the
cosmos. Other aspects of the world, however, are subject to change.
Feasting, for example, is typical of the age of the heroes. Any reader
of the *Iliad* will be struck by the lavish communal meals consumed by
gods and heroes. In fact, ancient audiences were fascinated by the diet
of the heroes: they seemed to nourish themselves exclusively with
meat.[68] Primitive gods such as Heaven and Earth in the *Theogony*
show little sign of a developed social life, let alone the kind of elaborate feasting familiar from the divine assemblies of the *Iliad*. The
preconditions for communal meals are gradually established with the
emergence of Olympus and the long drawn-out process, narrated in
the *Homeric Hymns*, whereby the house of Zeus gradually fills with its
Olympian guests: each new god who arrives on Olympus is given his
or her seat at the table. Progress in the divine sphere is reflected by
progress at the human level, where communal feasting becomes
equally important.

The heroic-age feast, then, together with the type scene that
describes it, marks a specific moment in the overall history of the
cosmos. Already in the *Odyssey*, divine and human feasts are far less
prominent than in the *Iliad*. The Phaeacians live in a rather old-
fashioned world of their own, while the suitors who constantly feast in
Odysseus' palace seem oblivious of the fact that they are destroying
someone else's livelihood.[69] Finally, in the impoverished world of the
Works and Days, mortals must eke out their living by working the land.
Meat is no longer abundant. Time needs to be spent not at dinners but
in the fields, tilling the soil.

We could quote many other typical activities, expressed in traditional
type scenes, which come in and out of fashion in the course of cosmic
history. Odysseus must systematically unlearn the Iliadic practice of
gloating over a defeated foe: it is not appropriate in the post-war world
through which he travels. Pre-Olympian gods do not yet use the kinds

of weapons and clothes appropriate for elaborate dressing or arming scenes: such items become fashionable after Zeus' accession to power. Seafaring, as a method of transport associated with the heroic age is described in the *Iliad*, where it takes the form of an elaborate and smoothly-running type scene.[70] In the *Odyssey* we learn about the difficulties of sea journeys: storms and the concomitant problems of navigation break up the formulaic pattern of seafaring scenes such as the one described in *Iliad* 1.[71] In Hesiod's *Works and Days*, the problems associated with sailing have become almost insurmountable and the heroic-age type scene has been transformed into a complicated bundle of warnings and precepts.[72]

Homeric type scenes, like traditional epithets, do not describe a static world: they reflect the unfolding history of the universe. As the cosmos evolves, so do the activities in which gods and humans typically engage. Traditional scenes and epithets function as a reminder of the overall shape of the universe, not only as a timeless structure but also as a dynamic process. In fact, one of their main functions seems to be that of keeping that chronological dimension fresh in our minds, so that we may view the Homeric poems *in medias res*, as part of a larger history of the cosmos.

Conclusion

Throughout this chapter we have suggested that the Homeric poems can be read as a form of history. They outline what happened in the past and show a keen awareness of what took place before and after the events told within the main narrative. The traditional words and formulations used across the epic tradition serve to place a particular story within a wider context. In fact, they can be seen as a kind of historical method: they capture the essence of the cosmos as it develops through time. They are, in a sense, the most appropriate way to talk about the history of the cosmos, and for this reason they strike audiences as true. If we return, one last time, to Alcinous' words in *Odyssey* 11, we see that he is inclined to trust Odysseus' account because his words have the right 'shape', *morphê*. This shape, we have argued, reflects a precise understanding of the cosmos and its history. Achilles is swift-footed, Zeus is the son of Cronus, banqueting is what heroes and gods do at a particular stage in the history of the world. These insights are shared across poems and cannot be randomly changed or manipulated by individual bards: this is how things are and this is how bards sing them. If a bard started confusing things by calling Odysseus swift-footed, we would be inclined to dismiss him as unreliable. Alcinous would complain that his words have no shape, that they are lies, and that we can learn nothing from them.

We have used the term resonance in order to describe the connection between traditional words and phrases and the overall shape of the cosmos. The traditional aspects of Homeric epic, the stock epithets, repetitive phrases, standardised type scenes do not usually undergo conscious manipulation at the time of composition or performance, and yet they are neither fortuitous nor irrelevant to the meaning of the poetry. They were developed in order to capture precisely the history of the cosmos and human society. To this day, formulaic language is used when precision matters: in the court room, at church services.[73] In these contexts, formulas help to link the individual situation to a larger context: mass on a particular Sunday is linked with proper Christian worship through time, an individual legal case with the overall legal system within which it is judged. The formulas of ancient epic had a similar function: they linked a particular story to an overall understanding of the cosmos and its development through time.

It may seem that we are not making much allowance for the exceptional contribution of individual bards. After all, there can be exceptional legal cases, not to mention musical performances or political speeches, all of which may contain a high proportion of formulaic material. The point is that these happen within a framework, and that their framework needs to be understood as culturally meaningful. There is an implication, in some Homeric scholarship, that the language of epic arises 'naturally' from the constraints of oral performance.[74] In its most extreme version this view has long since been refuted, yet it lingers in the work of scholars who seek to establish universal parameters of oral poetry on the basis of an analysis of the Homeric texts. By contrast, we suggest that Homeric language is best understood as a specialised medium that expresses perfectly the *contents* of Greek epic poetry.[75] It is no coincidence that early audiences talked about Homer and Hesiod as authorities who could describe to the Greeks the precise character of the gods, and give an account of early human history. Archaic audiences were not interested in the mechanics of oral composition, they wanted to know how their world had come into being and how it 'worked'. In keeping with their focus, in the second part of the book we examine some resonant patterns in the Homeric poems. We begin by looking at the overall world depicted in the poems: nature, fate and the gods, then move on to observe how human society was organised within that world, and finally interpret the stories of the two main characters in the *Iliad* and the *Odyssey*, Achilles and Odysseus, within the wider framework outlined in the previous chapters.

Part II

Resonant Patterns

We have seen in the first part of this book that there is a tendency to read the Homeric poems in relation to later literature: it is a platitude of Homeric scholarship that the *Iliad* is 'the first Greek tragedy', and that the *Odyssey* is a precursor to the modern novel. The problem with this kind of reading is that it tends to decontextualise the poems or, rather, to discuss them in the context of later developments which cannot have been of any concern to early bards and audiences. In the first two chapters, we have tried to outline some ways in which one can resist the temptation to read the poems teleologically; that is to say, we refused to start from a perspective which sees them as the first works of European literature, the first tragedies, the first novels, the first works of genius. Focusing on ways in which early audiences conceptualised Homer, and on how the poems resonated within a wider epic tradition, helped us to develop an approach to Homeric epic which makes sense of it in an early Greek context, rather than in relation to later literature.

In the second half of this book, we offer an interpretation of some major aspects of the Homeric poems: the gods, fate, human society, life in the city, the stories of the protagonists of the *Iliad* and the *Odyssey*. In approaching these themes, we aim to identify some resonant patterns which shape Homeric epic: the fate of individual characters, it will emerge, resonates with the overall social and theological framework outlined in the poems, as well as with the wider epic tradition to which the poems belong. In order to identify and discuss these patterns, we believe it is useful to move from the general to the particular: in this way, the significance of a specific episode or character can be explored within a wider framework.

We begin by asking what kind of world is depicted in the Homeric poems, what kind of divine and social forces help to shape it, and then ask how the stories of individual characters are played out against this wider setting. Even a superficial reader of the *Iliad* will quickly be aware that Achilles is no ordinary mortal and that, in some important ways, he tests the limits of what it means to be human. Similarly, Odysseus' home-coming is anything but ordinary: many have seen in the return of Odysseus a deliberate and painful journey from the extra-ordinary and magical (the cave of a goddess, the promise of eternal youth) to the mundanely human (a wife and child, the prospect of old age). In order to approach the stories of these exceptional characters, we begin by asking in what kind of world they live, and what kind of assumptions and limits their stories are designed to test. Just as the *Iliad* and the *Odyssey* can be read as exceptional poems which rely on, and test the resources of, a wider epic tradition, so the stories of their main characters can be said to explore the overall theological and social framework outlined, or taken for granted, in the poems.

3

Gods, Animals and Fate

The impact of the gods on the stories told in the *Iliad* and the *Odyssey* is clear from the beginning. In the *Iliad*, after the invocation to the Muse (herself a goddess) the poet asks 'which god' caused the quarrel between Achilles and Agamemnon – a quarrel whose consequences span the rest of the poem. At the beginning of the *Odyssey*, we are told that the gods took Poseidon's momentary absence from Olympus as an opportunity to send Odysseus back home. These opening references serve to place the particular themes explored in the poems – 'the wrath of Achilles', 'the man of many turns' – within a wider framework shaped by the will and power of the gods. It thus seems that the gods provide a good starting point for exploring the overall setting of the Homeric poems, the world within which the story of individual characters unfolds.

Perhaps because the gods are so prominent, and their intervention dramatically shapes the poems, readers have often asked whether there are limits to their power. In order to explore this question, we discuss two aspects of the Homeric world which do not seem, at first sight, to be subject to the will of the gods: fate and nature. This chapter, then, aims to provide an overall introduction to the world of the *Iliad* and the *Odyssey* by investigating the connections between the gods, nature, fate, and the poet's narrative.

The 'frivolity' of the gods

The Homeric gods have shocked and inspired readers from antiquity to today. They are dazzling and unforgettable, but also deeply problematic. Already in the sixth century BC Xenophanes complained that the gods of early Greek epic are immoral: as we have seen, he claimed that 'Homer and Hesiod ascribe to the gods every action that causes shame and reproach among human beings: theft, adultery, and mutual deception.'[1] Some ancient readers interpreted the gods as allegories for impersonal powers, such as love or war, in an attempt to solve the problem of their immorality.[2] This tendency can also be traced in some modern approaches to the Homeric gods: some scholars, for example, identify Athena's intervention in *Iliad* 1 with Achilles' own better judgement.[3] But this kind of interpretation, though perhaps tempting in some instances, is not convincing as an overall strategy for dealing with the Homeric gods: they are described in too much detail to be easily reduced to impersonal cosmic, or psychological, forces.

The problem of the gods' behaviour thus remains with us. Passages where they appear to be more light-hearted or, we might say, 'frivolous' than human beings tend to cause the worst difficulties. The first book of the *Iliad*, for example, closes with the image of Hephaestus bustling about the house of Zeus offering nectar to the other gods and making them laugh – this while on earth the anger of Achilles is destined to cause 'countless sorrows' to the Achaeans.[4] In *Odyssey* 8, Aphrodite is caught cheating on her husband Hephaestus: when the gods see her in bed with her lover Ares, they burst out laughing.[5] Needless to say, adultery in the human realm is no laughing matter: the Trojan War is caused by an unfaithful wife, Agamemnon returns home only to be killed by his wife and her lover, the suitors on Ithaca are a serious threat to Odysseus' return and are treated accordingly. The standard way in which modern readers respond to these scenes is to say that the behaviour of the gods highlights, by contrast, that of human beings. Seth Schein succinctly summarises this approach: 'in the *Iliad* the actions and nature of the gods emphasize by contrast the seriousness of what human beings do and suffer.'[6] In fact, the idea that the gods provide a contrast to the stature and dignity of mortals can be traced a long way back into antiquity. 'Longinus', in one of the most famous ancient pieces of literary criticism, states that 'as far as possible Homer made the humans in the Trojan War gods and the gods humans'.[7]

For many centuries, the Greek gods remained symbols of easy-going pleasure. One only has to think of the way they were painted in the Renaissance to feel vindicated in interpreting them as joyful and carefree counterparts to the tragedy of human life.[8] Karl Reinhardt famously wrote of the 'sublime frivolity' of the Homeric gods:[9] his phrase applies equally well to the divinities painted in the Italian Reinassance. And this, we suggest, is precisely the problem: interpretations which present the Homeric gods as frivolous counterparts to mortals see them in the light of their later reception, with little regard for early audiences.

Unlike later painters and writers, early Greek audiences did not contrast the Homeric gods with Judaeo-Christian concepts of the divine. They worshipped the very gods that were described in the Homeric poems: they looked to Apollo for advice about what to do, prayed to Artemis before childbirth, thanked Hephaestus for his crafts.[10] For them, the Homeric gods could not be viewed as literary devices created in order to highlight the suffering and dignity of mortals, they had to be understood within the context of their own religion. It would be very interesting to know how an early critic of the Homeric gods such as Xenophanes went about doing this, but unfortunately most of his poems are lost to us, and it is very difficult to reconstruct his thought. All one can say about him with any certainty is that he was a very unusual thinker, especially when it came to religion, and that his views cannot be seen as representative of early Greek responses to Homer.[11]

Another ancient Greek thinker, Herodotus, may prove to be more helpful in our attempt to place the Homeric gods within an early Greek context. As we have seen already, Herodotus identifies Homer and Hesiod as the founding fathers of Greek religion: 'It is they who established the theogony for the Greeks. They gave epithets to the gods, defined their due honours and spheres of expertise and described their appearance.'[12]

Herodotus' short statement proves to be an excellent starting point for our investigation. In the first place it shows that Homer's depiction of the gods was not considered subversive or even marginal to Greek religion: on the contrary, it was an important aspect of it, its foundation no less. Modern scholars echo Herodotus' emphasis on Homer and Hesiod when they discuss the distinctive nature of Greek religion. Walter Burkert, for example, writes: 'The authority to whom the Greeks appealed' in order to create order among their different religious traditions 'was the poetry of Hesiod and, above all, of Homer. The spiritual unity of the Greeks was founded and upheld by poetry.'[13] It follows that, whatever we make of the Homeric gods, we cannot dismiss them as literary fictions entirely divorced from the religious life of their audiences. If, moreover, we bear in mind that festivals in honour of the gods, such as the Panathenaea, were an important context for the performance of Homeric epic, this point becomes all the more obvious. Whatever we make of the gods' behaviour in the Homeric poems, they cannot be seen as straightforward comic relief: they have to be approached within a wider cultural context which is shaped, in part at least, by religion.

Herodotus, in fact, gives us an important clue concerning the role of the Homeric gods when he mentions Hesiod together with Homer as the founder of Greek religion. For Herodotus, the two poets, taken together, define the images, epithets, and spheres of expertise of the gods. Once again, many historians of religion echo his views. Walter Otto, for example, notes that the Homeric gods are essentially the same as those depicted in Hesiod, and in fact in earlier sources such as the Linear B tablets. He concludes that the portrayal of the Homeric gods relies on a wider tradition, and that each god 'possessed clearly defined lineaments, which were well known to all hearers.'[14] This is true, and yet there are some important differences in the way Homeric and Hesiodic gods are portrayed: most strikingly, perhaps, the gods in the *Theogony* appear to be in no way as light-hearted as they are in the Homeric poems.

Two main questions arise from this: in the first place, we may want to account for any differences in the way the gods are portrayed in Homeric as opposed to Hesiodic epic. Secondly, we may ask why Herodotus chooses to disregard these differences and present the two poets as offering, together, a coherent picture of the gods.

Both these questions can be answered if we bear in mind that the Greek gods have a history: they are born at a particular point in time, they grow up and seek to establish their authority among the other gods. Eventually, they become the recipients of human worship according to their particular sphere of influence and place in the divine hierarchy. Often, the age at which the gods 'freeze' reflects their position in the family tree: those who belong to an earlier generation, e.g. Zeus, Poseidon, Demeter, are depicted as older than those who were born in the next generation: Apollo is forever a young god, Artemis is permanently at the threshold of puberty, Athena remains forever, and above all, a daughter.[15] We have seen in Chapter 2 that the history of the gods, from the time in which there was only Void (*Theogony* 116) to the world as it is now (*Works and Days*), spans early Greek epic. The *Theogony* tells how the gods were born and how Zeus managed to establish his supremacy; many *Homeric Hymns* describe how a particular god was born and his/her powers defined in relation to those of the other gods; the *Catalogue of Women* recounts how the gods had sex with mortal women and gave rise to the heroes; the *Iliad* and the *Odyssey* explore the stories of the heroes but make it clear that the time in which gods and mortals mingle freely is coming to an end. By the time we reach the age depicted in the *Works and Days*, the gods are very distant from daily life among mortals. The way in which the gods are portrayed in each of these poems depends in no small measure on the particular stage of divine history the poem in question portrays.

In the *Theogony*, the gods compete with one another for supremacy. The insubordination of a child is no laughing matter: it can lead to the overthrowing of the father and to a revolution of power in the divine hierarchy. Similarly, disagreements between husband and wife have serious consequences: Heaven is castrated and deposed as a result of his wife's 'cunning plan';[16] Cronus loses his power because his mother, wife and children are united against him;[17] Zeus has to swallow his own wife Metis in order to secure his rule for ever; moreover, he allows only his daughter to be born: an announced son never sees the light of day.[18] After Zeus has secured for himself the rule of Olympus, the *Theogony* quickly mentions the birth of other gods, for example, Apollo, Artemis and Hermes,[19] but does not linger on those births: the poem is above all concerned with the establishment of the rule of Zeus. Some *Homeric Hymns* explore how the birth of a particular god affects the balance of power on Olympus,[20] but it is above all the Olympian scenes in the *Iliad* that tell us how the gods relate to one another under the rule of Zeus.

As we shall see, the 'sublime frivolity' of the Homeric gods is a direct result of the rule of Zeus. The first Olympian scene in the *Iliad*, which is often quoted as the ultimate example of divine frivolity, in fact makes this quite clear. When Hera expresses her anger at Zeus, Hephaestus begs her not to do so, and suggests that no god could protect her if she did. He reminds her of an earlier occasion on which he tried to take her side and, as a result, almost lost his life (1.586-600):

'Have patience, my mother, and endure it, though you be saddened,
for fear that, dear as you are, I see you before my own eyes
struck down, and then sorry though I be I shall not be able
to do anything. It is too hard to fight against the Olympian.
There was a time once before when I was minded to help you
and he caught me by the foot and threw me from the magic threshold,
and all day long I dropped helpless, and about sunset
I landed in Lemnos, and there was not much life left in me.
After that fall it was the Sintian men who took care of me.'
He spoke, and the goddess of the white arms Hera smiled at him,
and smiling she accepted the goblet out of her son's hand.
Thereafter beginning from the left he poured drinks for the other
gods, dipping up from the mixing bowl the sweet nectar.
But among the blessed immortals uncontrollable laughter
went up as they saw Hephaestus bustling about the palace.[21]

It may seem strange that Hera responds to Hephaestus' unsettling speech with a smile, and yet she does not have much of a choice. It is clear that Zeus is the strongest god and that she could not successfully oppose him, even with the help of the other gods: Hephaestus has already pointed out to her that Zeus could hurl all the gods from their places, if he so wished. The alternative she faces, therefore, is simple: either a humiliating defeat or a banquet in which she is an honoured guest. No wonder that she, and the other gods, invariably choose the latter.

We have already seen that the banquets of the heroic age are splendid affairs, and this is particularly so on Olympus. However, that does not mean that they are bereft of any social function. Agamemnon in *Iliad* 4 rouses Idomeneus to fight by reminding him that he is honoured at the banquet. Conversely, he berates Menestheus and Odysseus for being the first in the banquet but the last in battle.[22] In book 12, Sarpedon reminds Glaucus that they enjoy a place of honour in the banquet, and should therefore fight in the first line of battle.[23] Drinking and dining is not only a way of indulging oneself; it provides a context in which the Achaean leaders negotiate their status and forge alliances. Divine banquets serve a similar purpose: it would be a mistake to see the feasting of the Homeric gods as 'mere entertainment'. As the *Homeric Hymns* make clear, to become an Olympian god is to claim one's seat in the house of Zeus. Although the tone may seem frivolous, the underlying principle is not: the distribution of divine honours, which forms the backbone of cosmogony, is reflected in the proper distribution of food and wine at the banquet.

There is, then, an important connection between the feasting scenes of the *Iliad* and the violence of earlier times. However, it is of course true that the situation of the gods has changed dramatically since the time when each of them tried to take their share by force. The foot of Hephaestus is the perfect symbol for the shift from conflict to mirth: the passage we just quoted implies that he is lame because he was hurled from Olympus 'by the foot'. Yet by now his lameness has become the source of 'uncontrollable laughter' among the Olympians.

In order to understand the Homeric portrayal of the gods, it is important to be sensitive to their overall history as it is outlined in early Greek epic. From the perspective of the *Iliad*, open challenges to the power of Zeus are a thing of the past. By now, it is clear to all the gods that they cannot successfully oppose him or, more precisely, that they can only lose from an open confrontation: their decision to smile, drink and be merry stems directly from that realisation. In place of violent confrontations, we see incessant feasting. The Olympian feast has become the prime context in which the order of the universe under Zeus can be celebrated and enacted. The gods as the guests of Zeus owe their status and position in the world to his continuing good will. Not everyone finds this easy to accept. Apart from Hera, there is another god who deeply resents the power of Zeus: Poseidon. In book 15, he claims that the world was divided equally between three brothers: the sky to Zeus, the underworld to Hades, and the sea to Poseidon himself.

Zeus, therefore, should not boss him around, as he does with his own children on Olympus.[24] This challenge to Zeus is perhaps the most serious in the whole of the *Iliad*; and yet, in this case too, it is resolved without any actual, physical, confrontation. Iris asks Poseidon whether he really wants her to deliver this 'unyielding and strong' message and reminds him that respect is due to an eldest brother. In response, Poseidon backs down.

At this point, Zeus smugly comments that this was best for all involved, including Poseidon himself. He points out that Cronus and 'the other gods who are with him under the earth' know what it means to come into conflict with Zeus.[25] The *Theogony*, of course, tells precisely how Zeus established his rule by overthrowing Cronus, and depicts the defeated gods as being held under the earth.[26] The Hesiodic poem also makes it clear that, although Zeus is, to begin with, the youngest son, he becomes the eldest because his siblings are swallowed by Cronus and need 'to be born again'.[27] In order to understand the import of the exchange between Zeus and Poseidon in book 15 of the *Iliad* it is necessary to bear in mind its wider theogonic resonance: the larger context explains, among other things, why Zeus can be considered the eldest brother. The overall history of the gods is in fact important in order to understand all divine interactions in the *Iliad*. Not every reference to the past is as close to the *Theogony* as the one we have just discussed: scholars have often emphasised contradictions and inconsistencies between the two poems.[28] Yet, it is significant that in the *Iliad* all episodes of violence among gods, except for one to which we shall return, belong to the past. In the overall context of early Greek epic, this is easy to understand: by the time in which the *Iliad* is set, the pantheon has reached a stable hierarchy under the rule of Zeus and the gods know that they can only lose from a confrontation with him.

An awareness of the overall history of the gods can also help to make sense of another aspect of their portrayal in the *Iliad*: in this poem, the gods often remark that it is not worth fighting over mortals. For example, in order to persuade Hera to make up with Zeus, Hephaestus not only reminds her about an earlier crisis, but also points out that the gods should not give up a good feast for the sake of mere mortals (1.573-81):

'This will be a disastrous matter and not endurable
if you two are to quarrel thus for the sake of mortals
and bring brawling among the gods. There will be no pleasure
in the stately feast at all, since vile things will be uppermost.
And I entreat my mother, though she herself understands it,
to be ingratiating toward our father Zeus, that no longer

our father may scold her and break up the quiet of our feasting.
For if the Olympian who handles the lightning should be minded
to hurl us out of our places, he is far too strong for any.'

Hephaestus' consideration that the gods should not fight over mortals
becomes important at a specific point in the history of the cosmos. By
the time depicted in the *Iliad* and the *Odyssey*, divine relations have
reached a permanent if carefully calibrated balance: Zeus is in power,
and each god is granted his or her place in relation to the other gods. As
a result, there is little reason for disagreement among them: 'their
honours and spheres of expertise', to use Herodotus' phrase, have been
established. The main source of conflict is what happens to human
beings on earth, and especially what happens to the mortal sons of gods.

In terms of the overall logic of Homeric and Hesiodic epic heroes
come into existence precisely so as to ensure the permanent stability of
the Olympian world order under Zeus: mortals come and go, while Zeus
and the other gods remain.[29] This, however, implies a learning process
on the part of gods as well as humans: several episodes show that the
gods must learn to abandon mortals – all mortals, even their favourite
ones – to their fate.

In *Iliad* 1, the quarrel between Zeus and Hera is caused by Thetis'
request that Achilles, her son, be granted special honour.[30] Likewise,
most other divine conflicts in the poems are caused by the gods' involvement in human affairs. This, of course, was not the case earlier in their
history: in the battles of the *Theogony*, human beings played no role. In
book 14, Hera sets out to seduce Zeus, so that Poseidon may help the
Achaeans undisturbed.[31] When Zeus wakes up, he realises that the
Trojans are losing and feels great pity for Hector. This feeling prompts
him to threaten Hera and demand her obedience. He reminds her of an
earlier occasion in which he hung her from a golden chain between
heaven and earth because she was persecuting his son Heracles. At that
time, he adds, all the other gods and goddesses felt great pity for her but
could not help her.[32] On the strength of this warning, Zeus goes on to
ask her to act as his messenger and make sure all the gods comply with
his wishes. She does so, once again, by laughing off her embarrassment,
although the narrator makes sure we realise her laughter is the result
of coercion (15.101-12):

> ... Hera laughed
> with her lips, but above the dark brows her forehead
> was not at peace. She spoke before them all in vexation:
> 'Fools, we who try to work against Zeus, thoughtlessly.

> Still we are thinking in our anger to go near, and stop him
> by argument or force. He sits apart and cares nothing
> nor thinks of us, and says that among the other immortals
> he is pre-eminently the greatest in power and strength. Therefore
> each of you must take whatever evil he sends you.
> Since I think already a sorrow has been wrought against Ares.
> His son has been killed in the fighting, dearest of all men
> to him, Ascalaphus, whom stark Ares calls his own son.'

Again, we encounter two familiar themes: first of all, human beings, and in particular mortal sons of gods, are the cause of strife on Olympus; secondly, conflict among the gods is curbed by the consideration that Zeus is strongest and must, therefore, be obeyed. The only alternative to strife and defeat, as Hera well knows, is a smile. A little later, we are also told that gods should not upset harmony on Olympus for the sake of mortals. Hera's speech prompts Ares to join the war on the side of the Achaeans; but Athena restrains him (*Iliad* 15.138-41):

> 'I ask of you to give up your anger for your son.
> By now some other, better of his strength and hands than your son was,
> has been killed, or will soon be killed; and it is a hard thing
> to rescue the generation and seed of all human beings.'

Even an exceptional man, the son of Ares no less, should be seen as belonging to 'the generation and seed of all mortals'. This point is of crucial importance to the *Iliad* as a whole. Achilles himself, the best of the Achaeans, the son of Thetis, by the end of the poem sees himself as sharing the fate of all human beings.

Three themes, then, are intertwined in the Iliadic portrayal of the gods: in the first place, because the Olympian hierarchy is established, gods no longer violently challenge Zeus or one another. Whereas in the *Theogony* and, to an extent, in the *Hymns*, they come into conflict with one another for the sake of their own position on Olympus, in the *Iliad* tensions among them are caused primarily by their involvement with human beings, particularly their own mortal sons. The poem then shows that they must ultimately learn to abandon all mortals to their fate: they should not disrupt harmony on Olympus for the sake of beings who are destined to die. The one and only physical conflict among gods, the theomachy of book 21, confirms the impression that divine violence no longer reaches the seriousness and intensity which characterise it in the *Theogony*. Moreover, it is caused by involvement with human affairs and, for that very reason, quickly dies down.

At *Iliad* 20.56-65, we are told that when the gods line up for battle against one another, the whole earth shudders and Hades fears that it might split open above him. It has often been pointed out that the passage resembles very closely the beginning of the conflict between Zeus and Typhoeus in *Theogony* 847-52.[33] And yet the differences are equally important. In the *Theogony*, Zeus finally establishes his rule by defeating Typhoeus and, with him, the goddess who had given birth to everyone else: Gaia, 'Earth'. The mighty battle between Zeus and the youngest son of Gaia is of cosmic significance since, from that moment onwards, Zeus will rule for ever while Gaia will never again generate a god. In the *Iliad*, the battle of the gods has no such significance. Zeus does not even take part in it; in fact, we are told that the whole episode is a source of amusement to him.[34] The gods soon stop fighting and their relationships and powers remain fundamentally unchanged after the conflict. Indeed, some even refuse to fight. At *Iliad* 21.461-67 Apollo declares that all mortals must die and are therefore not worth a fight among gods. He says to Poseidon:

> 'Shaker of the earth, you would have me be as one without prudence
> if I am to fight even you for the sake of insignificant
> mortals, who are as leaves are, and now flourish and grow warm
> with life, and feed on what the ground gives, but then again
> fade away and are dead. Therefore let us with all speed
> give up this quarrel and let the mortals fight their own battles.'

This observation prepares us for the somewhat anti-climactic conclusion of the scene. The gods simply go back to Olympus once they have had enough. The war among mortals, of course, carries on relentlessly.

In a sense, then, scholars are right in suggesting that the existence of the Homeric gods is directly contrasted with human suffering on earth. This, however, does not mean that the gods should simply be understood as counterparts to human beings, literary fictions created for comic relief and as a foil for the suffering of mortals. The episodes of conflict between Zeus and Hera, for example, should not be seen as mere squabbles between husband and wife: the *Iliad* makes it clear that they hark back to a time in which confrontations between the king and queen of the gods could lead to revolutions in the cosmic order. The overall effect of the portrayal of the gods, then, is not just that of highlighting the suffering – and perhaps the dignity – of mortals, but also that of presenting the *Iliad* as an exploration of a particular stage in the history of gods and men.

The observations we have made so far are not intended to replace readings which focus on the lack of conflict and suffering on the part of the gods; rather, we try to place those readings within the wider context of the epic tradition to which the *Iliad* belongs. This broader perspective has some repercussions for the overall interpretation of the poem. The tensions which used to characterise relationships among gods at an earlier stage in the history of the cosmos have now largely shifted onto the human plane. The gods still quarrel for the sake of mortals but must ultimately learn not to care for them to the point of upsetting harmony on Olympus. Conversely, mortals inherit the preoccupations of the gods: as we shall see in the next chapter, their quest for *timê* (honour) is part of their divine heritage.

The divine geography of the *Odyssey*

If the *Iliad* depicts a particular stage in the history of gods and men – the time when the gods must learn that all human beings, even their sons and favourites, share a fate of death – it makes sense to ask whether the *Odyssey* describes later developments in divine-human relations. Chronologically, the story of Odysseus takes place after the end of the Trojan War: Achilles is long dead; in fact, Odysseus meets his soul when he travels to the underworld. As we shall see in Chapter 5, there are other ways in which the *Odyssey* presents itself as a post-Iliadic poem, but for now we focus on a more specific question. It has long been pointed out that the portrayal of the gods in the *Odyssey* is different from that in the *Iliad*; what remains to be seen is whether these differences can be explained in terms of a gradual development in the history of the gods and their relationship with mortals.

Like the *Iliad*, the *Odyssey* begins by outlining the divine context of the story told in the poem: after the invocation to the Muse, we are told that, in the tenth year of his wanderings, the gods established that it was time for Odysseus to return home. All the gods, we hear, felt pity for him (*Odyssey* 1.19), except for Poseidon who was angry because Odysseus had blinded his son Polyphemus (*Odyssey* 1.20-1, 68-73). In several respects, the opening Olympian scene in the *Odyssey* is quite different from those we have encountered in the *Iliad*. In the first place, the gods are not divided into two roughly equal camps: they all agree that Odysseus should go home, except for Poseidon. Secondly, there is no open confrontation between Poseidon and the other Olympians: they wait until he has gone to have a banquet with the Ethiopians before discussing Odysseus' homecoming. In this way, peace on Olympus is not upset by the plight of Odysseus: the gods discuss his fate without much drama, and even Poseidon is allowed to rejoice in a banquet – albeit away from Olympus. Thirdly, Zeus does not have to assert his power against Poseidon or any of the other gods; he simply comments that Poseidon will have to fall into step with the unanimous decision of the Olympians: there is no confrontation between the two brothers either in book 1 or in the rest of the *Odyssey*.

A final and very important point is that the gods discuss Odysseus' case by focusing on merit, rather than on any special relationship he might have with them. Zeus begins by pointing out that human beings should not blame the gods for their own misfortunes, and cites Aegisthus as a case in point: it was his own wickedness which brought about his end. At this point, Athena observes that Odysseus has done nothing to deserve a bad fate. Zeus agrees and adds that he is intelligent among mortals and generous in his sacrifices to the gods. For these reasons, all the gods agree that he should be allowed to return home. The divine support for Odysseus, then, does not stem from a close blood relationship between him and a god. Rather, he happens to display qualities to which all human beings can aspire: intelligence in his dealings with mortals, and piety in his relationship to the gods.

The overall thrust of the first Olympian scene in the *Odyssey* is an insistence on the separation between gods and mortals. Whereas in the *Iliad* the gods tend to intervene in human affairs for the sake of their own sons or otherwise favourite mortals, at the beginning of the *Odyssey* Zeus argues that mortals determine their own fate and should not blame the gods. His speech can almost be read as a polemical comment on a phenomenon which has attracted the attention of many readers: the fact that in the Homeric poems an event can simultaneously have a divine and a human explanation.[35] Although Zeus knows that the gods can influence what happens on earth, he insists that mortals should not focus on divine causes for their suffering, but rather see their fate as the result of what they themselves do. Paradoxically, the decision to intervene in favour of Odysseus stems precisely from a desire to safeguard this principle: because he has done nothing to deserve a bad fate, he should be allowed back home. It is important, in this respect, that the gods intervene simply in order to ensure that Odysseus is able to do what he wants and deserves.[36] After their debate on Olympus, they send Hermes to tell Calypso that she should release him and let him sail home.

The gods, then, become dispensers of justice (they argue that Odysseus deserves to go home) in order to enforce a distinction between the human and the divine plane. Zeus argues in favour of Odysseus because his merit lies, among other things, in respecting the difference between the divine and the mortal realms. But the main motivation for ensuring that he sail back home is that, in this way, he will have no reason to blame the gods. Just like Aegisthus, Odysseus should explain his fate by looking at what he himself has done, rather than by invoking divine intervention. It follows that by safeguarding justice for mortals, the gods become less visible as agents on earth.

The first Olympian scene in the *Odyssey* suggests that the separation between gods and mortals is further advanced than in the *Iliad*: the gods no longer fight one another in order to support their favourite mortals. Neither do they seek to enhance their own honour by championing that of a mortal: rather, they ensure that each man meets the fate he deserves, so that mortals may have no reason to blame them for their own fate. Not all the gods however are prepared to acknowledge, or help to establish, this divide between themselves and mortals. Calypso, we are told, wants to give Odysseus the gift of immortality and make him her husband for ever. The conflict of interests between her and the Olympian gods can be seen as symptomatic of the overall place of the *Odyssey* within the history of the world: the poem tells of a time in which unions between gods and mortals are no longer acceptable and must not be allowed to continue.

Similarly, gods no longer fight one another for the sake of their mortal sons: Poseidon, we have seen, is the one exception. In his determination to avenge the slight suffered by Polyphemus, he resembles the gods of the *Iliad*. Yet there is one complication: it is not clear, at least initially, whether Polyphemus really is a mortal. In the *Theogony*, the Cyclopes are sons of Heaven and Earth and belong to the earlier generation of gods.[37] The *Odyssey* apparently contradicts the theogonic account, yet in the *Odyssey* too the Cyclopes are primordial creatures. This is how Zeus describes Polyphemus when he first discusses the problem of Poseidon's hostility towards Odysseus (*Odyssey* 1.68-73):

'It is the Earth-encircler Poseidon who, ever relentless,
nurses a grudge because of the Cyclops, whose eye he blinded,
godlike Polyphemus, whose power is greatest
over all the Cyclopes. Thoosa, a nymph, was his mother,
and she was the daughter of Phorkys, lord of the barren salt water.
She in the hollows of a cave had lain with Poseidon.'

This passage, while not theogonic in any strict sense (Polyphemus is 'godlike', not 'a god'), yet recalls the way in which the birth of new gods is described in the *Theogony* and the *Homeric Hymns*: for example, Hermes, the son of Zeus and the nymph Maia, is conceived and born in a cave. The *Hymn to Hermes* goes on to say that the god eventually reached the peak of Olympus and was accepted by the other gods as one of their number.[38] If we bear in mind the wider resonance of this first description of Polyphemus, it becomes clear that the *Odyssey* opens with a question about the position of the Cyclops in the overall order of the cosmos: should he be accepted among the gods, like Hermes; be otherwise granted special consideration as the son of a god; or simply be left where he was born, in a cave?

The *Odyssey* negotiates a careful answer to these questions. When Odysseus describes the land of the Cyclopes, he remarks that 'putting all their trust in the immortal gods, they neither plough with their hands nor plant anything'.[39] A little later, he goes on to point out that the island off their coast has potential and could be cultivated properly (9.131-5):

> 'It is not a bad place at all, it could bear all crops in season,
> and there are meadow lands near the shores of the grey sea,
> well watered and soft; there could be grapes grown there endlessly,
> and there is smooth land for ploughing, men could reap
> a full harvest always in season, since there is very rich subsoil.'

Odysseus, then, assumes that the Cyclopes are fundamentally like mortals: they live in a good place for human habitation, even though they fail to exploit it properly. His observations suggest that they do not know how to found a proper human society.[40] There are more hints that he thinks of Polyphemus as a mortal: at 9.299-305, he says that he thought of killing him, thus assuming that he can die. We may also note that Odysseus calls Polyphemos a 'man', *anêr*.[41] Yet at the same time, he is also aware that the Cyclopes are no ordinary human beings: he points out that the reason why they can live without planting and ploughing is that they are especially close to the gods.

It has been observed that the lifestyle of the Cyclopes resembles descriptions of the golden age under the rule of Cronus, father of Zeus: this is true, yet it is important to realise that, in the *Odyssey*, the cyclopean golden age is presented as backward and primitive, almost as a negative foil to human civilisation:[42] 'it is not a bad place at all', observes Odysseus, 'it could bear crops in season ...'. Whereas in the *Works and Days* Hesiod presents the golden age as a wonderful time in which human beings lived 'like gods', did not suffer, and did not age,[43] the *Odyssey* relentlessly insists on progress and change: gods and mortals should stay apart, human beings should take responsibility for their own fate, Odysseus should go back home. 'Rocky Ithaca' may not be as wonderful a place as the land of the Phaeacians (or, potentially, that of the Cyclopes) but it is a proper, real place for human life. Penelope may not be an ageless goddess, but Odysseus craves for his mortal wife rather than blessed stagnation in the cave of a nymph.

In the context of the *Odyssey*, then, Poseidon and his son Polyphemus seem out of date.[44] While the other gods sit on Olympus discussing Aegisthus and Odysseus, and weighing the merits of each, Poseidon fights a personal battle for the sake of his son. He is still committed to enhancing his personal honour through his offspring, rather than ensuring justice on the basis of merit. Similarly, Polyphemus lives in a world which in crucial respects predates the rule of Zeus. In his case too, the idea of merit does not apply: the Cyclopes are close to the gods, and therefore need not work or rely on their own achievements.

The *Odyssey* places itself after the *Iliad* not only by recounting a journey which took place after the Trojan War, but also by describing a later stage in the relationship between gods and mortals. Whereas in the *Iliad* the gods must constantly be reminded not to fight one another for the sake of mortals but rather enjoy themselves on Olympus, in the *Odyssey* they have accepted that and, in fact, regret that mortals still hold them responsible for what happens on earth. Poseidon and Polyphemus are exceptions which serve to highlight, by contrast, the progressive thrust of the story. The positive counterparts to these two figures are Odysseus and Athena: he is the independent, resourceful man *par excellence*, while she is the goddess of progress and of justice for those who honour the gods and are self-sufficient in their dealings with fellow human beings.[45]

One important aspect of the *Odyssey* is that it presents the history of gods and mortals in geographical terms. In the course of the poem, Odysseus travels from the island of Calypso back to Ithaca. In doing so, he maps out the distance between gods and mortals: he begins as the sexual partner of a goddess, thus reminding us of the many relationships between gods and humans which gave rise to the generation of heroes; he stops by at Scherie, a land inhabited by the Phaeacians who, although mortal, are exceptionally close to the gods; and finally arrives back home at Ithaca, a place which is beset by many of the problems of a post-heroic existence as described in Hesiod's *Works and Days*: one cannot breed horses here, resources are limited, and issues of social justice are more pressing than ever. In some ways, Telemachus travels in the opposite direction: he meets some of the protagonists of the Trojan War – Nestor, Helen and Menelaus – and tries, through his acquaintance with them, to build a bridge between his own existence and that of his father.

If we look at Odysseus' own account of his travels, beyond those that are actually described in the main narrative, we see once again that history is mapped onto a geographical plane. Some pockets of Odysseus' world are remarkably primitive. Others come closer to the world of the audience in some ways but fall short in others. One could, of course, analyse in detail all the places Odysseus visits in terms of historical progress, but the main point is clear: the history of gods and men has, in the *Odyssey*, a geographical dimension. In some secluded places, gods still mingle with men, although on Olympus they insist on a separation between the two sides. Similarly, there are places in the *Odyssey* where mortals do not yet lead an existence that compares closely to that of the audience, while elsewhere the gap is far less pronounced. The earlier stages of the world are not simply blotted out. Rather, they have become marginal features in a universe that rapidly moves away from the concerns and values which dominated during the Trojan War.[46]

The gods and the bard

We have argued so far that the *Odyssey*, by and large, depicts a later stage in the history of gods and men than the *Iliad*, although the landscape it outlines is complex: some places are frozen at an early stage in the history of the cosmos while others, Ithaca in particular, relentlessly look to the future. Odysseus himself travels forwards in time as well as space, from communion with a goddess in a cave (Calypso), to a human society heavily dependent on the gods for its subsistence (Phaeacia), to rocky Ithaca: a hard, real place, where human beings live of their own work and resources.

What remains to be seen is whether in the *Odyssey* the gods are described in a similar way to that in the *Iliad*, or whether we detect some changes in terms of their behaviour. We argued in the first section of this chapter that, in the *Iliad*, life on Olympus is contrasted not only to the suffering of human life, but also to an earlier stage in the history of the gods where they openly and violently challenged one another. In the *Odyssey*, this earlier stage of instability and conflict is almost never recalled. Even the scenes of communal feasting which in the *Iliad* function as a natural extension of the struggle for cosmic honours are almost entirely absent from the text. The point is not so much that the gods no longer enjoy themselves, but that there is no longer a need for *Iliad*-style dinners: the distribution of shares, which, as we have seen, is a crucial aspect of communal feasting, is largely taken for granted in the context of the *Odyssey*. Whereas the *Iliad* explores the transition from direct violence to antagonism for the sake of mortals, to harmony on Olympus, the *Odyssey* assumes a more stable relationship among the gods themselves, and greater separation between gods and mortals.

This greater distance is made explicit in the text: for example, when Athena finally shows herself to Odysseus in book 13, he complains that he has not seen her since his departure from Troy.[47]

Generally speaking, the gods' personal involvement with humans becomes less intense: even Poseidon persecutes Odysseus only at a remove (he never actually encounters him in person) and only 'until his return to his own country': in the second half of the poem, Odysseus faces human rather than divine hostility.[48] Most importantly, perhaps, mortals are invited to see their fate as the result of their own behaviour: even if the gods intervene (and they certainly do), they are rarely as visible to ordinary mortals as they are in the *Iliad*. Athena does appear to Odysseus in book 13, of course, and she expresses a special fondness for him: he is as cunning and resourceful among mortals as she is among the gods. Yet, even in this affectionate speech, she teases him for his inability to recognise her.[49]

The issue of divine visibility seems to be at the heart of the only episode in the *Odyssey* where the gods do seem closely comparable to Iliadic descriptions. In book 8, the singer Demodocus performs three songs. The first (8.72-82) and last (8.499-520) are devoted to episodes from the Trojan War and are easy to interpret in the context of the book: Odysseus recognises himself in the performance of Demodocus and this self-recognition eventually leads him to reveal his identity to his hosts. The second song (8.266-366), which is also the longest and the only one reported *verbatim*, is more enigmatic.[50] It describes a scene of remarkable frivolity on the part of the gods: we are told how Hephaestus found out from the Sun that his wife Aphrodite was having an affair with Ares. Hephaestus then constructed a trap for the two lovers which was 'invisible to the eye' and through which he successfully caught them naked together in bed. At this point, he called all the other gods to have a good look at the humiliated couple. Eventually the lovers were released: Ares fled to Thrace, whereas Aphrodite went to Cyprus where she was given a bath and restored to her beauty.

It is not easy to see what might be the point of this song in the context of book 8. There are of course larger thematic parallels one might draw with Odyssean couples and, as usual, scholars have pointed out that the gods are presented as frivolous counterparts to human beings: whereas Agamemnon is killed by his wife's lover and Odysseus has to fight a crowd of depraved suitors, the unfaithfulness of Aphrodite has no major consequences.[51] Yet we have already seen that this approach is not, on its own, satisfactory; the gods in the *Odyssey* must be understood above all as gods, and not simply as foils to mortals.

One striking feature of the episode, which has not drawn much attention, is its insistence on visual language: Ares and Aphrodite meet in secret and, to begin with, only the Sun 'who sees everything' notices what is happening. Eventually, they are caught in a trap which they have failed to see, and are exposed naked in bed for the viewing of all the other male gods (goddesses refrain from looking out of modesty). The whole story, most importantly, is told by a blind bard who, with the help of the Muse, can describe for a mortal audience even something that the gods themselves want to conceal and initially fail to see.

It can be argued that the story illustrates above all the power of the bard, whose blindness is compensated by his ability to see and describe an episode which would otherwise be inaccessible to ordinary mortals and, in part, to the gods themselves. As we have seen in Chapter 1, ancient audiences were impressed by Demodocus and thought of him as an autobiographical figure. Homer, they reasoned, must have been like him: blind but gifted with the power of singing not only episodes from the Trojan War, but also Olympian scenes otherwise inaccessible to mortals.

That Demodocus' gift of seeing and describing the gods is unique to him as a bard is confirmed by the fact that no ordinary mortal in the *Odyssey* shares his ability. Not even Odysseus is able to say what goes on among the gods. For example, whereas we know exactly why Calypso suddenly lets him sail home, Odysseus never finds out: at 7.263 he wonders whether she simply made up her mind or whether she received a message from Zeus. Not only do we know that Hermes was sent to tell her to let him go, but we even heard word by word what the gods said about Odysseus and why they decided to let him go back.

There are many other instances in the *Odyssey* where characters are unsure about the identity or action of a god, whereas Homer tells us precisely which god is doing what at any given point in the narrative. For example, the bard tells us that Athena sends Odysseus to sleep when he arrives in Scherie (*Odyssey* 5.491-3), but when Odysseus tells the story himself, he simply says that 'a god' poured sleep over his eyes (7.284-6). Similarly, Homer says that Athena sent Telemachus a good wind for sailing (15.292), but Telemachus only recognises that 'the gods' did it (17.148-9). Even worse, the bard tells us that Poseidon sent a storm against Odysseus (5.291-4), but Odysseus, who knows no better, blames Zeus for it (5.302-5). One could think of many examples of this kind, but the main point is simple: ordinary human beings sometimes recognise divine intervention, but are unable to identify precisely which god did what: they can only mention 'a god', 'the gods', or 'Zeus'. By contrast, Homer is always able to identify the gods precisely and to describe how they relate to one another, as well as what they do to human beings.[52]

Part of the point of Demodocus' song in book 8, then, seems to be that of displaying what must have struck many members of Homer's audience as his most outstanding gift: to see and describe what cannot usually be seen. In the context of the *Odyssey* with its less developed Olympian scenes, this display of insider knowledge becomes particularly pointed. After the Trojan War we no longer 'usually' see the gods in their Olympian homes. The increasing separation between gods and men, it seems, is reflected in the relative scarcity of Olympian scenes.

It is all the more gratifying that we can still peep through the keyhole of Aphrodite's bedchamber, if only with the help of Demodocus, the singer within the song. The underlying motif of this tour-de-force of epic performance is still theogonic, and thus 'serious', in the sense that the union of two gods always has potentially threatening implications. For a start, we may wonder what would happen if Ares and Aphrodite had a child (Homeric gods rarely mate in vain): how would the birth of a new god affect the Olympian order? And even if they do not generate, how can Hephaestus be compensated for the slight to his honour? It seems, however, that the theogonic implications of the episode have all but disappeared underneath a thick layer of bravura and titillation. The point of the story, and the one highlighted by ancient readers, seems no longer to be that of reminding us of the historic background to the current Olympian order, but to advertise the bard's claim to a special kind of knowledge.

Demodocus, of course, gives no justification for his knowledge of Olympus. Similarly, Homer never says, 'I know that Zeus and Athena planned this when Poseidon was away because a nymph told me, and she heard about it from the messenger of the gods ...'. Both bards simply rely on their special relationship with the Muses, who are traditionally described as goddesses 'living on Olympus': this is how they know what goes on among the gods. It would be hard to overestimate the importance of this point. Odysseus has some privileged information because he was the lover of Calypso, but even he is kept guessing most of the time. The bard knows everything about the gods, even episodes which they themselves try to conceal. One consequence of this difference is that the bard sings with absolute authority and his account is objective and impartial: Scodel has pointed out that Demodocus does not pander to his audience,[53] but there is more to be said.

Several of the observations which have been made so far fall into place once we realise that the bard is the only mortal who commands a complete, clear and objective knowledge of the gods. For a start, Herodotus' statement that Homer and Hesiod were the first to describe the gods for the Greeks makes perfect sense: it was the bards alone who could do that. Secondly, the fact that the *Iliad* and the *Odyssey* are carefully placed within a wider divine history makes sense if we consider that bards know everything about the gods and can provide a larger context within which to place a particular episode. But there are even much more specific observations to be made about the epic bard and the gods.

We have seen that the history of the universe, for archaic Greeks, was first and foremost the history of the gods. The Homeric and Hesiodic bards as the chroniclers of early history therefore have to be experts in the matters of the gods. The very language of epic is shaped by the project of describing the gods to mortals. Apart from the epithets of the gods, which are singled out by Herodotus as something that Homer and Hesiod made known to the Greeks, there are specific words which are used to indicate divine presence or intervention. For example, in Homeric Greek, there are several words for 'arrow' or 'missile'; of these, one is exclusively used for arrows sent by a god: they are *kêla*. Similarly, the word *ouros* describes a wind sent by a god and taking a character to his destination. Audiences attuned to the language of epic can immediately detect the presence of a god. Even more radically, the bard knows the language of the gods and sometimes makes a distinction between mortal and divine speech. This is striking especially because the Homeric poems play down the differences between different human languages: the bard is much more concerned to point out differences in the way gods, as opposed to mortals, refer to things. At *Iliad* 14.290-1, for example, we hear of 'a singing bird whom in the mountains the immortal gods call chalkis, but men call him kymindis'. Several other instances in which the language of early Greek epic reflects the bard's special knowledge of the gods could be quoted. Yet the much more important point is this: the bard commands the tools to describe the gods. Through the Muses who dwell on Olympus not only does he see what happens on the holy mountain, but he can also describe it precisely to us.

Animals and fate

We have seen that the bard is uniquely able to see and describe the gods for ordinary mortals. In fact, his songs are shaped by the will of the gods at an even more fundamental level than has so far been suggested. The beginning of the *Iliad*, for example, makes it clear that the story told in the poem follows the 'plan' or 'will' (*boulê*) of Zeus. These are the first lines of the poem (1.1-7):

Sing, goddess, the anger of Peleus' son Achilles
and its devastation, which put pains thousandfold upon the Achaeans,
hurled in their multitudes to the house of Hades strong souls
of heroes, but gave their bodies to be the delicate feasting
of dogs, of all birds, and the will of Zeus was being accomplished
since that time when first there stood in division of conflict
Atreus' son the lord of men and noble Achilles.

There has been much debate about the exact meaning of the phrase
'and the will of Zeus was being accomplished'. In a fragment of a lost
poem of the Epic Cycle, the *Cypria*, the same phrase is used to describe
the whole of the Trojan War: Zeus wanted to exterminate the heroes
and caused the war for that reason.[54] Some ancient commentators
thought that the phrase was used in the same way in the *Cypria* and in
the *Iliad*:[55] their observation is astute, also because in both texts the
'will of Zeus' is linked to the death of the heroes. However, the proem
of the *Iliad* makes it clear that the phrase, while evoking the whole of
the Trojan War for some readers, has a more specific meaning too: the
will of Zeus, it says, was accomplished 'since that time' when Achilles
and Agamemnon first started to quarrel. One effect of this specification
is that it equates the 'will' or 'plan' of Zeus (the Greek *boulê* means
both) with the story told in the poem: the epic starts precisely with the
quarrel between Achilles and Agamemnon and this, we are told, is when
the plan of Zeus begins to be fulfilled.[56]

If this is the case, it makes sense to ask how much of the poem is
devoted to describing what Zeus brings about, and how much of the
story is independent of his volition. This is a complicated question
which cannot be worked out in every detail here. What we plan to do,
instead, is focus on two more specific issues. First, we ask whether the
natural world, and animals in particular, are independent of the will of
Zeus: is the story of the *Iliad* played out against a stable backdrop,
where animals, the seasons, the weather carry on as usual, or is the will
of Zeus inscribed even in nature? Secondly, we investigate whether Zeus
himself is subject to some higher power, which we might call Fate: this
is a question that has been much debated in Homeric scholarship.

The natural world is an interesting test case when investigating the
relationship between the will of Zeus and the story told in the *Iliad*. On
the analogy of modern literature, we might expect that nature is by and
large conceived as a 'setting' for the story told in the poem or, to put it
differently, for the plan of Zeus; and yet even a superficial reading of the
Iliad shows that this is not the case. We have already seen that, in the
language of epic, the word *ouros* is specifically used of a wind that takes

a character to his destination. By contrast, the word *anemos* describes winds with a specific geographical direction.[57] It is important to realise that an *ouros* is as 'real' as an *anemos*, in other words, that it is not a matter of what modern scholars call 'pathetic fallacy', the bending of the rules of nature to suit the needs of a story. Rather, the Homeric bard distinguishes between a wind sent by a god towards a specific goal, from a wind which may blow from east or west, clash with other winds, or create a storm. The distinction between a uniquely significant event and one that fits a predictable pattern, such as geographical direction, does not apply only to descriptions of winds. In fact, all aspects of nature can be presented by the bard either as manifestations of divine will or as timeless, and in that sense ordinary phenomena.

For example, the flight of birds can be explained in two ways: a bird is either sent by a god as an omen, or flies about for its own reasons, to feed its chicks, for example, or escape a predator. Sometimes, both explanations apply: a bird may be flying to its nest and, simultaneously, be sent by a god as an omen. Yet the important point is that very rarely is there any uncertainty about which of the two modes of explanation prevails. The question arises: in which cases are birds described simply as flying for their own reasons, and in what circumstances are they presented as manifestations of the will of a god? The answer to this question is surprisingly simple. In the main narrative, all birds have a divine significance: they tell us something about the direction of the story and, ultimately, about the will of Zeus. By contrast, in similes their movement has no such significance; it is rather presented as an example of the ordinary working of nature.

At *Iliad* 24.315, Zeus sends an eagle to Priam which the bard calls a *teleiotaton peteênôn*, a 'bird who most of all accomplishes *telos*'. The eagle carries a message which is duly decoded: Priam should go to the Achaean camp and retrieve the body of his son Hector. *Telos* is a difficult word in Homeric Greek, but broadly speaking, it refers to the accomplishment of a plan or action. For example, home-coming can be said to be the *telos* of one's journey, or death the *telos* of one's life. The related verb, *teleô*, is used in the proem of the *Iliad* to refer to the accomplishment of the will of Zeus. In all these cases, *telos* marks the end or purpose of a specific narrative sequence (a journey, a life, the story of the *Iliad*). Returning to *Iliad* 24, the connection between the movement of the animal, the will of Zeus, and the overall direction, or *telos*, of the narrative could not be clearer: the eagle sent by Zeus makes the *telos* of Priam's visit to the Achaean camp visible. In similes, by contrast, birds do not have the same significance. At *Iliad* 2.459-66, for example, the Achaeans and the Trojans are compared to a swarm of birds flapping about on a river bank. In this case, the animals are an image of a timeless aspect of nature, not a sign of the will of Zeus: certain birds always behave like that, and no particular message is to be deduced from their movements.

The fact that birds mean different things in the narrative and in the similes of the Homeric poems suggests that there is an important difference of perspective between the two. In the main narrative, the bard, with the help of the Muse, sings for us how 'the will of Zeus was accomplished', and shows the underlying direction of the story and how the divine will is mirrored in the natural world. In the similes, the bard illustrates a specific situation by referring, more often than not, to a familiar image. Here he describes nature as we ordinarily perceive it, that is to say, outside any specific divine narrative.

If we take into account the perceptions of characters inside the narrative, the flight of birds becomes all the more interesting. We said that, from the point of view of the bard and his audience, birds in the main narrative are always connected to the will of the gods. They say something about the ultimate 'aim' or *telos* of the story. But for ordinary mortals within the narrative this is not necessarily the case. In book 12, for example, Hector famously refuses to recognise an omen. He says that he cares nothing for birds and which way they fly; he only believes in one good omen: fighting for one's own country.[58] Hector, of course, is wrong: he fails to recognise that the eagle he sees is significant, whereas we do.[59] We have already seen that, through the bard, the audience has a privileged understanding of the gods: characters inside the poems do not know as much as we know from listening to the bard. This is also the case with bird omens: the bard makes the meaning transparent for us, the audience; but characters like Hector are not necessarily able to see the plan of Zeus.

It may be thought that birds are a very special case: after all they can function as omens in many cultures. Yet if we look at other animals, and at nature more generally, we see that the observations we have made so far still apply. In the main narrative, animals rarely display a will of their own. Horses, for example, are often said to run 'not unwillingly' towards whatever goal they are meant to be reaching: although they do not function as signs for the will of Zeus, they do not usually act contrary to his will or the overall direction of the narrative. Similarly, there is no problem with leading animals to the altar before sacrifice. All we hear is that they are killed. In similes, by contrast, animals often have a mind of their own and follow what we might call 'their instincts'. For example, farm animals may refuse to obey their master.[60] Sacrificial victims sometimes need to be dragged to the altar.[61] At *Iliad* 6.506-14,

Paris is compared to a horse which breaks free of its rope and gallops away to pasturing places. The overall image is one of beauty and freedom, but above all it suggests a world in which animals behave according to their own nature rather than following unproblematically some specific divine or narrative plan.

Similar observations to those we have made about animals apply to other aspects of nature. For example, in the main narrative of the Homeric poems there is little interest in seasons, and weather more generally: mostly what we get are storms or weather signs which are uniquely significant, and invariably linked to the will of a god. Similes, by contrast, often refer to the weather without implying that it should be read as a sign of direct divine intervention. The description of the shield of Achilles likewise portrays weather changes as natural phenomena without unique significance: the seasons succeed one another in a predictable and stable pattern, and are not presented as a communication from Zeus. One could add more examples to illustrate our main point, which is that in the main narrative the natural world quite directly expresses the will of Zeus and other gods, whereas in similes it does not. However, the much more pressing question concerns the overall effect of this portrayal of nature in the poems.

To take the *Iliad* first, the bard begins his poem with an invocation to the Muse. He summarises the contents of his story and claims that it shows how 'the will of Zeus was accomplished'. When he tells the story, he describes a world that is imbued with divine meaning: the flight of birds speaks of the will of Zeus; weather signs are uniquely significant and thus indicate the direction of the story. The bard, of course, is also able to look at animals and nature as an ordinary human being might do, but he reserves that kind of perspective for the world of the similes, or the description of the shield of Achilles. When he wants to give an illustration of ordinary, present-day life, he depicts birds flapping about on a riverbank, horses breaking free of their rope, seasons succeeding one another in a stable and predictable pattern. In historical terms, this is the world of humans 'as they are now', struggling to survive in a potentially hostile environment and, above all, struggling to make sense of their existence. In this post-heroic world, nature behaves according to fixed rules, even where it is apparently chaotic (the flapping birds) or exceptional (e.g. a mountain fire). In all cases there is a generic explanation and the will of the gods remains invisible. Characters inside the poem sometimes view nature in the same way as it is presented to us in the similes: Hector, for example, protests that he has no time for birds who randomly fly this way or that. He does not see the divine significance of nature as clearly as we do when we are listening to the bard. Likewise, Glaucus compares the races of man to leaves that sprout and wither with the seasons.[62] Iliadic characters clearly see their lives as being to some extent informed by the patterns that we find in the similes. From the perspective of the narrator, however, such patterns remain subordinate to the larger divine plan.

The picture drawn in the *Odyssey* is slightly more complicated, and here we recall what we said earlier about the *Odyssey*'s geography. Just as there are places in the *Odyssey* where gods and humans are not yet clearly separate, we also find places where people still live entirely without seasons: for example, the garden of Alcinous continually bears fruit.[63] This detail fits in well with the general depiction of Scherie as a place that belongs to an earlier, more luxuriant age. In Ithaca, where gods and humans lead more separate lives, we also find clearer indications that the weather plays an important part in human life. For example, we hear at 14.457-8:

A bad night came on, the dark of the moon, and Zeus rained
all night long, and the great west wind blew, which always brings rain.

These lines are very different from descriptions of nature found in the *Iliad*: the narrator does not hint at any divine plan behind the blowing of the west wind and the rain which it brings on. Although Zeus is still involved, there is little sense that he is pursuing his own plans. In fact, the west wind, which 'always' brings wet weather, appears here as the real cause behind the rain, a cause which is entirely independent of the narrative plan of the poem.

The *Odyssey*, then, describes a world in which the seasons, and natural phenomena more generally, are more clearly patterned and thus closer to the world 'as it is today'. The west wind blows on some occasions, on others it does not; wet weather comes and goes. Such things are not random (e.g. the west wind always brings wet weather), but they are no longer the result of *ad hoc* divine planning. The world that the bard describes for us in the *Iliad*, by contrast, is imbued by divine presence: the gods are visible, as is their effect on characters, on the shape of the story, on the very workings of nature. Nothing is left to chance, and there is no room for randomness. We may ask ourselves, then, what conceptions of fate apply in this transparent world.

For the sake of argument, let us start by saying that an event can be explained in one of three ways: either it follows a predictable pattern (for eaxample, after winter comes spring), or it is uniquely significant (for example, an omen), or it means nothing at all (a freak occurrence). In ancient Greek, different words are used to describe these three types of explanation: *moira*, along with related words, refers to what is 'allotted' and therefore describes a well-established pattern; *telos*, 'aim', 'end', refers, as we have indicated already, to the direction a particular story is taking and is often linked to the will of a god; *tychê*, 'what occurs', refers to chance.[64]

In the Homeric poems, and especially the *Iliad*, there is little room for chance; and, in fact, the word *tychê* is never used. Events tend to be presented either as part of a plan or a story, or as part of an established pattern. Sometimes, the same event can be seen either as the ultimate aim of a narrative or as part of what is decreed by fate. So for example, death is the allotted portion for all mortals, it follows a predictable pattern (*moira*, cf. *moros* 'death'); yet it can also be seen as the ultimate 'end' in the story of an individual (*telos thanatoio*). The issue, once again, is one of narrative perspective: we may look at an event either as what is set down as a fixed and stable pattern (*moira*) or as part of a particular intention (*telos*).

The *Iliad* dramatises and explores the tensions between *moira* and *telos*. We have seen that the poem illustrates how the 'will of Zeus was accomplished', how it reached its *telos*. At the same time, the poem also shows that events follow an allotted pattern, *moira*, which has little to do with divine will, human intentions or narrative direction. Occasionally, the will of Zeus comes into conflict with *moira*. The most famous case concerns the death of Sarpedon. It may be useful to focus on this episode as a way of concluding this chapter not only because it sheds light on the relationship between fate and the will of Zeus, but also because it brings together all the main themes which we have discussed so far.

In book 16, Zeus sees his own son Sarpedon on the battlefield and realises he is about to be killed by Patroclus. He is overcome by pity and considers rescuing him, thus acting against *moira*. He discusses this possibility with Hera who warns him against it (16.431-49):

> And watching them the son of devious-devising Cronus
> felt pity, and spoke to Hera, his wife and his sister:
> 'Ah me, that it is destined [lit.: it is *moira*] that the dearest of men, Sarpedon,
> must go down under the hands of Menoetius' son Patroclus.
> The heart in my breast is balanced between two ways as I ponder,
> whether I should snatch him out of the sorrowful battle
> and set him down still alive in the rich country of Lycia,

or beat him under at the hands of the son of Menoetius.'
In turn the lady Hera of the ox eyes answered him:
'Majesty, son of Cronus, what sort of thing have you spoken?
Do you wish to bring back a man who is mortal, one long since
doomed by his destiny, from ill-sounding death and release him?
Do it, then; but not all the rest of us gods shall approve you.
And put away in your thoughts this other thing that I tell you;
if you bring Sarpedon back to his home, still living,
think how then some other one of the gods might also
wish to carry his own son out of the strong encounter;
since around the great city of Priam are fighting many
sons of the immortals. You will waken grim resentment among them.'

It may be tempting to read this passage as showing that Zeus is not
omnipotent: he too has to comply with the decrees of fate. Yet the
passage suggests a more complicated relationship between the will of
Zeus and what is established by *moira*.[65] Zeus presents the possibility
of rescuing Sarpedon as a real one: the implication of his words is that
he could snatch him from death if he so chose. Hera's answer confirms
that Zeus could save his son, if he decided to do so: she does not
mention any objective limits to his power; rather, she points out that
the other gods would not approve if he rescued Sarpedon. Worse, she
reminds him that the gods would then feel tempted to save their own
mortal sons from their fate of death. Her argument must, by now,
sound familiar. We have already seen, for example, that Athena begs
Ares not to upset harmony among the gods for the sake of his mortal
son Ascalaphus: he should die like all other mortals, the gods should
not make exceptions for their own offspring. Hera is essentially
making the same point. In the case of Sarpedon too, harmony among
the gods – and hence the stability of the universe – can only be ensured
if all mortals are abandoned to their own fate.

The passage, then, does not define the limits of Zeus' power or deny
his omnipotence; rather, it dramatises the reasons why Zeus decides to
respect *moira*. More generally, it can be said that the *Iliad* shows us
when and why the *moira* of human beings, their fate of death, is established and respected by all the gods thereafter. The exchange between
Zeus and Hera makes particularly good sense if we are attuned to its
wider resonance in the history of gods and men. In the *Theogony* and
the *Catalogue of Women*, Heracles, a mortal son of a god, is granted
immortality.[66] In the *Iliad*, no such exception is conceivable: human
beings are mortal, gods are gods.[67] The *Iliad* depicts a crucial moment
of transition: Zeus considers snatching Sarpedon from his fate of
death, but decides against it. This is because the stability of the

91

universe is more important than the fate of a single individual on earth. The *Iliad* shows us that the establishment of *moira*, what is allotted to each human being, is inextricably bound up with the problem of harmony on Olympus, and hence with what Herodotus called the Greeks' 'theogony'.

Conclusion

Relationships among the gods evolve through time. When Earth first emerges from Void, and in the first generations which follow from her union with Heaven, divine relations are characterised by a ruthless struggle for power. Eventually, Zeus establishes his rule for ever, through a combination of might and justice. The other gods become his honoured guests on Olympus: each has his or her share of power and honours and a stable hierarchy is established. The *Iliad* shows that the gods eventually learn not to upset that hierarchy by seeking to protect their own mortal sons on earth: as a result, the gap between gods and mortals widens, and the gods start to view all mortals as ordinary and similar, no matter who their parents might be. Fate too seems to have a history: the discussion over Sarpedon's death in book 16 shows that Zeus learns to respect *moira* in order to avoid conflict with the other gods. Although it may appear strange to us that early Greek epic traces the origins and establishment of fate, it is interesting that Jack Lawson, in his study of fate in ancient Babylonian literature, also suggests that the gods' relationship to fate changes over the course of time.[68]

If we compare the depiction of the gods in the *Iliad* to their characterisation in the *Odyssey*, some interesting differences emerge. It is above all clear that in the *Odyssey*, the gods avoid direct confrontation for the sake of mortals: Poseidon and his son Polyphemus are presented as rather primitive figures who hark back to modes of behaviour which prevailed in the earlier history of the cosmos. By and large, the gods adopt a behaviour which encourages mortals to view their destiny as a consequence of their own action, rather than of divine intervention: this emerges with particular clarity from the debate among the gods in book 1. One consequence is that the gods, their wishes and interventions become less visible to ordinary mortals. It is through the performance of the bard Demodocus that ordinary human beings can see the gods most clearly. Like the main character, who knows the cities and the minds of many men, the *Odyssey* is interested above all in the world of mortals. The gods are more remote than in the *Iliad*, and the figure of the bard emerges as an important intermediary between the divine and the human world. In the next chapter, we explore how human society, just like divine relations, evolves through time.

4

Men, Women and Society

In the last chapter, we investigated some major forces which shape the Homeric world: the gods, fate, the laws of nature. We saw that the concept of 'fate' is in the making at the time in which the *Iliad* and the *Odyssey* are set: the gods must learn to leave mortals to their own devices. Zeus, we have seen, could snatch his son Sarpedon from the grip of death but, as Hera points out, 'the other gods would not approve'. For this reason, Sarpedon is abandoned to his fate or, to put it differently, fate emerges as an impartial principle which does not depend on the preferences and wishes of individual gods, nor on their blood ties with particular mortals. Similarly, nature, in the Homeric poems, is intimately linked to the will of the gods: in the main narrative, there seem to be few regular, predictable seasonal changes, but rather storms and weather signs which express the plans of the gods. The impression is that of a world in transition, where the gods learn to respect the boundary between themselves and their human offspring, and start viewing all mortals as ephemeral beings who live and die like leaves on a tree. Patterns emerge: leaves sprout and wither, spring is followed by autumn, all mortals live and die, the gods learn to respect the rules of destiny and nature.

In this chapter, we look in greater detail at the society of mortals in the *Iliad* and the *Odyssey*. We investigate the norms which underpin the behaviour of men and women in the Homeric world, and examine the social structures and institutions depicted in the poems. This analysis of human society is intended to provide an overall context within which we can, in the next chapter, interpret the personal stories of Achilles and Odysseus: we argue that the challenges faced by these two characters are shaped not only by the divine forces we have already discussed in Chapter 3, but also by the social norms and structures which are the focus of this chapter.

Homeric society is a vexed topic in modern scholarship. Historians have devoted a lot of energy to investigating how people relate to one another in the Homeric poems, what considerations motivate individual action and risk-taking, how the individual relates to the community, how public life is organised, whether the poems depict embryonic *poleis*, city-states, and, if so, what is the nature of these cities.[1] There is no great consensus regarding these questions, but most scholars approach the poems as reflecting pre-classical social structures. Like other 'primitive' systems, Homeric society is thought to be based largely on the competitive pursuit of status. Scholars focus on key concepts such as *timê*, 'honour', *geras*, 'gift of honour', and *kleos*, 'fame', in order to show that Homeric society, as a whole, values individual achievement more than collaboration.[2] Put negatively, Homer's (male) characters appear to care little about others; their main preoccupation seems to be with their own prestige, which they acquire and defend in a perennial zero-sum game: what one man gains is lost by his opponent. The Homeric heroes are standardly portrayed as individualistic, competitive, and brave to the point of cruel inhumanity. Brooks, for example, claims that Homeric men are 'trained to meet every emergency by an act of reckless bravery', without any consideration for others.[3] More generally, some scholars have claimed to have reconstructed a 'heroic code' which lies at the heart of the Homeric poems: individuals face death with little concern for their own or other people's safety in order to gain fame and social prestige.

In this world of primitive and undiluted self-assertion there seems to be little space for cohesive social structures, though, on the face of it, that is precisely what the Homeric poems show us: people in Homer live in large-scale communities and go to war in pursuit of common goals. Yet scholars disagree profoundly about how to evaluate communal life in Homer. The existence and nature of the Homeric *polis* has been the subject of a particularly heated debate: Finley famously argued that the Homeric poems reflect historical social structures dating to the ninth or tenth century BC, and that the *polis* in anything like its classical sense is largely unknown in the poems.[4] Others have taken different views. According to Morris, the poems were composed at a time in which the aristocracy was losing power and were intended to promote aristocratic values in the face of competing social forces, including the *polis* itself.[5] Raaflaub, on the other hand, sees in the poems many positive examples of emerging *poleis*.[6] Despite these different views, many scholars accept one important and, to our mind, questionable assumption: the Homeric poems reflect real, historical social structures in the pre-classical period.

It is unsurprising that no consensus has been reached regarding Homeric society: the poems in the form we have them are dated to different centuries by different scholars and, in any case, stem from a long tradition of re-composition in performance which developed over many centuries. It is therefore extremely difficult to establish quite what social structures, and from what period, they might be reflecting. The problem is compounded by our own ignorance of dark-age and archaic societies: the Homeric poems are often used as crucial sources of evidence for those periods, and arguments about the historical background of the poems tend to fall into some form of circularity. Problems do not end here. It seems to us that discussions of Homeric society often underestimate one important point: from the perspective of historical audiences, the Homeric poems depict a specific stage in the development of the world, the age of the heroes. Scholars have often asked whether 'Homer' and his audiences were familiar with the *polis* as a fully developed social structure: this question often turns out to conflate two separate issues. We can ask whether early Homeric audiences lived in cities and what they thought about social structures in their own day; and we can also ask whether they thought that the heroes lived in cities. The gods clearly do not inhabit a *polis* in the Homeric poems: they live in houses, *Olympia dômata*. What we would like to investigate is whether human beings inhabit a more developed social world than the gods at the stage in the history of the cosmos which the Homeric poems depict.

In this chapter, then, we are going to view Homeric society not as a reflection of real social structures in the dark age or the archaic period, but rather as a phenomenon which, in the Greek imagination, took place at a specific time within the overall history of the cosmos. It is possible and interesting, of course, to speculate about particular historical circumstances or memories from the distant past which may have influenced the portrayal of human and, indeed, divine societies in the Homeric poems. Yet it is also important not to divide the Homeric poems into 'literature' (the gods, narrative structures, allusion) and 'history' (social structures, warfare, artefacts): the world depicted in the poems is a coherent whole which made sense to early audiences. In this chapter, we seek to investigate the norms which govern the behaviour of men, women and society at large by placing Homeric society within the wider history of the cosmos as depicted in early Greek epic. In the last chapter we often looked back to the early history of the universe in order to explain the behaviour of the gods. In this chapter we more often look ahead to the world of the audience ('human beings as they are now'). As a result, we will be confronted with a different kind of resonance: the correspondences and differences between society as it was at the time of the Trojan War and the world as it is 'now', i.e. when the poems were performed in the archaic period.

Men, women and mortality

We have seen in Chapter 2 that the history of the cosmos was conceived as a huge family tree stemming from Earth's union with Heaven and branching out to the generations of mortals as they are now. Zeus becomes the supreme ruler of the universe after the demise of his father Cronus and his grandfather Heaven. One of the most persistent formulas which describes Zeus in early Greek epic, 'father of gods and men' (*patêr andrôn te theôn te*), expresses the supremacy of Zeus in genealogical terms. This formula is of crucial importance if we are to understand the development of the history of the cosmos. The power of Zeus is intimately connected to his role as a father: at *Iliad* 15.197-9, Poseidon links Zeus' supremacy to the fact that he can order around his sons and daughters at will. Erika Simon has argued that the power of Zeus is linked to his innumerable children on Olympus and on earth,[7] but the formula 'father of gods and men' seems to have very precise gender implications. The word *theos*, god, can be used both of male and female divinities, but the word *anêr* is usually applied to men as opposed to women. Other terms, *anthrôpos* (human being), or *brotos* (mortal) refer to both men and women, irrespective of gender. The implication is that Zeus is the father of gods and goddesses on the divine plane, but above all of men in the human sphere. This may seem strange, at first sight: we all know that Helen, for example, is described as the daughter of Zeus, though there is always some doubt about his paternity.[8] Clearly, the formula is not to be taken too literally. Still, it alerts us to a deep-seated assumption about men and women in early Greek epic. There is an unbroken line between gods and men: the *Theogony* and the *Catalogue of Women*, taken together, outline an enormous family tree which includes, as relatives, both gods and men. Women, by contrast, are separated from the divine sphere: Pandora, the first woman, is created out of earth and water, she has no divine ancestry.[9] In the *Catalogue of Women*, she appears at the beginning of the process whereby gods mate with mortal women and give rise to the heroes: she symbolises the separation between the sexes, and the beginning of mortal life.[10]

The divide between men as descendants of gods and women as separate from the divine affects the very form and nature of the epic universe as a whole. We have already seen that epic history is cast as the history of the divine family. In practice, that makes it a history of sons succeeding their fathers. As we have seen, Zeus manages to retain power by swallowing Metis, who otherwise would have generated a son stronger than himself. The other half of his strategy, however, is to populate the world with sons who speak of his power as 'the father of gods and men' without being in a position to challenge his supremacy.[11] Although Zeus is not literally the father or even the ancestor of all men, conceptually he is envisaged as the head of a huge family tree which includes gods and men but, leaving aside very few and explicable exceptions, does not include women. Other formulas emphasise this difference between the sexes. As far as females are concerned, there are goddesses, *theai*, and there are women, *gynaikes*. The male line, by contrast, includes gods, heroes and men. The heroes, in fact, are often called *andres hêrôes*, 'man heroes', an expression which emphasises their gender.[12] We should note that there is no equivalent formula to describe 'woman heroes', nor a Homeric word or expression which translates the English 'heroine'.[13]

In the last chapters, we have seen that, at the time in which the *Iliad* and the *Odyssey* are set, the pantheon is largely complete: the gods have stopped generating new gods, and the relationships between them have reached a stage of relative stability, as compared to the earlier revolutions of power described in the *Theogony* and the upheaval caused by the birth of new gods recounted in the *Homeric Hymns*. The concept of *timê* is absolutely crucial to the gradual process of settlement and stability on Olympus. In the *Theogony*, line 885, we are told that Zeus grants to each god his due honours, *timai*; the *Homeric Hymns* investigate in far greater detail how this is done and show how the proper distribution of *timai* vouchsafes the stability of the Olympian system. There is one issue, however, which still creates tensions among the gods: the honour and fate of their mortal sons on earth. Thetis entreats Zeus so that her son, Achilles, might receive his due honour, *timê*, on earth. She points out that since he is fated to die young, he should at least not be refused *timê*. The example of Heracles, which is discussed at *Iliad* 15.14-33 and again at 19.95-133, clearly shows that the gods care for their own sons partially as a way of asserting their own power in relation to other gods. Hera persecutes Heracles because she considers his existence an insult to her honour; Zeus champions him as a great son who represents the power of 'the father of gods and men'. In each and every case, the gods are concerned with their own male offspring: Helen may be the daughter of Zeus, but it is clear that the god has no special concern for her.[14]

If we now view the situation from the point of view of the male protagonists of the Homeric poems, we see that many of their concerns and motivations are connected to their status as descendants of the gods. For a start, the story of Achilles is intimately linked to the power of Zeus as father. As Laura Slatkin has argued, behind the predicament faced by

Achilles, and his terrible anger, lies the story of Thetis' unrealised union with Zeus.[15] According to Pindar, *Isthmian Ode* 8, Poseidon and Zeus both wanted to have sex with Thetis, but when they found out that her son would be stronger than the father, they changed their mind, and married her off to a mortal instead. We need not assume that the Homeric narrator is specifically alluding to this story in order to appreciate that the *Iliad* makes much of the humiliation inflicted upon Thetis.[16] The behaviour of Achilles and Thetis moreover suggests that Zeus owes them something: Achilles is the best of the mortal heroes and should at least be granted *timê*, given that he is in any case destined to die young. This is how Achilles himself describes the situation at 1.352-4:

> 'Since, my mother, you bore me to have a short life,
> therefore Zeus of the loud thunder on Olympus should grant me
> honour at least. But now he has given me not even a little.'

Achilles is speaking not so much as an exceptionally ambitious man, but as a member of the divine family who claims his rightful place within it. He regards the fact that he is short-lived as an affront that entitles him to compensation in the form of *timê*. Yet the requisite amount of compensation is not forthcoming. For Achilles, the mortal god, that means that Zeus is no longer distributing the cosmic honours 'well': all the gods received their *timai*, thus ensuring stability on Olympus, but what about short-lived Achilles? He claims that Olympian Zeus should grant him *timê* but fails to do so. This is a potentially dangerous claim, and Zeus takes Achilles' complaint very seriously.

The situation at the beginning of the *Iliad* prompts the supreme god to devise a plan which ensures that Achilles is granted *timê* by Agamemnon and the other Achaeans, though it remains doubtful whether the *timê* Achilles finally receives is an adequate compensation for a short life: there is a strong suggestion, in the poem, that it is not. It has to be said that not all men in the Homeric world have the same claim to honour as Achilles, nor can other heroes bring the same amount of pressure to bear upon Zeus. Achilles is in many ways special. Yet the problem he articulates is essentially the same for all the heroes: how can they, as divine yet mortal beings, find their appropriate place in the order of things?[17] What *timê* is due to the mortal sons of gods? In a sense, from the point of view of the audience, this question has a straightforward answer: heroes become the objects of cult after their death, that is their *timê*.[18] But the Homeric poems singularly fail to adopt the perspective of the audience in this important respect: hero cult is almost completely absent from the epics; instead, we are forced to adopt the heroes' own perspective on death. As far as they can see, there is no adequate compensation.

In their quest for honour, *timê*, the heroes resemble the gods: it is significant that both gods and goddesses are obsessed with their own *timê*, whereas women are not. Again, the *andres hêrôes*, the man heroes, are close to their divine ancestors but are fundamentally different from women. Other considerations also suggest that the preoccupations and aspirations of the heroes are to a large extent a result of their divine ancestry. *Mênis*, for example, the terrible anger felt by Achilles, is a sentiment that he shares with the gods but not with women. As Muellner has shown, the word *mênis* marks the break-down of cosmic order on a grand scale: things are not as they should be, and reparations have to be made quickly.[19] In the *Homeric Hymn to Demeter*, the goddess feels terrible anger, *mênis*, because her daughter has been taken away from her. She starves out humankind until the gods promise her *timê* and human beings begin to worship her as she deserves.[20] The parallels with the story of Achilles are obvious: his *mênis* is provoked by Agamemnon's appropriation of his slave Briseis, and as a result of this prevarication he behaves in a destructive manner towards the Achaeans, demanding that his *timê* be restored. But here the parallels end: when Agamemnon offers to give Briseis back, together with many other gifts, Achilles declines the offer and claims that nothing is as sweet to him as his dear life. For a moment at least, he does not seem prepared to face death on the battlefield on any grounds.[21] Eventually, he does return to the fighting, but out of grief for his own dead friend, Patroclus, rather than any sense of the honour that is due to him, as the best of the Achaeans, the son of the goddess, and the might-have-been son of Zeus.

The story of Achilles is exceptional yet at the same time paradigmatic. Just as his motivations shift from a godlike demand for *timê*, to a realisation of loss, so Homeric epic more generally shows us how the heroes learn what it means to be mortal. One important aspect of this process is the acceptance of women, and their role in human life. At the beginning of the *Odyssey*, Odysseus lives with a goddess and is promised eternal life:[22] instead, he chooses to return to his aging wife, and to an ordinary human existence on a rocky island, the emblem of present-day life. Similarly, in the *Iliad*, it is women who have the last word: book 24 closes with the ritual lament, *goos*, which Andromache, Hecuba and Helen perform at the funeral of Hector. Pat Easterling has shown that this form of lament is, in important ways, an alternative to the male quest for *kleos*.[23] Heroes often express the desire that their name and exploits may be known far and wide after their death: *kleos* is literally 'what is heard', and is an objective form of fame, memorialised in song and known to distant and future communities: epic poetry itself is a form of *kleos*. The ritual lament performed by women, on the contrary, emphasises the links between the deceased man and his immediate community: his wife, parents, and children, and all those who depended on him. In essence, every human being can hope to be remembered and memorialised by those who loved him: so the women's *goos*, which draws the *Iliad* to a close, represents an entirely human way of dealing with death which is appropriate to all men: *andres hêrôes*, but also *andres* more generally.

In short, the Homeric poems show us how the heroes learn to understand their own mortality and how they eventually come to view it in human terms. The compensation they seek, in terms of *timê*, associates them with their divine ancestors: both gods and men are sorely concerned with their own honour. Similarly, fame in the form of *kleos* is invoked as some sort of compensation for death, but it is not something to which all men can aspire. Penelope tells us that the bard sings the *klea* of 'gods and men':[24] clearly, through their *kleos*, some exceptional mortals enter the repertoire of bards to which the gods also belong. Not all mortals, however, can aspire to *kleos* and even the heroes suggest that it is no adequate compensation for death. In the end, they come to accept their own mortality in ordinary, human terms. In this process, women play a crucial role. They offer the last words at the funeral of Hector and, more generally, they are a symbol of ordinary human life. Odysseus leaves a goddess to return to his own wife, an exceptional wife to be sure, but a mortal one none the less. In itself, the association between women and mortality is not surprising. It pervades many ancient narrative traditions. Hesiod associates marriage with the drudgery of ordinary human life, and berates the need for women in a typically misogynistic way.[25] Other accounts are more sympathetic to women as a compensation for, or marker of, mortality. In the Old Babylonian *Poem of Gilgamesh*, the ale-wife Siduri says to Gilgamesh:

> 'You will not find the eternal life you seek.
> When the gods created mankind,
> they appointed death for mankind,
> kept eternal life in their own hands.
> So, Gilgamesh, let your stomach be full,
> day and night enjoy yourself in every way,
> every day arrange for pleasures.
> Day and night, dance and play,
> wear fresh clothes.
> Keep your head washed, bathe in water,
> appreciate the child who holds your hand,
> let your wife enjoy herself in your lap.'[26]

4. Men, Women and Society

This is the task of the ordinary man. Like Gilgamesh, the Homeric heroes hover between their divine ancestry and the future generations of mortals. In order to understand their behaviour and the nature of their social interactions it is crucial that we keep in mind this overall genealogical trajectory.

Men, women and war

In many ancient accounts of the history of the cosmos there is a traumatic event in which gods turn against mortals: the event creates a gulf between the two races, and defines the human condition. In some Near-Eastern traditions, a flood marks this transition. For example, in the poem of *Atrahasis*, the Babylonian account of the flood, we read that the gods were angry at the great quantity of human beings which populated the earth: their noise disturbed the gods' sleep. As a result, Ellil, the supreme deity, decided to send a flood and wipe them out.[27] In the Greek tradition, the gods also resent the growing human population and, for this reason, destroy them. However, in order to wreak their destruction, they choose a different method: they inflict the Trojan War, which causes the death of many men. The account is given most explicitly in the first fragment of the *Cypria* (fr. 1 Davies):

> Once upon a time the countless tribes <of mortals thronging about
> weighed down> the broad surface of the deep-bosomed earth.
> And Zeus, seeing this, took pity, and in his cunning mind
> devised a plan to lighten the burden caused by mankind from the face of
>   the all-nourishing earth,
> by fanning into flame the great strife that was the Trojan War,
> in order to alleviate the earth's burden by means of the death of men.
>   So it was
> that the heroes were killed in battle at Troy and the will of Zeus was
>   being accomplished.[28]

There are some obvious similarities between this account of the Trojan War and Near-Eastern stories of the flood:[29] in both cases, the gods want to relieve the earth (and themselves) of the burden of human beings. Yet the differences are equally telling. For a start, whereas a flood wipes everybody out, a war is especially deadly for men. The *Cypria* makes it clear that the Trojan War kills the heroes, not humankind in general. Thus, just as early epic distinguishes between 'man heroes' and 'women' in terms of birth and genealogy, so it draws a sharp distinction between them with respect to death. In the Homeric poems, it is specifically men who have to face death, women almost always survive. It is in fact remarkable how little is made of female death in the Homeric poems: even a superficial comparison with tragedy, where women often meet violent deaths, throws this characteristic of epic into relief. In the Homeric poems, women provide continuity in human life: we have already seen that they memorialise Hector after his death. They also continue to live, and look after children, after the death of their husbands.

There are other telling differences between the Trojan War and Near-Eastern flood narratives. A natural catastrophe such as a flood leaves very little room for personal choice, individual response, or social interaction and decision-making: human beings are no fish, and when faced with a torrential floodwave there is little left for them to do.[30] By contrast, in war, men are constantly asked to participate actively, to risk their lives consciously, to choose to die. Homeric epic shows us how warriors interact with one another in the face of death, how they question the value of a (male) life, and consider the rewards which might make it attractive to risk it.

When asked why warriors fight in the Homeric poems, scholars tend to quote a famous passage from *Iliad* 12, where Sarpedon tells Glaucus why they should fight in the first line of battle (12.310-28):

> 'Glaucus, why is it you and I are honoured before others
> with pride of place, the choice meats and the filled wine cups
> in Lycia, and all men look on us as if we were immortals,
> and we are appointed a great piece of land by the banks of Xanthus,
> good land, orchard and vineyard, and ploughland for the planting of
>   wheat?
> Therefore it is our duty in the forefront of the Lycians
> to take our stand, and bear our part of the blazing battle,
> so that a man of the close-armoured Lycians may say of us:
> "Indeed, these are no ignoble men who are lords of Lycia,
> these kings of ours, who feed upon the fat sheep appointed
> and drink the exquisite sweet wine, since indeed there is strength
> of valour in them, since they fight in the forefront of the Lycians."
> Man, supposing you and I, escaping this battle,
> would be able to live on forever, ageless, immortal,
> so neither would I myself go on fighting in the foremost
> nor would I urge you into the fighting where men win glory.
> But now, seeing that the spirits of death stand close about us
> in their thousands, no man can turn aside nor escape them,
> let us go and win glory for ourselves, or yield it to others.'

James Redfield has called this passage 'the most lucid statement of the hero's role and task'.[31] More generally, scholars have seen in Sarpedon's speech the clearest formulation of 'the heroic code' – a set of principles and motivations which lie at the heart of Homeric heroism: honour is gained from risking one's life in the first line of battle. Now, the reasons given by Sarpedon for why one should fight in battle are complex, ranging from a sense of obligation to one's community ('why is it you and I are honoured') to an equally marked sense of the futility of human existence ('But now, seeing that the spirits of death stand close about us'). Despite this complexity, some recent studies have focused on the ruthlessness of the Homeric hero *qua* warrior, speaking for example, of 'an anticommunity of combat' where heroes 'must overcome mercy and terror and learn to value their honor above their own lives or another's'.[32] It seems to us that a spirit of community can be detected even on the battlefield, and emerges clearly also in this passage.

It is first of all important to note that Sarpedon does not talk about heroes at all in his speech to Glaucus: he tells him what they should do as 'kings', *basilêes* – a social term. This is an important detail because it points to a fundamental difference between ancient and modern concepts of heroism. In English and other modern languages, the term 'hero' tends to denote a single individual of exceptional bravery. We talk about 'heroes of war', we may jokingly claim 'you are a hero', or even urge 'be a hero!'. None of these uses has its equivalent in Homeric Greek. The Homeric term *hêrôs* is never used in normative contexts in order to tell people how to behave towards one another. *Hêrôs* denotes primarily an individual who lived long ago, in the heroic age, somebody who died and whom the audiences may now worship in hero cult. One could say that the Greek term *hêrôs* immediately opens a historical perspective and encourages comparison between *hêrôes* of old and men as they are now. In the Homeric poems themselves, the term *hêrôs* is used relatively rarely, and often in contexts which offer a historical perspective on the narrative. In the proem of the *Iliad*, for example, we are told that the anger of Achilles 'hurled to the house of Hades the strong souls of heroes': the historical resonance of this passage is unmistakable. The *Iliad*, like many other heroic epics, promises to tell us how the heroes met their end. It is not surprising that ancient readers compared this opening to the beginning of the *Cypria*: both texts suggest that the plan of Zeus leads to the destruction of the heroes.[33]

Since the term *hêrôs* implicitly draws a comparison between the epic world and the world of the audience, it is unsurprising that characters which belong to the heroic age use it sparingly. In tragedy, which shows the famous heroes of old interacting with one another on stage, the word *hêrôs* is all but absent.[34] Within the Homeric poems, characters do occasionally address each other as 'heroes', but they never tell one another to 'be heroes' or talk about heroic codes of behaviour. We have seen that even the passage which, according to modern scholarship, represents the clearest expression of the 'heroic code' does not talk about *hêrôes* at all, but rather outlines the duties and privileges of leaders. Generally speaking, it seems that when Homeric characters want to discuss or define proper social relationships among themselves they invoke two sets of concepts: they may tell one another to 'be men', or they may remind themselves how leaders should behave towards their people. In other words, if we are interested in studying Homeric society, the concept of 'hero' is close to useless. It is much more promising to analyse the language of masculinity and leadership, since both are repeatedly used to define how men should behave towards one another.

In the Homeric dialect, there are two different words which are standardly translated as 'manliness' but which have very different connotations: *ênoreê* denotes proper masculinity, whereas *agênoriê* is best understood as 'excessive masculinity', usually in a negative sense.[35] If we ask ourselves what characterises the behaviour of 'excessively masculine' men, we soon realise that they tend to behave in an antisocial and/or self-destructive way: for example, they tend to have no concern for their own safety and that of others. According to Diomedes, Achilles is an extreme case of excessive manliness. When he refuses the gifts that Agamemnon offers him and decides not to return to the battlefield, Diomedes thinks that this is the ultimate example of *agênoriê* (*Iliad* 9.697-700):

'Son of Atreus, most lordly and king of men, Agamemnon,
I wish you had not supplicated the blameless son of Peleus
with countless gifts. He is *agênôr* (excessively manly) at the best of
    times,
but now you have driven him far deeper into his *agênoriai* (extreme
    masculinity).'

Achilles refuses to consider the needs of his fellow Achaeans who are in very serious danger without him. His refusal to fight with and for them is taken by Diomedes as a sign of selfish, hypermasculine behaviour. Other passages in the poem confirm that Achilles has to learn to be a proper man, that is, care for others, rather than be solely concerned with his own *timê*, as a god might be.

Hector too is accused of being 'too manly', though on slightly different grounds. In a famous passage in *Iliad* 6, he refuses to listen to

Andromache who asks him to stay behind the walls of Troy. 'War is of concern to men', Hector replies, and adds that it is his concern above everyone else's.[36] He appears to be striking a careful balancing act between a proper, that is, socially responsible form of masculinity (*ênoreê*) and reckless bravado (*agênoriê*). Andromache is not convinced, and when she hears the wailing for Hector, she immediately suspects that it was his reckless courage (*agênoriê*) which killed him, 22.454-9:

> 'May what I say never come close to my ear, yet dreadfully
> I am afraid that noble Achilles might have cut off bold Hector
> alone, away from the city, and be driving him towards the plain,
> and that he will have put an end to the bitter *agênoriê* (excessive manliness)
> that always was on him, for he would never stay back where the men
> were in numbers, but break far out in front, his strength giving way to no one.'

Andromache spells out the main danger implicit in excessive manliness: it threatens to cut off an individual from other men, thus making him vulnerable and endangering those who rely upon him for support, including his family and city. Now, Hector would probably disagree with Andromache's analysis of the situation and so would many readers of *Iliad* 22: Hector's decision to face Achilles on his own is dictated by a complex set of reasons, it is not simply an act of reckless self-destruction. Yet it is clear that the language of masculinity itself highlights the importance of solidarity among men: Andromache's use of the term *agênoriê* is not tendentious, even if her analysis of the situation may be. In the *Iliad*, the words *agênôr* 'very/too manly' and *agênoriê* 'excessive manliness' typically refer to an isolated individual who fails to co-operate with others for the common good and often damages himself as well in the process.

If we look at injunctions to 'be men' in the *Iliad*, we see once again that proper masculinity involves care for and solidarity with other men. Never, in the course of the poem, is an individual told to 'be a man', in the singular. Rather, warriors are addressed collectively and told to 'be men', as a group. Injunctions of this kind are common in the *Iliad*: they follow a standard pattern and resonate through the poem. This is an example of such an injunction, uttered by Agamemnon at 5.529-33:

> 'Be men, dear friends, and take up the heart of courage,
> and have consideration for each other in the strong encounters,
> since more come through alive when men consider each other,
> and there is no glory when they give way, nor strength either.'

The idea expressed in this, and other similar passages, is simple: 'being men' involves looking after one another on the battlefield.

In the *Odyssey*, definitions of proper masculinity are rather different. This is unsurprising, since the war is over and there is no need for cohesion and mutual care on the battlefield. Yet, in this poem too there is a clear sense that 'being a man' entails proper consideration for other men and their role in society. The adjective *agênôr*, 'excessively manly', is standardly used to describe Penelope's suitors.[37] This use of the adjective may, at first sight, seem strange. In the *Iliad* it is almost always used in the singular, and it tends to describe an isolated individual who rushes forward into battle on his own, thus endangering himself and others. The suitors are neither isolated nor excessively brave. And yet, the use of the term *agênôr* to describe them makes sense. Their excessive masculinity is displayed, above all, in the fact that they covet someone else's wife. A man, or more precisely 'the man' of the proem, desires his own wife: we should remember that in ancient Greek *anêr* means both 'man' and 'husband'. The hypermasculine suitors, by contrast, reveal their lack of manly restraint by wooing another man's wife: in their lack of consideration for proper, respectful and caring relationships between men, they resemble the recklessly individualistic warriors of the Iliadic battlefield. The parallel makes sense on more than one count. In the first place, the behaviour of both the suitors and reckless warriors is self-destructive. Secondly, and perhaps more importantly, it is antisocial, in that it fails to take into account the needs and rights of other men. In both poems, therefore, normative definitions of masculinity emphasise the importance of proper relations among men: on the battlefield, they seek to ensure solidarity for the sake of safety and glory; in times of peace, they safeguard the role of the man/husband within the family.

Like the language of masculinity, the language of leadership also emphasises the individual's duties towards a wider society of men and, indeed, women. We have already seen that Sarpedon links the social rewards accorded to kings, *basilêes*, with the special responsibilities and expectations that are attached to that role. More generally, in the Homeric poems, leaders are repeatedly called 'shepherds of the people' and, in that role, they certainly have very precise duties towards their 'flock'.[38] The trouble is that leaders regularly fail to look after their people: in fact, they are consistently held responsible for destroying them. In *Iliad* 9, Agamemnon has a moment of despair when he realises he has 'destroyed many people' and that, for this reason, he will have to sail home with a bad reputation, or bad *kleos*.[39] Similarly, Achilles' decision to withdraw from the battlefield has disastrous consequences for the people;[40] Hector too is worried that he might be said to 'have destroyed the people',[41] and Odysseus' relationship to those who followed him to Troy is anything but straightforward: after all, he returns home on his own, having lost all his people.[42]

The fact is that 'shepherds of the people' consistently fail to protect their flock in the Homeric poems. Sometimes they try hard, as in the case of Hector, but ultimately none of the more important Homeric leaders is successful as a shepherd of the people. This failure of leadership is embedded in the very language of epic: a complex system of formulas expresses the thought 'he destroyed his people' in many different metrical and grammatical contexts.[43] There is no equivalent system which expresses the thought that the leader saved his people or looked after them like a good shepherd: the suspicion arises that there is no reason to express this thought precisely because epic leaders very rarely act successfully. This consideration should make us pause. It is remarkable that the people, or *laoi*, to use the Greek term, are invariably depicted as a vulnerable group, dependent on their leaders and doomed to be let down by them. The reasons why this is the case should be sought, we think, in the overall history of the cosmos.

We have seen that, as descendants of the gods, the heroes are deeply concerned with their own mortality, for which they seek compensation in terms of honour, *timê*, and fame, *kleos*. In their quest for compensation, they are fundamentally uninterested in the needs of others, or in society more generally: we have seen that Achilles' quest for *timê* is, and is meant to be, damaging for the rest of the Achaeans: like a god, he strikes down on mortals until his powers are recognised. Other Homeric characters also strike us as selfish, individualistic, and bent on their own self-assertion.[44] Yet we have also seen that as 'men', the Homeric heroes are repeatedly urged to look after one another, to fight together for common safety, and to respect one another's role in the family. It is as 'men' rather than demigods that the heroes are asked to abide by the rules of human society. Similarly, as leaders, the heroes have very precise duties: they are presented as shepherds who should look after their flock. This role of shepherd of the people is conceived as entirely human in Greek epic: it is important to note that no god is said to be a shepherd, or to have a people, *laos*, for whom he or she should care.[45] The trouble is that just as the Homeric heroes often fail to behave as 'men' should, so they fall short of their duties towards their people: Achilles causes the destruction of the Achaeans; Odysseus loses all his companions (who are sometimes called his people, *laoi*);[46] moreover, when he arrives in Ithaca, he causes more destruction by unleashing a civil war. It seems that here as elsewhere the Homeric poems depict a world in transition: as men, the heroes are expected to care for one another; as leaders they should look after their people; but in fact, we often see them entirely concerned with their own mortality, and the rewards they can reap from life. In their quest for *timê*, they behave like their ancestors, the gods, and the gods are neither 'men', nor 'shepherds of the people': the social expectations aroused by both these terms do not apply to them.

The city

We have seen that Homeric epic depicts a society in a phase of transition. There is a clear sense that men should co-operate with one another for the sake of the common good, yet individuals often behave in a selfish, antisocial and ultimately self-destructive manner. Similarly, the poems offer a clear sense of how leaders should behave towards their people: we have seen that the metaphor of the 'shepherd of the people' implies that leaders should look after their people and ensure their well-being. However, leaders typically fail in their role as shepherds: Agamemnon, Achilles, Hector and Odysseus are all, at some point, accused of having 'destroyed the people'. In general, it is possible to detect a tension between the behaviour of individuals as descendants of the gods, and their duties as members of a human society. This tension is played out above all in the figure of Achilles: we have seen that in order to ensure that he obtains the *timê* he deserves, he is willing to inflict endless suffering on the Achaeans. His wrath, *mênis*, has been compared to that of Demeter in the *Homeric Hymn to Demeter*: the goddess is so angry and pained by the loss of her daughter that she inflicts death by starvation until she is appeased with the promise of *timê* among gods and mortals.[47] The trouble for Achilles, however, is that he is not a god: in *Iliad* 9 he suggests that no amount of *timê* can compensate for his death, and later he decides to join the battle again not because he receives his due honour (though he does, in as much as a mortal can do), but because he has lost his companion Patroclus, and wants to avenge him.

We have also seen that women play an important role in the assertion of human values and institutions. Through their ritual lament, *goos*, they memorialise the dead in an entirely human way: the emphasis is not on *timê*, nor on everlasting fame, *kleos*, but rather on the depth of loss for those who loved and depended upon the deceased. In other words, the women's ritual lament emphasises the importance of social relationships among human beings belonging to the same family, city and society. There are many other ways in which women help to form and promote social relationships. We have seen, for example, that Andromache is quick to accuse Hector of excessive masculinity when he dies: he has failed to stay together with the other men, thus making himself, and those who depend on him, vulnerable. If we consider that women have no strong genealogical link with the gods, it becomes all the more clear why they come to symbolise human life and society.

If we now step back for a moment and consider the overall trajectory of epic history, it seems that as the history of the cosmos progresses, individuals become less strong: for example, in terms of individual prowess the heroes are inferior to the gods but superior to present-day humans. Conversely, however, social norms and structures only emerge in the course of cosmic history. This is already clear in the transition from the rule of Heaven to the reign of Zeus. Heaven is vast, almost omnipresent, and he seems to rule entirely by might. In later generations, however, the world becomes more complex: more and more gods are born, and power needs to be negotiated between them. Zeus has supreme power, but it is clear that he does not simply rule by force: he distributes different honours among the gods and rules with the help of *dikê*, justice – a social concept if ever there was one.[48] The society of the gods, however, remains fairly primitive. The overall social framework, on Olympus, is that of the family: as we have seen, the concept of leadership in a non-biological sense is largely alien to the gods and, for this reason among others, the formula 'shepherd of the people' is never applied to a god.[49] Another important difference between the Olympian family and human societies on earth concerns the institution of the city. Gods live in 'Olympian houses', *Olympia dômata*; human beings, by contrast, live in cities. If we look at the distribution of the word *polis* in early Greek epic, an interesting pattern emerges: it is absent from the *Theogony*,[50] and makes its appearance in the age of the demigods as described in the *Catalogue of Women*, the *Iliad*, and the *Odyssey*. Finally, the *Works and Days*, for all its focus on country life, is firmly set in a world of the *polis*.[51] Like other social institutions, the *polis* emerges gradually in the course of history. The myth of the ages, as it is told in the *Works and Days*, shows this very clearly.[52] The emphasis there is of course on the degeneration of man. Yet, a counter-history of institutional progress can also be detected. There is little evidence of social organisation in the golden age, and golden-age men are tellingly said to roam the earth as perennial nomads after their death.[53] Families and houses are first mentioned in the silver age.[54] Bronze-age men too are explicitly said to live in houses, both before and after death (lines 150 and 153 respectively). Cities make their first appearance in the times of the heroes, if we assume that 'Thebes of the seven gates' is envisaged as being one.[55] The word *polis* and related terms are not used at this stage; yet it does finally appear in Hesiod's description of the iron age.[56]

It seems that Aristotle follows the logic of epic when he describes the development of human society from the house to the city.[57] The gradual transition from one to the other as a focus of social life coincides with the transition from a purely divine world in the *Theogony* to the world of mortals in the *Works and Days*. The *Iliad* and the *Odyssey* depict a crucial moment of transition, and in this section we look at the *polis* as it is depicted in these two poems. We begin by investigating the attitude of the gods towards this human institution.

Bluntly put, in the *Iliad*, the gods do not seem to care much for cities. There are, to be sure, cities that are dear to them: Hera, for example, is the patron goddess of Argos, and the walls of Troy were built by Poseidon, with some help from Apollo.[58] However, when it comes to it, the gods seem to care very little about cities, and are ready to destroy them in order to make a point vis-à-vis other gods in internal Olympian struggles for power. Representative, in this respect, is the exchange between Zeus and Hera in *Iliad* 4.50-68. Hera hates Troy, ever since Paris failed to choose her as the most beautiful goddess. In this passage she pleads with Zeus for the destruction of Troy, arguing that he should let the city perish since Hera too is a daughter of Cronus, and deserves honour and respect. In return, she is willing to give up her three most beloved cities: whenever Zeus feels like it, he is welcome to destroy Argos, Sparta and Mycenae.

This exchange is symptomatic of the overall attitude of the Iliadic gods towards the cities of mortals. On the whole, the fate of cities is embroiled in the gods' assertion of their own power, and with the overall distribution of *timai* in the cosmic order. Poseidon is the Olympian god most obsessively concerned with his own *timê*: he is also the most consistently hostile to cities. He works for the destruction of Troy, although he originally helped to build it; he feels personally challenged by the Achaean palisade and insists on its being obliterated beyond a trace;[59] and he precipitates the demise of Scherie, another heroic-age polity.[60] In the case of Scherie, the logic of 'family above city' is abundantly clear: Poseidon turns against the Phaeacians and their city, whom he previously cherished, because they help Odysseus return home. If we ask why he resents Odysseus' return the answer is clear: the hero blinded Poseidon's son Polyphemus and should be punished for it. As far as the god is concerned, the rights of his own son clearly override his patronage of the Phaeacians and their city.[61]

Other episodes demonstrate that the gods are more interested in individual heroes than in human cities. Hera and Athena are hostile to Troy because Paris offended them.[62] Zeus is a more complex figure, yet he is certainly not a city god in any straightforward sense. We know that he has destroyed many cities in the past and will do so in the future.[63] By contrast, we hear little about him saving or founding cities. This is particularly remarkable when we compare his stance vis-à-vis the household and family. As *herkeios*, Zeus protects the farmstead.[64] As *xenios* he protects the rights of family guests.[65] Whereas these two epithets link the god to the concerns of the household, no attribute of Zeus speaks of his protection of cities. Under the influence of the gods, heroes too seem to privilege the house and immediate family over the city and the wider community: Aphrodite carries Paris off to his palace and wife in book 3, thus nullifying the settlement that has been reached between the warring parties.[66] Achilles too abandons the common cause and leaves the assembly place to withdraw to his own tent: his mother Thetis supports him.[67]

The most blatant case in which personal considerations override the protection of the city can be seen, perhaps, in Athena's response to two prayers in *Iliad* 5 and 6. The prayers frame Diomedes' moment of glory, his *aristeia*, and are clearly complementary. Diomedes prays to Athena to assist him as he enters into combat with his spear (5.118). By contrast, the Trojan women pray to her to 'break the spear' of Diomedes (6.306). Structurally, the prayer of Diomedes marks the beginning of his rampage, whereas that of the Trojan women coincides with its end. By then, Diomedes has exchanged armour and completed his *aristeia*. It is all the more striking, therefore, that Athena does not heed the prayer of the Trojan women. The sequence is constructed far too carefully to suggest a trivial explanation, such as that the plot 'demanded' it. Whatever else the two passages may mean, they clearly make a point about the nature of the Homeric *polis*. And in doing so, they simultaneously make a point about the concerns of the Homeric gods.

Diomedes and the women of Troy invoke Athena in strikingly different ways. Diomedes reminds the goddess of the loving relationship she had with his father, Tydeus (*Iliad* 5.116) and asks her to support him in turn (line 117). Athena recognises the ancient bond and agrees to fill Diomedes with the fighting spirit of his father (line 125). The basis of Diomedes' successful prayer is thus a relationship between a heroic household and a god, which passes from one generation to the next rather like the relationship of guest-friendship. This model of divine-human interaction contrasts sharply with that evoked by the women of Troy. They address Athena as (*e*)*rhysiptolis* (*Iliad* 6.305), 'she who saves the city', asking her to take 'pity on the city, the wives of the

Trojans and their helpless children' (lines 309-10). In turn, they promise a communal offering. The attitude and expectation of the Trojan women reminds us of many rituals and offerings to the gods in 'the world as it is now'. As we shall see in the next section, the Athenians, for example, offered a robe to their patron goddess Athena at their most important city festival, the Panathenaea. Within the *Iliad*, however, the prayer and offering of the women of Troy is doomed to fail: the links between gods and heroes are just too strong to be counteracted by the communal prayers of women. We have seen in the previous section that women speak for the bonds between members of the community and that men are often urged to take care of one another. Similarly, leaders should look after their people, yet in practice the social norms embedded in the language of leadership and masculinity often fail to be respected: individual concerns over one's own personal honour and prestige undermine social cohesion and the well-being of the larger community. In the *Iliad*, the gods care for their own *timê* and for their personal relationship with individual heroes more than they care about the safety of cities or the communities which live within them.

There are, however, some episodes in the Homeric poems which point to a future time in which the gods no longer involve whole cities in their personal struggles for power and prestige, but rather begin to act as distant and fair protectors of human communities. This is perhaps most clearly the case at the end of the *Odyssey*. In the last books of the poem, the question of succession in Odysseus' house draws the whole of society into a spiral of violence. The crisis of the heroic-age city, we note, is again associated with family concerns. Yet the dispute over the house of Odysseus does not lead to wholesale destruction. The decisive turn of events comes about in *Odyssey* 24, when Odysseus is on the verge of massacring the Ithacan *laoi*.[68] In this last episode, Zeus finally has his mind set on saving the city. Athena is despatched down to stop Odysseus, and sanctions a permanent settlement. Though Athena is the champion of Odysseus throughout the poems, she does not act out of a whimsical preference for him: rather, she obeys her father and seeks a solution to the conflict which is based on the justice of Odysseus' position and which benefits the whole community. In the later stages of the history of the cosmos, the gods are often presented as guarantors of justice, *dikê*, in the city: this view is prominent, for example, in the *Works and Days*. What we seem to find at the end of the *Odyssey* is a first example of a goddess acting in order to preserve social justice, rather than in order to assert her own power and prestige or that of her family and friends. In Chapter 5 we shall see that the end of the *Odyssey* depicts a world that is remarkably close to that of the audience in other respects too.

As we mentioned at the beginning of the chapter, scholars have endlessly debated the nature of the Homeric *polis*, without paying sufficient attention to the fact that, from the perspective of the audience, the Homeric poems depict a very specific moment in the history of the world. It is not surprising that the Homeric *polis* and Homeric society more generally seem primitive to modern observers who are trained on the classical *polis*: in a sense, this is exactly how it is meant to appear. Institutions such as the *polis* are only beginning to develop in the age of the heroes and are constantly threatened by the gods, and the heroes themselves, who are more concerned with their own power and prestige than with the well-being of the community. We have seen that gods and heroes are not simply primitive but that their concerns are dictated by the overarching narrative of how the world came into being. In a sense, the Homeric poems tell a story of decline: the heroes are stronger than ordinary mortals. On the other hand, however, they outline a story of institutional progress, and of a gradual increase of social stability and justice. This general development emerges most clearly if we consider the contexts in which the Homeric poems were performed.

The world of the audience

As we have already seen, the Homeric poems say nothing specific about their intended audience. The only thing we are told explicitly is that the world of the poet and his audience is later than that depicted in the poems themselves. The poems repeatedly compare the heroes of old to mortals 'as they are now', not, we note, mortals 'as they really are'.[69] The distinction, then, is primarily drawn between different historical ages, rather than between reality and fiction, or 'myth' and 'history'. In a sense, in order to interpret the Homeric poems, we do not need to know anything more specific about their context of performance, as long as we remember that it belongs to the 'present', and that it is populated by mortal beings as they are 'now'. Ancient listeners would have known how to decode the contrast, both in terms of the degeneration in physical prowess (from the heroes to lesser mortals) and in terms of the unfolding structures of society (from rudimentary families to cities). However, depending on the particular context in which the poems were performed, the comparison between the world 'then' and the world 'now' acquired further significance and led audiences to view the poems in a particular light.

We know that the poems were performed in many areas of Greece and in a variety of different contexts, but in the case of one particular city, Athens, we happen to have more detailed information about the performance of Homer. We know that the poems were performed, at least from the sixth century onwards, at the Great Panathenaea, the main city festival in honour of the patron goddess Athena. In the remainder of this chapter, we look at how Homeric society resonates with the world as it is 'now' in the particular context of the Great Panathenaea. It seems to us that the festival context is so important for our understanding of Homeric society that we might meaningfully speak of a 'production' of the poems analogous to theatrical performances. Just as each production of, say, Shakespeare's *Hamlet*, crucially affects our response to the play on any given occasion, so did the way the Athenians collectively staged the Homeric poems – with the important difference that the Panathenaic 'production' remained largely unchanged for a long period of time.

The Panathenaea was the most important festival of the Athenian calendar year.[70] It celebrated the birthday of Athena and the history of her city from its beginnings to the present day. The festivities featured various kinds of displays, athletic contests and, above all, a lavish procession from the city gates to the Acropolis, which culminated in a communal sacrifice to the patron deity, Athena Polias ('Athena of the city'). The Great Panathenaea, a more extensive version of the festival which was celebrated every four years, featured, among other attractions, the performance of Homeric epic. In fact, the performance of Homer – and Homer only – was a legal requirement from early on.[71] The participants in the festival and also in the procession were, in theory at least, all those who lived in the city: men, women, children, foreign residents and guests. It follows that the Homeric poems were deemed to be of interest to the entire community.

As a festival that celebrated Athens, the Panathenaea encouraged comparison between the society described in the epics and present-day Athens. This could be done from a variety of different angles. For example, Athenian audiences could compare the heroes they honoured in cult, chiefly Theseus and Erichthonius, with the race of heroic men as the Homeric poems describe them. They could compare their own fate as the people of Athens to that of the Homeric *laos*, a people perennially threatened by disaster; and they could also compare their city, Athens, with the heroic-age cities described in the Homeric texts, chiefly Troy. In all these instances, Homeric epic resonates meaningfully with the context of performance.

At the beginning of this chapter we suggested that the Homeric heroes as a race of men descended from Zeus were almost as obsessed with their own place in the system of divine honours as the gods themselves. As with the gods, their preoccupation manifested itself in an often destructive self-interest. By contrast, Athenian heroes, and above all Theseus and Erichthonius, whom the Athenians honoured at the Panathenaea, were often linked to social progress. They were remembered for having advanced human society, and their era marked not so much the end of cosmogony but rather the beginning of civilisation as we know it. In recognition of their contribution to the advancement of society, men like Theseus were venerated in cult: unlike their Homeric counterparts, they did not lack proper honours. The relationship between the Homeric race of heroes and the founders of Athens can thus be described in terms of a contrast between two views of social history, one where the collective crisis of the heroic age leads to death and disruption and one that emphasises continuity and progress.

Similar observations can be made about the second aspect of Homeric society which we have been studying, the people and their leaders. We have seen that the *laoi* of the heroic age depend for their well-being on individual leaders who do not usually act as they should. One of the resonant phrases of heroic epic is 'he destroyed the people', a formula that encapsulates the failure of the shepherd of the people. An Athenian audience at the Panathenaea would have thought of itself as a *laos* who, with the help of stable institutions and a new relationship with the gods, had made the transition to better times. They no longer had to rely on heroic-age 'shepherds of the people' but, every time the herald called them together as a *laos* (or rather *leôs*, in the Athenian dialect), they could hope for a secure and prosperous future.[72]

Finally, we can see a similar contrast at work between heroic-age Troy and present-day Athens. As a celebration of the city of Athens, the Panathenaea encouraged listeners to focus on the Homeric *polis*. More specifically, it encouraged audiences to compare their own relationship with their patron goddess Athena to that between Athena and 'her' city in epic: Troy. Comparison invariably worked in favour of Athens and so helped to reinforce the festival's patriotic message. More generally, Homeric epic helped the Athenians to pinpoint a critical moment in their own political history; and to understand the reasons why Athens succeeded where powerful, glorious Troy had failed. The crisis of the heroic city described in Homer is overcome at Athens through the stable relationship with the gods which the Panathenaea celebrates. If we ask how exactly this might have worked in practice, we may usefully start by considering *Iliad* 6 against the background of the Panathenaic procession. Comparing the garment that the Athenians offered to their patron goddess with that offered by the Trojans will have had the effect of rooting political reflection in the context of divine history. Athena in *Iliad* 6 is invoked as *(e)rhysiptolis*, 'saviour of cities', the epic equivalent of the Athena *Polias* worshipped at the Panathenaea.[73] It is all the more telling that the heroic-age city of Troy cannot persuade the goddess, whereas Athens proudly considers itself her favourite city. There is no obvious reason why Athena should accept the Athenian *peplos* but refuse the Sidonian robes she is offered in the *Iliad*; but this does not mean there is no reason at all. As has long been observed, the Sidonian robes offered by the Trojan women serve as a poignant reminder of the human entanglement in divine history (the judgment of Paris and all that follows from it).[74] The Athenian *peplos*, by contrast, has no such connotations. It has been acceptable to Athena in the past and, for this reason, it is assumed that it will be acceptable in the future. Athena's refusal to grant the prayer of her Trojan worshippers characterises her as a heroic-age Olympian who values personal relationships more than the needs of the city. By contrast, Athena Polias has truly become a city goddess.

It is important to emphasise that the Homeric poems were not performed only at the Panathenaea; there is, moreover, no clear evidence to suggest that they were composed or heavily manipulated to suit that context.[75] In other situations, ancient audiences will have drawn slightly different comparisons between the world depicted in the poems and their own lives. In a more private setting, for example, such as a classroom or an individual tutorial, the poems were used for moral edification and as studies of exemplary characters: we know, for example, of a father who insisted that his son learn the whole of the *Iliad* and the *Odyssey* by heart in order to acquire the best possible aristocratic education.[76]

All these readings are important and relevant for the interpretation of the poems, but it seems to us that, as far as a study of Homeric society is concerned, the performance of the poems at public festivals such as the Panathenaea is particularly significant, in that it encouraged a collective response. We know that the Homeric poems were performed widely at city festivals other than the Panathenaea, though most of our evidence comes from Athens. In other cities, comparisons between heroic society and present-day institutions will have worked somewhat differently. Yet some of the observations we have made remain relevant. In particular, audiences at other city festivals will have been in a position to appreciate the development of social institutions, such as the *polis*, and the communal worship of the gods as protectors of entire communities.

Conclusion

We have seen that, in the course of cosmic history, individuals become gradually less powerful, while social institutions grow in complexity and stability. Heaven rules by sheer might and is eventually replaced by Cronus and then Zeus, who establishes a patriarchal rule based not only on the power but also on the justice of the father. In the age of the heroes, we witness an even more complex set of social institutions. Whereas the gods live in 'houses' and their relationships are basically familial, the heroes live in cities. The Homeric poems leave no doubt that male characters have a number of obligations not just as family members and husbands, but also as members of a social group: they should look after one another on the battlefield and respect one another's role as husbands in the home. Men also have precise responsibilities as leaders. The fact is, however, that they tend to fall short of all these obligations and to follow their divine ancestors in valuing their own power and prestige above the needs of the wider community.

The Homeric poems, then, depict a crucial moment in the development of human society. Women play an important role in this gradual process which transforms the cosmos into the world as it is now. They are, from the beginning, separate from the gods: they are never, as a group, treated as privileged daughters of Zeus. As a result they tend to be associated more readily with the present day: Achilles considers whether to fight for immortal *kleos*, or go home and get married – an alternative which would make his life much more similar to our own. Hector, for all his dreams of *kleos*, is ultimately remembered in the *goos* of the women. Odysseus rejects life with a goddess and immortality in order to return to his wife. To 'be a man' is to live with women in the families that make up human cities. It is also to recognise one's responsibility to other men and to the people one leads. The Homeric heroes are 'men' in this sense. But as sons of the gods they are also caught in the logic of cosmogony which dictates that they secure for themselves a place of honour in the larger order of things. In this respect, as in so many others, the Homeric poems depict a world in transition: social norms, aspirations and institutions can only be understood if we take into account the earlier and later development of the cosmos. In the next chapter, we explore how the overall history of the cosmos resonates through the personal stories of Achilles and Odysseus.

5

Death, Fame and Poetry

In the last two chapters, we have looked at some major aspects of the world depicted in the Homeric poems: the gods, fate and nature in Chapter 3; the structures, aspirations and development of human society in Chapter 4. The overall impression that emerged from those chapters was that of a world in transition: the gods have stopped directly challenging the authority of the 'father of gods and men', and live in a fairly stable hierarchy. However, their concern for their mortal sons on earth still upsets divine relationships on Olympus. This is particularly obvious in the *Iliad*; but the *Odyssey* too shows how Poseidon, a god still linked to an earlier logic of violence and self-assertion, cares for his own son Polyphemus more than for his relationship with the other gods. As far as human society is concerned, we have seen that the 'godlike' heroes still think like gods, at least to an extent: in particular, their preoccupation with personal honour, *timê*, is a trait that they share with their divine ancestors. At the same time, the poems show that men are developing a sense that 'as men' they should care for one another on the battlefield and respect the norms of human society, such as guest friendship and marriage, in times of peace. A more collaborative system of values is in the making.

One aspect of the Homeric poems to which we have so far paid little attention is the depiction of individual characters. Readers of Homer have often been struck by the subtlety of Homer's character portrayals and the pathos of their suffering. Diomedes, Eumaeus, Andromache, Nausicaa and countless others are all fully drawn personalities each with their own deeply felt hopes and fears, triumphs and anxieties. If we were to attempt an in-depth discussion of Homer's characters, this book would have to be at least twice its current length: even the most anonymous victims of battle usually receive some attention from the narrator, if only in the form of a fleeting epithet or a brief simile. The overall impression is one of unusual complexity and richness, and it is no coincidence that epic in time gave rise to the most character-conscious of all Greek genres: Athenian tragedy. In this chapter, we do not aim to discuss the overall effect of character portrayal in Homer partly because the topic goes well beyond the scope of the book, and partly because there are other good studies of the subject.[1] We would, however, like to suggest that an awareness of the overall tradition of Homeric and Hesiodic epic, and the history of the cosmos which it describes, is relevant to the understanding of individual life stories. For reasons of space, we focus on the protagonists of the Homeric poems, Achilles and Odysseus, but we believe that our approach is useful for the interpretation of other characters too.

In the first part of this chapter, we show how the personal stories of Achilles and Odysseus are rooted in the resonant order of the epic cosmos. It is not just coincidence, or simply a matter of literary fiction, that Achilles is prone to extreme, uncompromising anger and that Odysseus is cunning and adaptable: their character traits speak, among other things, of their place within the unfolding history of the universe. In the second part of the chapter, we explore the connection between individual character and overall tradition from a different perspective: we argue that the individual stories of Achilles and Odysseus evoke the overall history of the cosmos from the beginning to the present. In the course of the poems, these two characters undergo developments which bring them closer to the world of the audience. What emerges from the discussion is a complex connection between mortality, fame, and epic poetry itself. Individual characters shape their own *kleos* as a means of transcending, at least in part, their death. *Kleos*, we have seen, includes epic poetry; so the characters' own reflections on personal fame beyond death and the songs that we hear about them are intimately connected. Before we investigate the complicity between individual characters and the Homeric audience, we must however look one last time at the overall picture of the epic tradition.

The death of the heroes: two perspectives

We have seen that the texts of the Homeric tradition mark points of crisis and transition within the wider context of cosmic history. At a very general level, the *Homeric Hymns* ask how the Olympian gods find their place in the overall order of things. Similarly, the major epics can be read as stories of heroes struggling to find their place in the world. The *Iliad* explores what it means for Achilles to be the son of a divine mother and a mortal father; whereas the *Odyssey* asks what it is to be a 'man' with a wife, a family, a home and people. Both Achilles and Odysseus thus appear to be engaged in timeless and culturally unspecific pursuits: all human beings must come to terms with death (whether or not they have divine ancestors), and they almost all live in a society and family context in some way comparable to those of Odysseus. Achilles and Odysseus, then, can be seen as exponents of an abstract problem which we might call 'the human condition', and this is how they have often been understood. Yet it is our contention that not only do the historical circumstances of the Trojan War form the 'setting' and necessary backdrop to the suffering of individuals, but that their suffering is inextricably woven into the fabric of history as Homeric audiences saw it. In other words, where modern readers separate historical fact from literary drama, early Greek audiences saw the drama of the heroes as a necessary part of the history of the cosmos.

In order to understand what is at stake in the stories of Achilles and Odysseus we must first of all return to the fate of 'heroic men' at the time of the Trojan War. We have already discussed several aspects of their existence in Chapters 3 and 4, such as their quest for honour and their attempt to find some form of recompense for death. In this section we propose to start from the downfall of the heroes as a race, and then narrow the discussion to some basic choices and problems faced by Achilles and Odysseus. The characteristic tone and perspective adopted in the Homeric poems emerges most clearly from a comparison with Hesiod. In the *Catalogue of Women*, the Hesiodic poem that recounts the rise and fall of the demigods, we hear (fr. 204.96-103 M-W):

> For at that time high-thundering Zeus planned grandiose things,
> stirring up <quarrel> throughout boundless earth.
> Already he was eager to make away with the copious race of mortals,
> all the while pretending to destroy the demigods,
> lest they, the gods' children, seeing [the light (?)] with their eyes (i.e.
>   being alive), waste (?) away [together] with the earthly people,
> but blest [and strong (?)] as formerly,
> they would have their life and their seats apart from human beings.[2]

The text of the passage is poorly preserved, and some details of the restoration are uncertain.[3] However, the overall gist is clear enough. Zeus has in mind 'grandiose things'. His apparent purpose is to destroy the demigods. Yet, what he really plans is to remove the 'children of the gods' from contact with ordinary humankind and ensure that they continue to live in bliss as they did before the war was inflicted upon them.[4] What the poem describes is a time of great confusion and suffering. In a line shortly after the passage quoted we hear of 'suffering upon suffering' resulting from the plan of Zeus.[5] However, the text insists that there is a deeper purpose behind the turmoil: the children of the gods need to be saved from an ordinary human fate. As 'demigods' they deserve better than what the miserable mortals will soon experience, once the climate changes, the seasons start succeeding one another, and a new (i.e. the present) age of toil and woes begins.[6] Immediately after the passage quoted above, we find a description of the beginning of seasonal change and the suffering that ensues for humankind. The heroes are spared this fate: their apparent destruction is, in fact, a gigantic rescue operation.

The Hesiodic account of the Trojan War highlights the family relationship between gods and heroes and plays down the heroes' connection with the rest of humankind. Once removed from ordinary mortals, the heroes become closely assimilated to the gods by being called *makares*, 'blessed ones', a term with unmistakable divine connotations.[7] For all the suffering it entails, the crisis of the demigods thus has a strikingly positive outcome: the Hesiodic heroes are spared the miserable conditions that are in store for the rest of us. The Homeric account could not be more different: the heroes are themselves presented as 'miserable mortals', and the Trojan War is seen as the cause of their downfall. Except for one passage, Homer's heroes are never called *hêmitheoi*, 'demigods'.[8] We have already seen how one poem, which was attributed to Homer in the archaic period, views the death of the heroes. This is how the *Cypria* began (fr. 1 Davies):

> Once upon a time the countless tribes <of mortals thronging about
> weighed down> the broad surface of the deep-bosomed earth.
> And Zeus, seeing this, took pity, and in his cunning mind
> devised a plan to lighten the burden caused by mankind from the face of
>   the all-nourishing earth,
> by fanning into flame the great strife that was the Trojan War,
> in order to alleviate the earth's burden by means of the death of men.
>   So it was
> that the heroes were killed in battle at Troy and the will of Zeus was
>   being accomplished.[9]

The *Cypria* recounts the beginning of the Trojan War and the first nine years of fighting. While the text itself is lost, a late summary of the plot survives, as well as some fragments, including the one we have just quoted.[10] It is not difficult to see certain parallels between this opening fragment and the Hesiodic account cited above. In both cases, Zeus plans a cosmic disaster. In both cases, the disaster is nothing but the Trojan War itself: it is the conflict that leads to the disappearance of the heroes. However, despite these parallels, the Homeric passage invites us to adopt a very different perspective. The heroes of the *Cypria* are not distinguished from (other) 'human beings': they are simply called *anthrôpoi*. They are not assimilated to the gods either, and their disappearance does not result in a life of bliss. We have seen that Hesiodic epic separates the cosmic disaster that befalls humankind from the Trojan War that is fought by the heroes. In the Homeric passage the two events coincide. The Trojan War, in other words, is itself the disaster. The heroes have little to gain: fame may be one consolation for death but, as we shall see, it remains at best an inadequate reward.

The fragment from the *Cypria* illustrates well the overall outlook of the Homeric tradition, including the *Iliad* and *Odyssey*. Rather than elevating the heroes to the status of gods, Homeric epic emphasises the doom that overhangs their existence. Scholars have long been aware that the Homeric account differs from the Hesiodic one in this important respect, though they have not always agreed on the precise nature of the relationship between the two traditions. Griffin, for example, suggests that, unlike Hesiod, Homer is simply uninterested in fitting the disappearance of the heroes into a universal scheme of human history.[11] Seth Schein adds an important qualification: Homeric audiences will have been aware of narratives which emphasised the afterlife of heroes and their blessed and powerful status after death: after all, the cult of the heroes and their tombs is well attested from the eighth century onwards. Audiences, therefore, will have been struck by the perspective adopted in the Homeric tradition: 'in the *Iliad*, regardless of what the audience may have expected from their familiarity with the traditional conceptions of an afterlife, Homer suppresses all mention of any continued or posthumous existence for mortal warrior-heroes.'[12] Schein goes on to explain that death as an absolute boundary is crucial for the *Iliad*'s approach to human life. The decisive issue, in other words, is not so much Homer's refusal to consider the bigger picture: after all, we have seen that the *Cypria* can present the Trojan War as the cosmic event which destroys the heroes, and the proem of the *Iliad* also insists that as a result of the war, and Achilles' anger in particular, countless souls of heroes have been sent to Hades.[13] The point is rather that the Homeric tradition chooses to focus on the moment just preceding the downfall of the heroes. Homer and Hesiod do not describe two different realities but rather adopt different viewpoints. Hesiod is interested in the structures that make up our world. In Hesiodic epic, it is important that the 'children of the gods', whose births constitute the bulk of the *Catalogue of Women*, are not just left to disappear without a trace: we are told what place they have in the present order of things. Once dead, they are blessed forever. The Homeric narrator, by contrast, concentrates not on what remains after death, but on what is lost. His prime focus is not the structure of the universe but the suffering of individual characters.[14]

125

Achilles and the rift between gods and men

The Homeric poems do, of course, emphasise that the heroes are closer to the gods than ordinary mortals are, yet the perspective adopted is mainly that of the heroes themselves, who are forced to realise that, unlike the gods, they must die. From their point of view, the limitations of mortality are far more striking, and more difficult to accept, than their relative proximity to the gods – which in any case becomes obvious mainly in comparison with later generations of mortals. Many traditional epithets applied to the heroes describe them as 'equal to the gods', 'divine', 'godlike', 'born of Zeus'. Yet, in the Homeric poems, these expressions are not always used in a straightforward way: in particular, the phrase *daimoni isos*, 'equal to a god', is employed precisely in contexts where a hero must realise his own human limitations. There is a tension, in other words, between our perception of the heroes as close to the gods, and their bitter realisation that there is an insurmountable gulf between themselves and their divine ancestors.

When Achilles decides to withdraw from battle, several heroes try to take on his role as the best of the Achaeans. They are forced, in the course of the story, to face their own limitations as human beings, just as Achilles must eventually accept his own humanity and mortality. It is typical of the resonant poetry of Homer that the scenes in which Diomedes and Patroclus are confronted by Apollo and forced to back down anticipate the confrontation between the god and Achilles himself, even at the level of single words and expressions. As will become obvious, in each case the phrase *daimoni isos*, 'equal to a god', is used to describe a situation in which the hero is forced to recognise just how unlike a god he actually is.

In *Iliad* 5, Diomedes experiences his *aristeia*, his moment of greatest power and glory on the battlefield. In the course of his rampage, he even manages to wound Aphrodite and Ares, thus momentarily blurring the line between gods and mortals. It is Apollo, the god most pressingly concerned with safeguarding the distinction between human and divine,[15] who eventually brings him to his senses. When Diomedes charges against Apollo, the god reminds him of his proper place in the order of things (5.438-42):

> But as he charged a fourth time equal to a god (*daimoni isos*),
> Apollo who strikes from afar cried out to him in the voice of danger:
> 'Take care, retreat, son of Tydeus, and strive no longer
> to make yourself like the gods in mind, since never the same is
> the breed of gods, who are immortal, and men who walk upon the
>   earth.'

5. Death, Fame and Poetry

After Diomedes' achievements – he is at the apex of his *aristeia* – the god's warning constitutes a particularly stern lesson: human beings are 'never' like the immortal gods. This message resonates throughout the *Iliad*. In book 5, Diomedes acts as the main Achaean champion in the absence of Achilles;[16] later in the poem, Patroclus plays the same role: he goes back to the battlefield wearing Achilles' own armour, and leading the Myrmidons while Achilles still refuses to join the battle. Patroclus acts with great valour but Apollo, once again, makes sure that he does not overstep his limits (16.702-11):

> Three times Patroclus tried to mount the angle of the towering wall,
> and three times Phoebus Apollo battered him backward
> with his immortal hands beating back the bright shield.
> But as he charged a fourth time equal to a god (*daimoni isos*)
> Apollo called aloud, and spoke winged words in the voice of danger:
> 'Give way, illustrious Patroclus: it is not destined
> that the city of the proud Trojans shall fall before your spear
> nor even at the hand of Achilles, who is far better than you are.'
> He spoke, and Patroclus gave ground before him a great way,
> avoiding the anger of him who strikes from afar, Apollo.

Patroclus, like Diomedes, is called *daimoni isos*, equal to a god, precisely at the moment when he is confronted by a real god, Apollo, and told to back down. This is no coincidence. The phrase is used again when Apollo thwarts Achilles himself, as he attempts to kill Hector at 20.444-8:

> ... But Phoebus Apollo caught up Hector
> easily, since he was a god, and wrapped him in thick mist.
> Three times swift-footed noble Achilles swept against him
> with the brazen spear. Three times his stroke went into the deep mist.
> But as he charged a fourth time equal to a god (*daimoni isos*)
> Achilles called aloud, and spoke winged words in the voice of danger.

There is an obvious irony in describing Achilles as a man 'equal to a god' (*daimoni isos*) at the very moment when Apollo snatches Hector away with the ease that only a real god possesses (*rheia ... hôs te theos*). The two phrases look similar, yet they have very different connotations: whereas *daimoni isos* describes an illegitimate attempt on the part of a mortal to arrogate for himself superhuman status, *hôs te theos* is used in contexts where the superiority of gods over mortals is made apparent. The two ideas, though related, are expressed in different formulaic shapes. Readers attuned to the resonant patterns of epic thus find the ambivalent status of Achilles encapsulated in the very language of our passage. By frustrating Achilles' attempt to kill Hector there and then, Apollo frustrates his attempt to arrogate for himself the strength and status of a god. The language in which this is put quietly underlines the point.

There is no doubt that the three scenes we have just considered are linked. Diomedes substitutes for Achilles and is reminded by Apollo of the limitations of the human condition. Patroclus substitutes for Achilles and is reminded by Apollo that neither he nor Achilles himself is fated to capture Troy. Finally, Apollo meets Achilles and, again, asserts the gulf between gods and mortals. The encounter between Achilles and Apollo leads up to another confrontation between them, which we have already discussed. In book 22, swift-footed Achilles fails to catch up with the god who, being immortal, runs even faster. Apollo makes him realise the irony of the situation (22.8-20):

'Why, son of Peleus, do you keep after me in the speed of your feet,
being mortal while I am an immortal god? Even yet you have not
seen that I am a god, but strain after me in your fury.
Now hard fighting with the Trojans whom you stampeded means
    nothing to you.
They are crowded in the city, but you bent away here.
You will never kill me. I am not one who is fated.'
Deeply vexed, swift-footed Achilles spoke to him:
'You have balked me, striker from afar, most malignant of all gods,
when you turned me here away from the rampart, else many Trojans
would have caught the soil in their teeth before they got back into Ilion.
Now you have robbed me of great glory, and rescued these people
easily, since you have no retribution to fear hereafter.
Else I would punish you, if only the strength were in me.'

There is a deep-seated antagonism between Achilles and Apollo throughout the *Iliad*, and indeed in the wider epic tradition. This tension can be explained in part by the fact that Apollo is the Homeric god most concerned with upholding the divide between gods and humans, whereas Achilles is the human being who most consistently challenges that divide.[17] The antagonism which underlies all the scenes we have discussed so far in a sense foreshadows the moment in which the god actually kills Achilles. It is important, however, that the *Iliad* does not recount that moment: it lies in the future.[18] Instead, the poem presents us with scenes in which Achilles must come to realise his own limitations as a mortal: he may strive to be equal to a god, *daimoni isos*, but he is forced to see that he is not. The point of view adopted is that of Achilles himself: this is one of the reasons why his death is not included in the poem. We are not made to view the death of Achilles at the hands of Apollo as third-party observers; rather, we see how the god confronts the hero and makes him realise his own mortal limitations while he is still alive.

Viewed from the perspective of the heroes, questions about the value of a human life and the possible rewards for death are unavoidable. We may think of the heroes as demigods who are long dead, whom we worship in cult, and who act as protectors for us ordinary humans in the iron age. But this is not what the heroes themselves were thinking when they faced their own extinction. We have seen in the last chapter that Homeric men inherit from the gods a need to be given an adequate place in the order of things, that is, to be accorded the *timê*, the honour, they deserve. We have also seen that their preoccupation with status is complicated by the fact that they must die. We now come to the same problem from a different angle: given that, in Homer, we share the perspective of the heroes to a large extent, we must ask, with them, what kind of *timê* is appropriate for a mortal. The question quickly becomes one of adequate recompense. Since death has little appeal in itself, there has to be, from the point of view of the protagonists, something that makes it worthwhile to risk their lives.[19]

The issue is raised above all by Achilles who, as we have seen, embodies with most urgency the predicament of all the heroes. Agamemnon precipitates a crisis in Achilles' existence by taking away his token of honour, Briseis. Achilles responds with anger, withdrawing from the Achaean war effort and blackmailing his overlord, until the humiliated king agrees to return Briseis, together with countless other gifts. The women, cities, tripods, and other goods that Agamemnon promises in *Iliad* 9 betoken a transferral of honour on an unprecedented scale. However, Achilles' position has hardened. He points out that no amount of gifts could bring him back to life once dead. It is because Achilles knows that he must die that Agamemnon's offerings are unacceptable to him (9.406-9):

> 'Cattle and fat sheep are things to be had for the lifting,
> and tripods can be won, and the tawny high heads of horses,
> but a man's life cannot come back again, it cannot be lifted
> nor captured again by force, once it has crossed the teeth's barrier.'

Achilles' speech in book 9, from which the above lines are taken, is among the most hotly debated passages of all Greek epic. It continues to raise a number of difficult issues: is Achilles justified in rejecting

Agamemnon's offer? Should he have accepted the gifts even though Agamemnon still appears to be interested above all in his own standing as a leader? Achilles' speech may even seem disingenuous: is he really concerned with the value of a human life or is he simply vying for supremacy?[20] Without wishing to underestimate the complexity of Achilles' motivations, we would like to make one specific point. Achilles rejects as flawed a mechanism that underpins much of Homeric society: the appropriate allocation of honour, *timê*, among humans. It may be that Agamemnon is simply failing to offer Achilles the right *kind* of recompense, as has been argued recently.[21] Yet, if that is so, Achilles uses the opportunity to develop a far more radical line of criticism: nothing that Agamemnon could offer makes up for his death. Indeed, ever since the quarrel of *Iliad* 1, Achilles has been looking for a different way of acquiring status: the kind of permanent *timê* that Zeus can grant and which ensures a stable order to the divine universe in perpetuity.[22]

In the course of the poem, Achilles' honour is in fact gradually restored, but only at the cost of social catastrophe. The pattern is familiar from earlier episodes in the history of the cosmos. In the *Hymn to Demeter*, the goddess is granted proper honours after she has displayed *mênis* and caused starvation among human beings. Similarly, Achilles' quest for *timê* is linked to the devastation of the Achaeans on the battlefield. However, whereas Demeter is able to bestow prosperity on humankind once her honour has been restored, it is very unclear that Achilles is in a position to do the same. As a mortal, his role is not that of bestowing divine gifts on humankind for ever more, but rather that of behaving as a responsible man and leader during his own life-time. The issue of Achilles' honour thus comes into direct conflict with the developing norms and structures of human society which we have described in the last chapter. Indeed, by book 16, the hero famously expresses the wish that everyone might perish and only he and Patroclus be left alone to conquer Troy.[23] In the same context, Achilles acknowledges that Zeus has honoured him by smiting the very people who, as a heroic-age leader, he is supposed to protect (16.237):

'You did me honour and smote strongly the people of the Achaeans.'

At this point, it becomes clear that the logic of honour, *timê*, which was a crucial principle in the formation of a stable divine system, has become deeply problematic. In Chapter 4 we saw that the emerging world of human beings depends to a large extent on a sense of social obligation. Human beings do not live alone, and it is not acceptable for leaders to destroy their own people, the *laos*, under any circumstances. While Achilles tries to rectify a perceived breach in the divine order, which traditionally rests on well-distributed *timai*, he becomes himself a threat to the emerging order and stability of human society.

The problem resurfaces when Patroclus dies. Again, Achilles sets out to gain redress by appealing to concepts and modes of behaviour which were appropriate at an earlier stage in the history of the cosmos. Again, he fails to find satisfaction. This is what he tells Hector when he kills him (22.271-2):

> '... Now you will pay in a lump for all those
> sorrows of my companions you killed in your spear's fury.'

There are various words for revenge in Homer. The one that underlies Achilles' threat to Hector is *tisis*, which may derive from the same root as *timê* and is closely related to it in meaning.[24] Whereas *timê* is the status one acquires, *tisis* is the retribution one exacts. Like *timê*, *tisis* is crucial in the making of the epic universe. It is used of the conflict between Heaven and his children, as well as that between Cronus and Zeus.[25] Achilles undertakes to avenge the death of his companion, just as Zeus had avenged the transgression of the Titans. Yet, unlike Zeus, Achilles fails to bring about a solution that is satisfactory to him and acceptable to others. Like his quest for honour, Achilles' act of revenge puts him on a collision course with the emerging values of human society. In a famous speech in *Iliad* 24.33-54, Apollo points out the outrageousness of his behaviour and draws a sharp distinction between Achilles and the gods. According to Apollo, Achilles' reaction to the death of Patroclus is excessive and inexcusable. What is more, it makes him resemble an animal, not a god:

> 'You are hard, you gods, and destructive. How did not Hector
> burn thigh pieces of oxen and unblemished goats in your honour?
> Now you cannot bring yourselves to save him, though he is only
> a corpse, for his wife to look upon, his child and his mother
> and Priam his father, and his people, who presently thereafter
> would burn his body in the fire and give him his rites of burial.
> No, you gods; your desire is to help this cursed Achilles
> within whose breast there are no feelings of justice, nor can
> his mind be bent, but his purposes are fierce, like a lion
> who when he has given way to his own great strength and his haughty
> spirit, goes among the flocks of men, to devour them.
> So Achilles has destroyed pity, and there is not in him
> any shame; which does much harm to men but profits them also.
> For a man must some day lose one who was even closer

than this, a brother from the same womb, or a son. And yet
he weeps for him, and sorrows for him, and then it is over,
for the Destinies (*Moirai*) put in mortal men the heart of endurance.
But this man, now he has torn the heart of life from noble Hector,
ties him to his horses and drags him around his beloved companion's
tomb; and nothing is gained thereby for his good, or his honour.
Great as he is, let him take care not to make us angry;
for see, he does dishonour to the dumb earth in his fury.'

Achilles, the god points out, does not display proper human behaviour. Mortals know how to endure: they grieve for a while, but then they know how to overcome their sorrow, even if they lose a brother or a son. Apollo suggests that, in failing to conform to their behaviour, Achilles does not thereby become like a god, but rather like an animal, a lion who knows no pity and no shame.[26] The tendency to separate all mortals from the realm of the gods, which is crucial to the Homeric tradition as a whole, is nowhere clearer than in this passage. Apollo generalises Achilles' experience by comparing it to that of all human beings in distress. He mentions none of the mechanisms of revenge and recompense which have been important not only to Achilles' worldview but to the early history of the universe more generally. No amount of honour can help humans soothe their pain: they cry and wail, and eventually they stop. Endurance is their only possible response. Achilles must learn that there is no compensation for Patroclus' death or, indeed, for his own.

The logic of honour and revenge, which worked well for the gods when they had to settle their own conflicts, is simply not a viable model for Achilles in establishing his own place in the world. There remains one other way in which he can try to compensate for death. We have seen in the last chapter that the word *kleos* refers to what human beings hear, and is used of the contents of epic poetry itself.[27] In the *Iliad*, it can be accompanied by the epithet *aphthiton*, 'unperishing'. This qualification indicates why glory is so important to Achilles and the other heroes: *kleos* bridges the gap between the dead and the living.[28] One of the most famous descriptions of *kleos* in the *Iliad* makes this very clear: in book 7, Hector envisages himself as killing an enemy and predicts that the enemy will be buried by the sea. Future generations of men will sail past the tomb and remember for ever his glorious deed.[29] In some ways, Hector's vision is ironic: the *Iliad* closes with his own death, not that of a slain enemy, and in any case a tomb is supposed to memorialise the deceased, not his killer. Despite these ironies, the passage highlights some of the fundamental features of *kleos*: fame transcends death and spreads among future, distant people.

5. Death, Fame and Poetry

As we have seen, in book 9 Achilles is confronted with some difficult questions: what should he do with his life? Should he accept Agamemnon's gifts and return to the battlefield? It is in this context that he reflects most explicitly on the connection between *kleos*, life and death. He speaks of a precise choice between a long and obscure life and an early death accompanied by ever-lasting fame (9.410-16):

> 'For my mother Thetis the goddess of the silver feet tells me
> I carry two sorts of destiny toward the day of my death. Either,
> if I stay here and fight beside the city of the Trojans,
> my return home is gone, but my glory shall be everlasting;
> but if I return home to the beloved land of my fathers,
> my excellent fame is gone, but there will be a long life
> left for me, and my end in death will not come to me quickly.'

If Achilles' speech as a whole is full of problems, this passage is particularly enigmatic. We may ask whether Achilles' choice is in any sense realistic: are we meant to entertain the possibility that he might actually sail home, and thus suspend our knowledge of the tradition which dictated that he stay? Or should we see Achilles' speech as heavily ironic? Is Achilles making a specific point about the incompatibility of *kleos*, fame, and *nostos*, homecoming, for the benefit of his interlocutor, Odysseus? Should we see this speech as defining the *Iliad* itself against the tradition of the *Odyssey*?[30]

For the present argument, it is important to note that *kleos* is presented as a kind of compensation for death, but not necessarily as an adequate one. Although we know that Achilles is destined to stay, die young, and remain the object of song for future generations, we are forced, in book 9, to look at his existence from his own perspective, and consider the future, however fleetingly, an open question. He weighs two options and, momentarily at least, chooses in favour of a long, peaceful and obscure life. At one level, Achilles' decision is very personal. It is part of a polemical speech, calculated to hurt Agamemnon, Odysseus and the other Achaeans. Yet Achilles' temporary rejection of a glorious death and fame everlasting has a wider significance. Despite the fact that, in epic, *kleos* is presented as highly desirable, there are crucial moments where it appears merely as an imperfect substitute for a life that cannot last forever.[31] It has been rightly said that death in the *Iliad* is a creative as well as a destructive force.[32] Yet, Homeric *kleos* never entirely emancipates itself from the bereavement that comes with death and that is expressed in the lament or, as epic itself would have said, the *goos* of the survivors.[33]

Through the personal story of Achilles, his dilemma in book 9, we thus return to the unresolved problem of the heroes' place in the cosmic order. The honours accorded to the heroes after death in the Hesiodic tradition are not relevant, or rather do not appear to be relevant from the perspective of the heroes themselves, which is the privileged viewpoint within the Homeric poems. Instead, we are left with 'the glorious deeds of men', *klea andrôn*, as the sum of what is known – and told – among human beings in later times. This creates a peculiar complicity between the audience and the protagonists of Homeric epic. By spreading the fame of the heroes, we too become implicated in their quest for life: we know about Achilles because, in the end, he did not choose a long and obscure life, but died young on the battlefield. The complicity between the heroes and the audiences who listen to their *kleos* is far from unproblematic. As examples of *klea andrôn*, the Homeric epics convey a deep sense of regret which comes from the realisation that death cannot ever be properly recompensed. The heroes' failure to find eternal life lives on in our songs.

There is little sense of triumphalism in the Homeric account of the Trojan War. Nor is its characteristic pathos, and the ability to view things from the perspective of individual characters, simply a matter of poetic dexterity. There is dexterity of a different kind in the Hesiodic vision. What we argue, instead, is that the peculiar tone of the Homeric poems, and above all the *Iliad*, must be understood as part of their place in – and perspective on – the resonant order of cosmic history. Once we realise that the Homeric poems adopt a specific register appropriate to a particular moment in time, the moment just before the death of the heroes, we can begin to develop a more nuanced understanding of the different *kinds* of *kleos* appropriate to different phases in the history of the cosmos. The fame Achilles gains in the *Iliad* is not the same as the renown Odysseus wins in the *Odyssey*. The *Iliad*, which is set before the end of the Trojan War, contrasts *kleos* with a successful homecoming. In the *Odyssey*, which charts new pathways through the ruins of an old world, the fame of the protagonist becomes primarily a function of escaping the heroes' impending doom. For Odysseus, fame and survival are inseparable.

Odysseus: the fame of the survivor

There is at least one crucial difference between Achilles and Odysseus: whereas the Iliadic hero thinks of himself as having a choice between *kleos* and *nostos*, fame and a safe journey home, for Odysseus *kleos* and *nostos* go together. Nagy has argued convincingly that in this respect the *Odyssey* and the *Iliad* are complementary, indeed, that they compete with one another through their different conceptions of fame.[34] We would add that they also take a different stance towards the unfolding history of the cosmos: in the *Iliad*, the death of the heroes is seen as a final and unavoidable boundary which divides Achilles, Hector and the other victims of war from future generations (*essomenoi* – 'those who shall be'). The *Odyssey*, by contrast, tells a story of survival and transformation.

We have seen that, in *Iliad* 9, Achilles tells Odysseus, of all people, that he must choose between *kleos* and *nostos*. In *Odyssey* 11, the two heroes meet again, in the Underworld, and reflect on the value of life. At 11.482-6, Odysseus deprecates his own fate and tells Achilles that he should not grieve, even in death:

> '... Achilles,
> no man before has been more blessed than you, nor ever will be.
> Before, when you were alive, we Argives honoured you as we did the gods,
> and now in this place you have great authority over the dead.
> Do not grieve, even in death, Achilles.'

There are some Hesiodic echoes in this passage: Odysseus denies that anyone is 'more blessed', *makarteros*, than Achilles, just as the heroes are *makares*, 'blessed', in the *Catalogue of Women*.[35] Moreover, he claims that Achilles was honoured like a god while he was alive and continues to have special privileges after death; in other words, he tries to construct a narrative of continuity: Achilles, the best of the Achaeans, remains special before and after death. Achilles, however, refuses to accept Odysseus' account of bliss, honour, and continuity of status. He insists that nothing compensates for the loss of life (11.488-91):

> 'O shining Odysseus, never try to console me for dying.
> I would rather follow the plough in thrall to another
> man, one with no land allotted him and not much to live on,
> than be a king over all the perished dead.'

Achilles refuses to view himself as a privileged being, the best of heroes, and insists that life is the only thing that matters: even the life of a landless, hired labourer. In the *Iliad*, he repeatedly complained that Agamemnon did not accord him his due *timê*, and treated him instead as a migrant, dispossessed individual, the most wretched and dishonoured of beings.[36] In view of those statements, his present position is all the more remarkable: Achilles rejects the notion of honour, *timê*, altogether, and insists that it is life alone that matters, under any circumstances. Scholars have rightly seen in this passage the promotion of a specifically Odyssean ethos: survival is always worthwhile, even at the cost of humiliation.[37] For Odysseus, survival is itself a source of *kleos*: he must endure travel, poverty and abuse, but these difficult circumstances are part of his claim to fame. Whereas Achilles had to choose between unperishing *kleos* and returning home to an ordinary human life, Odysseus combines these two options in his own story.

Readers of Homer have often seen the different conceptions of fame promoted in the *Iliad* and *Odyssey* as a reflection of the character of the protagonists.[38] It is certainly right that both Odysseus and Achilles have very well defined characters which affect their views and choices: Achilles is straightforward, intense and uncompromising; Odysseus cunning, adaptable, bent on survival. Yet, we should not forget that their characters are in turn shaped by the circumstances in which they live. Odysseus and Achilles are, of course, roughly contemporaries; but Odysseus survives the Trojan War and, in the course of his journey, gradually travels towards an ordinary human existence, in a world that is recognisably closer to our own than that depicted in the *Iliad*. After all, members of a Homeric audience can aspire to enjoy many aspects of Odysseus' life in Ithaca: a stable marriage, a growing son, an aging father. In short, it can be said that in the *Iliad*, *kleos* bridges the gap between the heroes who die at Troy and the future generations who hear about them: *kleos,* and more specifically poetry itself, provide some continuity between the world of the heroes and our own. In the *Odyssey*, *kleos* is closely associated with Odysseus' *nostos*, a journey which in turn bridges the gap between the Trojan War and life in Ithaca: a rocky island ridden with problems, but remarkably close to post-heroic Greece.

In the next section, we look in further detail at the ways in which Odysseus' journey brings him closer to our own world, and to the experience of ordinary humankind, but for the time being we must address the connections between character, *kleos*, and cosmic history. There is no doubt that fame is conceptualised differently in the *Iliad* and the *Odyssey*: a comparison of two passages which define *kleos* and its function shows this most clearly. In *Iliad* 22.297-305, Hector reflects upon *kleos* shortly before dying:

> 'No use. Here at last the gods have summoned me deathward.
> I thought Deïphobus the hero was here close beside me,
> but he is behind the wall and it is Athena cheating me,
> and now evil death is close to me, and no longer far away,
> and there is no way out. So it must long since have been pleasing
> to Zeus, and Zeus' son who strikes from afar, this way; though before
>   this

136

they defended me gladly. But now my fate is upon me.
Let me at least not die without a struggle, inglorious,
but do some big thing first, that future generations shall know of it.'

Hector is sure that he is about to die: death is 'close' to him and 'no longer far away'. At this moment he resorts to *kleos* as a typically Iliadic way of transcending death. In doing something worthy of memory, Hector bridges the gap between himself and future generations (*essomenoi*). Let us now compare the following passage, *Odyssey* 9.16-20:

'Now first I will tell you my name, so that all of you
may know me, and I hereafter, escaping the day without pity,
be your friend and guest, though the home where I live is far away
    from you.
I am Odysseus son of Laertes, known before all men
for the study of crafty designs, and my fame goes up to heaven.'

This is how Odysseus introduces himself to the Phaeacians at the beginning of his long first-person narrative in *Odyssey* 9. The perspective is that of the survivor who builds new relationships in a changing world: the name, and with it Odysseus' claim to fame, establishes a basis for guest-friendship, *xeniê*, between himself and the Phaeacians, should he ever make it home. Note that Odysseus does not think about the resonance of his name among future generations; rather, he mentions his fame as a way of establishing a useful friendship. In a way, his very speech can be seen as an example of his 'crafty designs', in that it aims to ensure the support of the Phaeacians in his plan to return home. In both the *Iliad* and the *Odyssey*, definitions of *kleos* have a predictive force: the characters define their own claim to fame and simultaneously determine what kind of poem we hear about them. Conversely, however, the specific moment in history in which they live determines what character traits are most desirable, what kind of fame they can hope to attain, what stories will be told about them.

Iliadic and Odyssean conceptions of *kleos* are often directly contrasted in the Homeric poems themselves. We have already seen one of the most striking examples: Achilles in *Iliad* 9 characterises his 'undying fame' specifically in contrast to *nostos*. Achilles' speech is polemical. Of all people, he is addressing Odysseus, in anger, and with characteristic intransigence. The following passage from the *Odyssey* is more nuanced, but likewise suggests that *kleos*, and with it poetry, must change after the end of the Trojan War. This is how Telemachus remembers Odysseus at 1.231-43:

'My guest, since indeed you are asking me all these questions,
there was a time this house was one that might be prosperous
and above reproach, when a certain man was here in his country.
But now the gods, with evil intention, have willed it otherwise,
and they have caused him to disappear, in a way no other
man has done. I should not have sorrowed so over his dying
if he had gone down among his companions in the land of the Trojans,
or in the arms of his friends, after he had wound up the fighting.
So all the Achaeans would have heaped a grave mound over him,
and he would have won great fame for himself and his son hereafter.
But now ingloriously the stormwinds have caught and carried him
away, out of sight, out of knowledge, and he left pain and lamentation
to me ...'

At this early stage in the narrative, Telemachus is firmly committed to
an Iliadic notion of death and afterlife: he wishes that Odysseus might
have died in Troy and won great *kleos*. We recognise some of the
elements that were important in Hector's vision of *kleos* in *Iliad* 7, above
all the tomb as a visible memento for future generations. In the absence
of a tomb, Odysseus' existence remains poorly defined. He neither lives
nor is truly dead: he leaves behind him nothing but the bereavement of
his son. Once we have said that Telemachus' speech is indebted to Iliadic
notions of *kleos*, we must however add that it opens up new possibilities.
Might Odysseus one day emerge as a survivor and claim for himself a
new *kind* of fame? According to Telemachus, that is a remote possibility,
but the point is that without a tomb it cannot be ruled out. In short,
while the absence of a tomb precludes the attainment of *kleos* in an
Iliadic sense, it opens up the possibility of winning a new kind of fame.

Odysseus has to leave behind not only Iliadic *kleos* itself but also the
traditional means through which heroes try to secure their own fame.[39]
Trapped in the cave of the Cyclops, he must contain his urge to face the
monster with his sword.[40] Lying low in his own house he must learn to
let insults pass unchallenged and not to gloat over defeated foes. He
must take on precisely the role of the 'dishonoured stranger' which
Achilles – in the *Iliad* at least – found so unacceptable. On his way home
Odysseus makes mistakes, yet he rarely makes the same mistake twice.
Throughout the *Odyssey*, there is a palpable sense of learning and
change, a sense in which Odysseus adapts to new circumstances.[41] New
relationships are established from the shipwreck of the heroic period,
and new ways of conceptualising man's place in the world follow from
the new situation faced by Odysseus. Whereas we visit Achilles as a
shadow from the past, Odysseus reaches this new world order alive.
What we might call Odysseus' character traits, his flexibility, intelli-

gence and endurance, are appropriate, indeed necessary, in the new circumstances he has to face. They are also intensely desirable in the world as it is now: it is clear that any human being can profit from Odysseus' qualities of intelligence and endurance, whereas we would be less well served by a godlike desire for *timê* and *tisis*.

Achilles, Odysseus and the history of the cosmos

Throughout this book we have argued that the meaning of Homeric epic is in crucial ways determined by the shape of cosmic history. To the resonant order of things corresponds the resonant language of epic which assigns to each thing and person its precise place in relation to the larger whole: as Anne Carson puts it, 'Homer fastens every substance in the world to its aptest attribute and holds them in place for epic consumption.'[42] Homeric narrative is also sensitive to the passing of time: we have seen repeatedly that the very language and tone adopted in an individual poem depend on the historical circumstances it describes and the particular moment in which it is set.

What we are about to suggest in this last section may at first appear paradoxical, but is in fact a crucial part of the resonant art of epic: each surviving poem, as well as occupying a specific place in a much larger historical narrative, also incorporates that narrative within its bounds. In other words, individual hexameter texts tend to sketch the overall history of the cosmos as well as placing themselves at a particular point within it.

This is perhaps most obvious in the Hesiodic *Works and Days*, which incorporates a full account of past history from the golden age to the present.[43] In a similar vein, the *Theogony* can be read as a complete account of the world, which ends with the present, that is, with a stable Olympian hierarchy under the rule of Zeus. Of course, each poem depicts the history of the world from its own very specific perspective: thus, in the *Works and Days*, which focuses on the present, the history of the cosmos is essentially a history of humankind: we hear only incidentally that, in the golden age, men lived at the time when Cronus was king. Conversely, the *Theogony* looks at world history from the persepective of the Olympian order whose gradual emergence it describes. As a result, the narrative mentions human beings only in passing.[44]

The poems attributed to Homer follow a similar pattern, although their scope is narrower. The *Homeric Hymns* begin by describing the distant past, the time, for example, when a particular god was born, and end with an invocation to the god which is set in the present.[45]

Similarly, the *Iliad* and *Odyssey* describe developments which, conceptually, if not actually, lead us from the distant past to the present day. We have already seen that the poems allude to a remote past of cosmic upheaval and imply a difference between the heroes and 'men as they are now'. There is also another, more subtle way in which the poems trace the history of the cosmos: the personal stories of the main characters, Achilles and Odysseus, to some extent parallel the overall development of cosmic history. Whereas Achilles starts off as the powerful son of his divine mother, in the course of the *Iliad* he comes to accept his fate as a 'wretched mortal', and gradually begins to think of himself primarily as the son of Peleus. Through this development, the *Iliad* suggests a movement from a theogonic framework to the world of humans 'as they are now'. Similarly, at the beginning of the *Odyssey*, Odysseus lives together with a goddess in a cave (caves are frequent mating places in the early history of the cosmos), and is promised eternal life. Instead, he chooses to return to his rocky island and his mortal wife. As Achilles and Odysseus undergo the entire range of human history – and human experience – their stories come to transcend the historic moment in which they are set.

At the beginning of the *Iliad*, Achilles is presented as someone with close and powerful links to the gods. We have already seen that his encounter with his mother in *Iliad* 1 turns on the question of how he can be recompensed for his untimely death.[46] The plan devised by Thetis focuses on her son's need to be honoured – a concern he shares with the gods. It is part of Thetis' scheme that Achilles should respond to Agamemnon's challenge with *mênis*, a term which, again, reveals a godlike attitude, since the gods too react with *mênis* when they are not properly honoured. The success of Thetis' plan, moreover, depends very directly on the earlier history of divine relations. As Achilles reminds her, she once helped Zeus against a rebellious group of Olympian gods who had staged a coup against him.[47] This episode gives Achilles, as the son of Thetis, a powerful hold on Zeus and enables him to dictate the very course of world history.

At this early stage in the narrative, Achilles' father Peleus is only present in his son's traditional epithet, 'Achilles, son of Peleus'. Whereas Thetis appears in person on the seashore, her husband is far away, in Phthie, and seems to play no role in Achilles' life. In the course of the narrative the balance shifts, and Achilles eventually comes to think about his father with great intensity and to see himself primarily as his son.[48] This shift mirrors the overall development of cosmic history: in the distant past, men were godlike, offspring of the gods, now we are wretched mortals born of other wretched mortals.

5. Death, Fame and Poetry

In the course of the *Iliad*, Achilles experiences fully the crisis of *timê*
that we have seen to be characteristic of the heroic age more generally.
By the end of the poem, he accepts that he must live his life without
adequate compensation for death: even the *kleos* that humans bestow is
ultimately futile. It is at this point that he fully recognises himself as
his father's son and can sympathise even with king Priam, who is after
all another wretched mortal, just like his father Peleus. In a sense, we
could say that in the course of the *Iliad* Achilles comes to realise the full
significance of his standard epithet, *Pêleidês* or *Pêlêiadês*, son of Peleus.
His new ability to sympathise with the plight of all mortals is nowhere
clearer than in his words to Priam towards the end of the poem, at
24.525-38:

'Such is the way the gods spun life for wretched mortals,
that we live in unhappiness, but the gods themselves have no sorrows.
There are two urns that stand on the floor of the house of Zeus. They
   are unlike
for the gifts they bestow: an urn of evil, an urn of blessings.
If Zeus who delights in thunder mingles these and bestows them
on man, he shifts, and moves now in evil, again in good fortune.
But when Zeus bestows from the urn of sorrows, he makes a failure
of man, and the evil hunger drives him over the shining earth,
and he wanders respected neither of gods nor mortals.
Such were the shining gifts given by the gods to Peleus
from his birth, who outshone all men besides for his riches
and pride of possession, and was lord over the Myrmidons.
Thereto the gods bestowed an immortal wife on him, who was mortal.
But even on him the god piled evil also ...'

Achilles outlines a vision of human life which, in some ways at least, is
strangely at odds with the many claims about *kleos* found in the
Homeric poems. In typically Iliadic fashion, Achilles includes himself
among 'wretched mortals' (*deiloi brotoi*). Yet, in this case, the wretchedness of humankind is not balanced by the rewards of 'undying fame'.
The mortals that Achilles has in mind have no name, nor does he in fact
emphasise the fact that they must die. Instead, he insists that they lead
a life of misery.

Misery takes the form of restless wandering, and constant, aimless
travel seems to preclude the possibility of individual renown. The
human beings described by Achilles are faceless people, subject to the
inescapable logic of Zeus' two jars. The best that can happen to them is
a life of mixed blessings. The worst is not death but perennial and
anonymous nomadism. If the tomb is the ultimate embodiment of the

141

fixity of *kleos*, the picture sketched by Achilles represents the fleeting-ness of all human life. Historically speaking, this is the world of the post-heroic survivor, full of allusions to the *Odyssey*. Yet, Achilles teaches Priam a lesson about the nature of things which is appropriate for all time, and not just at a particular phase in the history of the cosmos. It affects us, the audience, as much as it affects Priam and Achilles himself. With the didactic tone and the present tense comes a set of typically Hesiodic images, above all the two jars, which make Zeus appear as a parsimonious farmer.[49]

Achilles' vision crucially depends on the role he assigns to death. In lines 525-6 we hear that the gods decreed that mortals live (*zôô*) in unhappiness. The point is not death but a miserable life. The difference may seem slight, but it is important. Without an emphasis on death, the historical distance between the world of the heroes and the present of the audience, carefully upheld and bridged by *kleos*, suddenly collapses. This last observation does not apply only to the last book of the poem. The *Iliad* as a whole has a strong tendency towards transcending the moment of the Trojan War and moving beyond the logic of *klea andrôn* into a world more akin to that described, for example, in the wisdom poetry of Hesiod. At the most basic level, we have seen that the similes constantly invite us to bridge the gap between past and present, and there are other ways in which the *Iliad* incorporates the post-heroic world into its narrative. In particular, we would like to single out one motif that is crucial to the story of Achilles.

Just as Achilles, in his speech to Priam, focuses on life rather than death, so the *Iliad* as a whole denies death to its main protagonist. Achilles' death is of course foretold at many points: we have already seen that his fatal encounter with Apollo resonates through the poem. Yet it is important to understand why the moment of his death is not actually told within the poem. One way of answering this question is to admire the *Iliad*'s poetic effectiveness in leaving us to imagine the most important events of the Trojan War: the sack of Troy, the death of Achilles. That is a consideration, but one can think of other implica-tions of this narrative choice.[50] The absence of Achilles' death changes not only the poetic effect of the text but also its meaning: instead of becoming the ultimate moment of *kleos* and transcendence, death in the *Iliad* is deferred and can therefore be generalised: like Achilles, we all have to face up to our own death, even if we do not know as much about it as he does. As a living person, rather than a dead hero, Achilles cannot unproblematically claim the special position for himself that *kleos* bestows. This is precisely what lies behind his speech in book 24. Of course, the words of Achilles are still framed by the situation of the

Trojan War. Yet, they also transcend the specific setting of the Trojan War and the logic of *kleos* as a recompense for death.

We have seen some of the ways in which the story of Achilles mirrors the overall trajectory of world history, starting with a situation of closeness between heroes and gods and ending with human life as it is 'now'. In a similar vein, the *Odyssey* incorporates into its post-Trojan setting elements of the wider history of the universe, from a time when humans lived in communion with the gods to the moment when they have well and truly parted company. We have already discussed Zeus' programmatic complaint at the beginning of the *Odyssey*, when he says that humans mistakenly blame the gods for their suffering.[51] We argued that the complaint sets the tone for a narrative in which the separation between gods and mortals is more advanced than in the *Iliad*. Nevertheless, the beginning of the *Odyssey* depicts a situation of close communion between gods and men. Calypso, the divine Nymph, has plans to keep Odysseus as her husband in Ogygie, the 'navel of the sea'. She does not accept that the time for such liaisons has passed and complains that the other gods are jealous of her love. Indeed, in defiance of the most basic distinction between gods and men, Calypso tells us that she wanted to make Odysseus immortal (5.135-6):

> 'I gave him my love and cherished him, and I had hopes also
> that I could make him immortal and all his days to be endless.'

In the event, Calypso has to yield to Zeus. She sends Odysseus back home and into the world of humankind, without any indication that their union has resulted in any offspring. This is not an altogether irrelevant detail: in the *Theogony* we hear that Calypso bore Odysseus two sons, Nausithoos and Nausinoos. Rather than dismissing this as 'a secondary development'[52] we note that the cosmogonic implications of Odysseus' union with Calypso are drawn out in the context of the *Theogony* but remain invisible from the perspective of the *Odyssey*. Not only can Odysseus no longer become a god, there will be no more births of demigods. Here as elsewhere, the Odyssean account is not simply a contradiction of what we are told in Hesiod. Rather, it adopts a different perspective, as a result of which we are encouraged to focus not on the making of the cosmic family tree, as in Hesiod, but on the separation between gods and humans.

Calypso disappears from the narrative when Odysseus leaves her island. After his encounter with the goddess, Odysseus is washed up on the shore of the Phaeacians. The Phaeacians are in important ways distinct from the gods; yet, for Odysseus, they are not distinct enough to offer an alternative to Ithaca. Once again, the problem of Odysseus' place in the world is expressed in terms of the cosmogonic leitmotif of marriage between unequal partners. When Odysseus meets Nausicaa for the first time, he addresses her as *'anassa'*, the traditional title of a Homeric goddess, and likens her to Artemis.[53] His fear that she might be a goddess proves unfounded: Nausicaa is a human being and, in fact, she herself thinks of him as godlike, thus suggesting a flattering reciprocity in the way the two look at one another. Yet, were Odysseus to marry her, he would break the rule that human beings, as opposed to gods, should form permanent attachments with only one woman at a time. Moreover, Odysseus would stay in his wife's place, rather than take her to his own home, as was customary in the world of mortals: his position would be subordinate to that of his wife and her family. Nausicaa is not Calypso, but she is not a suitable wife according to the social norms of the present day. The Phaeacians, we have seen, are a very special race who enjoy a close relationship with Poseidon and do not mingle with other human beings. As Nausicaa herself points out at 6.204-5:

> 'We live far apart by ourselves in the wash of the great sea
> at the utter end, nor do any other mortals mix with us.'

The Phaeacians occupy an intermediate position between the golden-age Cyclopes and the fully human world of Ithaca.[54] Nausicaa's words suggest that they are different from 'other mortals'. It is clear that Odysseus has travelled a long way since departing from the cave of Calypso. Yet, his journey through time as well as space must continue. Odysseus' place in the wider cosmic order, defined by his Ithacan household and encapsulated in his patronymic, 'son of Laertes', takes on paradigmatic resonance in view of the places he rejects: returning to Ithaca from Ogygie and Scherie involves a transition from past to present; goddesses and caves belong to the world described in the *Theogony* and the *Homeric Hymns*; while super-abundant crops, wealth and seclusion remind us of the golden age. Rocky Ithaca, not particularly wealthy, ridden with problems but essentially 'home', belongs to the real world or, to be more precise, a world that closely resembles that of the audience.

When Odysseus arrives in Ithaca, he must face the suitors of his wife Penelope and prove himself the legitimate master of his house. There are obvious parallels between the courtship of Penelope and that of Helen. At the beginning and at the end of the Trojan War, a crisis of family structures comes to represent a critical moment in the history of the cosmos. The suitors of Helen who, in the *Catalogue of Women*, represent the race of heroes, must vanish, so that the process of theogony can be brought to a close. Similarly, the suitors of Penelope must give way to the new political and social order of the post-heroic city. Amid the feasting and sporting suitors, who ape the heroes of the *Iliad* in a changed world, Odysseus takes the garb of an impoverished and displaced beggar who survives because of his 'enduring spirit'. In place of Iliadic injunctions to 'be men' and display valour in battle, Odysseus must admonish his heart to 'bear up' in the face of adversity (20.18-21):

> 'Bear up my heart. You have had worse to endure before this
> on that day when the irresistible Cyclops ate up
> my strong companions, but you endured it until intelligence
> got you out of the cave, though you expected to perish.'

Odysseus' stay in his house is cast as a test of the kind of virtue that Apollo defines as quintessentially human in *Iliad* 24: endurance.[55]

The ability to wait and suffer goes hand in hand with giving up claims to honour, *timê*. In the second half of the poem, Odysseus is repeatedly humiliated. For example, during the banquet he is almost struck with the hoof of an ox: what should have been his proper share in the meal – an important expression of a man's social standing (*timê*) in the *Iliad* – is here transformed into an insult.[56] More generally, Odysseus is constantly taunted by his opponents in a manner which no Iliadic hero would find acceptable. Achilles responded with divine wrath to far less objectionable behaviour. Odysseus must learn to endure in order to reclaim his place in the world. By implication, that place becomes a function of his ability to survive without friends, social status and material goods.

It is illuminating in this context to take a look at the lying tales which Odysseus tells in the second half of the *Odyssey*. As has often been pointed out, those tales echo closely the adventures that Odysseus undergoes in the main narrative. In them, he presents himself as a participant in the Trojan War, and a long-suffering seafarer. Moreover, he repeatedly claims that he either heard of or encountered Odysseus in person.[57] Much has been written about the character of Odysseus as a storyteller.[58] What we would like to stress here is that the Cretan tales can be seen as a complex alternative to Odysseus' life as the narrator describes it. One major difference concerns the tone of the narrative: the Cretan tales have often been called 'realistic', an impression which is easily substantiated when we look at their subject matter. The main characters are displaced figures who struggle to survive in a hostile environment. Few of them seem concerned with the pursuit of *timê* or *kleos*; instead, we find an insistent interest in material goods (*ktêmata*). Poverty, which is of no concern to the gods and does not worry the Iliadic heroes, poses a real and constant threat. Life is fluid, with characters drifting up and down the social ladder and even dropping out of human society altogether. The cohesion of the heroic age in which everyone knows everyone else, and in which people occupy a well-defined place in a stable system of genealogies and guest-friendships, is no longer there. In this respect, as in others, the world of the Cretan tales resembles that of the Homeric similes. Like the similes, the Cretan tales depict the gods as distant, and make little attempt to detect specific divine plans behind what happens on earth. In one tale, which is set in the Trojan plain, Odysseus mentions frost and snow as signs of the revolving seasons.[59] As we have seen, this is alien to the main narrative of the *Iliad*, where weather signs reveal the plans of the gods rather than the regular pattern of the seasons.[60] What emerges from the Cretan stories is a post-heroic or sub-heroic world, where human beings are left to fend for themselves, and where personal suffering illustrates the timeless truth that human life is hard and unpredictable. This is the world of 'human beings as they are now'.

Odysseus' story, then, transcends the chronological span of the *Odyssey*. In the form of disguises, lying tales, and ironic inversions, it integrates the post-heroic world into the heroic age, charting a transition from one cosmic era to the next. Yet, the most telling way in which Odysseus transcends the historical moment of the Trojan War lies, somewhat paradoxically, in the fact that he never, finally, arrives home. We recall that, by putting off Achilles' death, the *Iliad* carves out a space for reflection which enables us to see his existence as that of a wretched human being.[61] Odyssean *kleos* is crucially linked to return and arrival, not death. In that respect alone, the later setting of the *Odyssey* goes hand in hand with a more open-ended vision of a hero's life. Yet, the *Odyssey* goes one step further, suspending closure not only by aligning *kleos* with *nostos*, but also by putting off the ultimate moment of arrival. Odysseus remains a traveller even after returning to Ithaca, the 'end of his sorrows' has not yet been reached. As Teiresias tells him in book 11, and as Odysseus himself repeats in book 23, he will have to leave Ithaca one more time.[62] Putting off the ultimate end of the story is thus, again, linked to the acceptance of unending suffering.

The question of why Odysseus leaves Ithaca one more time has been the object of speculation for centuries.[63] We cannot try to solve the riddle of Odysseus' last journey, but we can say that it has important consequences for the *Odyssey*, in that the protagonist calls into question the logic of his own *kleos*. Odysseus' career becomes as open-ended as Achilles' view of human life in *Iliad* 24. In fact, there is a sense in which he becomes himself the eternal wanderer whom Achilles describes to Priam as the ultimate example of human wretchedness.[64] Among other things, this means that Odysseus' life can remain a symbol of suffering and endurance even after he has embraced his wife. One of his most insistent epithets, in the *Odyssey* and elsewhere, is *polytlas*, 'much-enduring'.[65] This epithet resonates through the texts and helps conceptualise the fame of Odysseus not so much as a series of impressive feats which eventually lead him to a reunion with his wife, but rather as an ongoing exploration of what is described in the *Hymn to Apollo* as the lot of human kind. In the *Hymn*, lines 190-1, we hear that the Muses sing about the following topics:

> They sing of the gods' immortal gifts and of human
> suffering ...

Suffering and endurance distinguish human beings from the gods. Because Odysseus never ceases to be a traveller, he continues to embody the suffering to which we are subjected and the endurance we must all develop.

Odysseus is of course not only a generic sufferer. As he himself boasts in book 9, it is his ruses as much as anything else that won him his renown,[66] and the recurrent descriptions of him as intelligent (*polymêtis*, *polymêchanos*) and versatile (*polytropos*) are amply borne out by his adventures. That Odysseus' crafty nature enables him to survive even in the most desperate of circumstances is well known and has been much discussed.[67] Odysseus not only suffers beyond all others but can also help himself in situations where average human intelligence would fail. Yet, for all his intelligence, he too falls short of achieving the final fixation of his *kleos* even in the more flexible, Odyssean form of a successful return journey. Odysseus neither dies nor unambiguously triumphs at the end of the *Odyssey*. Instead, he must travel again. In his case, as in the case of Achilles, the heroic era does not remain neatly secluded in the past but spills over into a world which we, the audience, recognise as our own.

Conclusion

In the course of this chapter, we have argued two complementary points. On the one hand, we maintained that the biographies and characteristics of individual heroes are informed by the particular historical circumstances in which they live. On the other, we suggested that the individual stories of Achilles and Odysseus encapsulate the history of the cosmos, from the time in which gods and humans lived closely together to the present day. These two observations, far from being contradictory, form a crucial part of what we mean by 'the resonance of epic'.

Since the work of Milman Parry in the 1920s, scholars have acquired an ever more sophisticated understanding of the processes of composition which lie behind early Greek hexameter epic. It is apparent that all the poems that were attributed to Homer and Hesiod in the archaic period share a common pool of stock epithets, type scenes, traditional narrative patterns and techniques. Much has been said about how these features helped bards to compose their poems but, from our point of view as readers, it is perhaps more important to ask how they affect the meaning and reception of the poems among ancient and, indeed, modern audiences. If we were to summarise our answer to this question, it could perhaps be formulated as follows. The language and compositional techniques of early Greek hexameter epic developed over a long period of time for the purpose of describing the deeds of gods and men *kata kosmon*, appropriately, as they should be described. Embedded in the traditional expressions used in Homeric and Hesiodic epic is a vision of the history of the cosmos, from the beginning, when Earth and Heaven gave rise to a genealogy of gods, to life in the present day. The system of formulas as a whole mirrors in its precision and stability the order of the cosmos itself. Small phrases such as 'Zeus the son of Cronus' or 'a stone that two men could not lift nowadays' contain within them a wider understanding of change through time. Conversely, they serve to fasten a particular story, character, artefact or situation to its place within the overall history of the cosmos: the gods start feasting together once Zeus is in power, human beings, at the end of the *Odyssey*, must learn that resources on earth are finite, and that one can only feast in moderation. The correspondence between the smallest element of traditional poetry and the grandest overall understanding of cosmic history creates a special resonance which is enabled by the traditional language of epic, as well as its narrative patterns. In the story of an individual character we can trace a historical trajectory which parallels that of the whole universe; while at the same time the life of that one character is but a small episode in the overall history of the cosmos.

Critics have often worried about the expressive possibilities of traditional hexameter poetry. Some have suggested that we cannot expect oral bards like Homer to have the same freedom of expression as those who enjoy the modern technology of writing. Others have insisted that

Homeric poetry is just as expressive as that of Virgil and of other great poets of later times; in so doing, they have sometimes failed to pay enough attention to the specific character of the early Greek hexameter tradition. These different approaches have enriched our understanding of Homer: scholars of oral poetry have offered penetrating insights into the composition of epic, and sometimes suggested interesting interpretative approaches; those who have insisted on reading Homer 'as literature' have often developed satisfying and enlightening readings unencumbered by too much technical jargon. It seems to us, however, that the expressive possibilities of traditional epic call for a more holistic approach. 'Tradition', for the Greeks, was not an abstract notion of how bards composed in performance. The fact that the Homeric poems belong to a rich tradition of epic means that they share not just compositional techniques with other texts but also a vision of the world which makes them uniquely resonant. One can detect an infinite series of echoes, allusions, tensions, shifts in perspective.

This is a short book, and many aspects of Homeric resonance have not been explored. In general, we have placed greater emphasis on the *Iliad* than the *Odyssey*, on men rather than women, and gods rather than mortals. These choices are never easy. Our main hope is that the book offers an interpretation of the *Iliad* and the *Odyssey* within the wider epic tradition to which they belong. The approaches of early audiences helped us to shape our own, and we hope to have communicated some of our interest in, and gratitude towards, the early Greeks who appreciated the Homeric epics and speculated about their author. We also hope that our overall interpretation may be of some use to readers when they turn to individual scenes or aspects of the poems which we have not discussed: it is of course from a direct engagement with the texts themselves that the pleasure, subtlety and wisdom of Homeric epic emerge most clearly.

Notes

Part I

1. Griffin (1987) vi; cf. Latacz (1996).

2. On the concept of 'literature' and the study of ancient Greek literary culture, see Ford (2002).

3. Schein (1984) 1 helpfully begins his study of the *Iliad* by pointing out that 'the *Iliad* is not a "first work"; rather it is an end product of a poetic tradition that may have been as much as a thousand years old by the time this epic was composed'. The ancient Greeks constructed genealogies for Homer: among his ancestors we often find poets like Orpheus and Musaeus, and even the god of poetry Apollo: see, for example, *Contest of Homer and Hesiod* 4 (West); Proclus, *Chrestomathy* I.4 (West).

4. For Oceanus as the river encircling the whole world see *Il.* 3.5, 18.489, *Od.* 12.1.

5. Herodotus 2.23.

6. In another passage, 2.53, Herodotus argues that Hesiod and Homer are in fact the earliest poets and that 'the poets who are said to have lived before those men in fact came later'. It seems that he can change his position depending on the point he is trying to make, but this need not concern us here: Herodotus' statements clearly show that Homer was not necessarily thought to be the most ancient poet in the tradition.

7. Metcalf (2002) explores the problem of cultural difference from an anthropological perspective. His observations at pp. 2-5 on different concepts of fiction, truth, lies, literature and sacred texts are particularly relevant to the present study.

8. See, for example, Gill and Wiseman (1993) and Pratt (1993).

9. Hellenistic commentators, for example, discussed at length Homer's reliability as a source of geographic, medical, and more generally scientific knowledge. Their work survives, in part, in the marginal notes found in medieval manuscripts ('scholia'), and is edited by Erbse (1969-88) and Dindorf (1855).

10. For an excellent recent study of Homeric audiences, to which we are much indebted, see Scodel (2002).

1. The Poet

1. The anecdote can be traced back to Mark Twain, 'English as she is taught', *Century Magazine* 33 (April 1887).

2. West (1998) v presents the *Iliad* as the work of one supreme poet; in

(1999) he argues that the name 'Homer' was invented in Athens long after the *Iliad* was composed.

3. Latacz (1996), especially the first two sections of ch. 2, pp. 23-30: 'The Source Situation: Nothing Authentic' and 'The Homer Legend: A False Track'.

4. See, for example, Lefkowitz (1981).

5. E.g. Burkert (1992), West (1997).

6. In Lucian, Babylon is chosen because it is a preposterous birthplace for Homer. It is also important, however, that elsewhere in Lucian the city has a place in narratives of transmitted wisdom from the Near East: cf. Lucian *The Runaways* 6-8 and Lightfoot (2003) 192. Modern interest in the connection between Greek epic and Near Eastern narrative has been prompted by the decipherment of Akkadian and other Near Eastern languages: a brief account of the history of modern scholarship on Greek and Near Eastern literatures can be found in the Introduction to Burkert (1992).

7. Goethe (1953) 478, reacting to the *Prolegomena ad Homerum*, for which see Wolf (1985).

8. The most important attempt to discriminate between the language of different early Greek hexameter texts is Janko (1982), who tries to date the textual fixation of the poems on the basis of such differences. Griffin (1977) tries to differentiate between the Epic Cycle and the *Iliad* in thematic terms, by suggesting that the poems of the Cycle are more interested in magic and the supernatural. It should be borne in mind, however, that the contents of the Cycle are known only from summaries: given the right emphasis, a summary of the *Iliad* could also sound fantastic (prophesying horses, warriors wrapped up in mist and whisked away form the battlefield ...).

9. The concept of a *Kunstsprache*, or 'artificial language', was first introduced into Homeric studies by Meister (1921). For an up-to-date assessment of the Homeric dialect see Horrocks (1997).

10. 'Catalogues' are essentially lists of items. As such, they are a characteristic aspect of the epic bard's claim to reporting events 'fully' and 'as is proper' (see further pp. 44-8). 'Ring composition' refers to the technique of structuring passages and whole texts in the form of concentric circles (a, b, c ... c', b', a'). 'Ekphrasis' is a detailed description of an artefact which attempts to capture its effect on the onlooker.

11. *Il*. 22.8-10.

12. E.g. Kirk (1962), Griffin (1977). An abridged and revised version of the latter can be found in Cairns (2001) 365-84.

13. E.g. Rutherford (1991-3), reprinted with minor revisions in Cairns (2001) 117-46.

14. This view was widespread in the nineteenth and early twentieth centuries but has since gone out of fashion; for discussion see Turner (1997), especially p. 134; for a (relatively) recent restatement of the 'kernel theory' see Bonfante (1968).

15. This does not necessarily mean that Homer himself could write: Lord (1953 = 1991, 38-48) and others after him envisaged Homer as dictating his poems.

16. E.g. Nagy (1990) ch. 2, esp. pp. 79-81.

17. This approach goes back to Finley (1977); a recent survey can be found in Crielaard (1995). There are useful introductory essays in Morris/Powell (1997): e.g. Raaflaub on social institutions (pp. 624-48), Donlan on the Homeric economy (pp. 649-67), van Wees on warfare (pp. 668-93); Morris (pp. 535-59) and Bennet (pp. 511-33) discuss material culture.

18. E.g. Burkert (1976), quoted in Taplin (1992) 34; West (1995).

19. Taplin (1992) 36 discusses earlier attempts to link the composition of the *Iliad* and *Odyssey* to the advent of writing. Powell (1991) and (1997) argues that the Semitic alphabet was adapted with the specific purpose of recording Homeric (and Hesiodic) epic.

20. For example, Nagy (1996).

21. See e.g. Pulleyn (2000) 8.

22. Preface to Cairns (2001); cf. also Introduction p. 56.

23. It is above all in this respect that comparative studies can be helpful, see Foley (2002).

24. E.g. Redfield (1994), Schein (1984), Taplin (1992) on the *Iliad*; Pucci (1987), Segal (1994), de Jong (2001) on the *Odyssey*.

25. Woolf (1929).

26. Butler (1897).

27. For a discussion of Butler see Whitmarsh (2002).

28. Any scholar studying the archaic period must rely on later sources. It is possible, however, to use later sources so as to gain some insight into an earlier period: see Dougherty and Kurke (1993), Introduction.

29. Graziosi (2002) ch. 4 discusses the sources and cites relevant bibliography.

30. Lefkowitz (1981) 23. The *Vita Herodotea* derives its title from the fact that it purports to be written by Herodotus. It is edited and translated in West (2003).

31. See, for example, Metcalf (2002).

32. Taplin recognises the problem in (1992).

33. *Od.* 8.62-86, 261-369, 471-522.

34. *Od.* 8.62-4; for further discussion of Demodocus' special gift see Chapter 3, pp. 81-2.

35. For Demodocus as a biographical figure see Graziosi (2002) 138-42.

36. *Theogony* 31-2, *Il.* 1.70. In addition to past and future Calchas is said to know the present; cf. *Theogony* 38 (of the Muses).

37. Latacz (1996) 29.

38. This point is made repeatedly in the Homeric scholia: for a collection of examples, see Snipes (1988).

39. *Il.* 5.302-4, 12.445-9, 20.285-7; cf. 12.381-3.

40. Cf. Edwards (1991) 35: '[The similes] give us a view of the world ... that existed in the poet's own day and long after him.'

41. For example, Wilamowitz (1884) 353, Pfeiffer (1968) 43-4; for discussion, see Graziosi (2002) 165-8.

42. Athenaeus 8.347e, quoted in Lamberton (1997) 40.

43. Nagy (1990) 414-16; Nisetich (1989) concedes that 'Pindar thought of Homer in broad terms' (p. 1) but argues that he '[preferred] the *Iliad* over the poems of the epic cycle' (p. 70).

44. Herodotus 4.32.

45. Herodotus 2.117.

46. The reasons why Homer's *oeuvre* was eventually defined as the *Iliad* and the *Odyssey* are complex. It is possible that these two poems were most suited to a Panhellenic audience, see Nagy (1990) 72-3; it also seems clear that the name 'Homer' spoke of beautiful poetry, and that the *Iliad* and the *Odyssey* were eventually singled out as the best poems. The rules which dictated that 'Homer and Homer only' be recited at the Panathenaea promoted a strict and consistent definition of the Homeric corpus: see Graziosi (2002) 195-9.

47. Graziosi (2002) 184-93.

48. Strauss Clay (1989) and (1997b).

49. Thucydides 3.104.

50. Aristotle, *Poetics* 1448b28-1449a2; a detailed discussion of the *Margites* with further bibliography can be found in Graziosi (2002) 66-72.

51. We should note, however, that this need not have been their only function: see Strauss Clay (1997b) 495-8. The longer *Homeric Hymns* are, of course, quite substantial compositions in themselves.

52. For the Homeridae, see Graziosi (2002) 208-17; for the name of Homer meaning 'the man who fits together the song' see Nagy (1979) 297-300; cf. West (1999).

53. Scodel (2002) illuminatingly discusses the 'rhetoric of traditionality' that enabled Homeric performers to communicate with their audiences.

54. *Works and Days* 640.

55. *Works and Days* 650-9.

56. Martin (1992) reviews the debate and argues that the persona of Hesiod should be seen as embodying the poetics of the *Theogony* and *Works and Days*. Griffith (1983) offers a brilliant analysis of Hesiod's persona in the poems. Graziosi (2002) 57-79 works out the implications of Griffith's argument for the definition of Homer's oeuvre.

57. Rosen (1997) 464-73 offers a useful overview of the debate.

58. Leckie (1999) xxxix.

59. Accius' remarks are quoted by Gellius, *Attic Nights* 3.11.4-5.

60. Graziosi (2002) 101-10.

61. Other ancient Greek sources present Homer and Hesiod as joining forces in giving an account of the gods: see, for example, Plato *Ion* 531c, discussed on p. 32.

62. The text is translated in West (2003); for discussion see O'Sullivan (1992), Rosen (1997), Graziosi (2001) and (2002) 168-80.

63. For a discussion of the date of the *Contest* and the origins of its material, see Graziosi (2001).

64. See Graziosi (2001).

65. See Graziosi (2002) 130-1.

66. Among the epic poets whose work has been lost, the most famous are Orpheus and Musaeus. They are discussed in West (1983). Of the others, the Corinthian poet Eumelos is of particular interest since he appears to have been credited with a fully-fledged account of the history of the universe that is comparable to the Hesiodic tradition: West (2002).

2. The Poems

1. See e.g. Edwards (1971), Janko (1982) for the language of Hesiod and Homer; Thalmann (1984) discusses the overall outlook and compositional technique of early epic; Ford (1992) 40-8 points out the thematic unity of early hexameter poetry.

2. Snell et al. (1955-).

3. See Arthur (1982).

4. The text repeatedly emphasises Zeus' regard for other gods; e.g. lines 392-403 (Styx), 411-52 (Hecate). More generally, Zeus distributes the gods' honours 'well': *Theogony* 73-4 and 885.

5. See West (1985).

6. The *Catalogue* uses both terms (cf. e.g. Hesiod fr. 204.100 and 119 (M-W)).

7. See West (1961) 133. The Elysian plain which becomes Menelaos' refuge from death is characterised at *Odyssey* 4.563-8 as not being subject to seasonal change. Likewise, the islands of the blessed at *Works and Days* 171-3 defy normal seasonal patterns; see further pp. 88-9.

8. Thalmann (1984) 75-7 considers the relationship between the two texts. For further discussion, see Strauss Clay (2003) 164-74.

9. E.g. West (1961). West argues that the end of the *Catalogue* represents a poor imitation of the *Works and Days*. By contrast, we suggest that its changed narrative style is entirely appropriate to the new cosmic era that is being described.

10. Rowe (1978) 8, quoting Finley (1975).

11. This is not simply a matter of what we would probably call today 'factual correctness'. For a discussion of 'vividness' as a crucial aspect of epic's account of the past see Ford (1992) 49-56.

12. See Janko (1982) for an early date: before 680 BC, and West (1985) 130-7 for a considerably later one: 580-520 BC.

13. Tsagarakis (1982).

14. Strauss Clay (1989) 15.

15. Compare *Homeric Hymn to Demeter* and *Theogony* 913-14; *Hymn to Apollo* and *Theogony* 918-20; *Hymn to Hermes* and *Theogony* 938-9; *Hymn to Aphrodite* and *Theogony* 1008-10.

16. Frr. 196-204 (M-W). The relationship between the account of the *Catalogue* and that of the Homeric poems is discussed on pp. 123-5.

17. The surviving fragments are translated in Davies (1989). For detailed discussion see Burgess (2001).

18. They are quoted and translated in Pulleyn (2000) 116.

19. Richardson (1993) 361.

20. The Theban cycle comprised an Oedipus epic (*Oedipodeia*), a *Thebaid* and an epic about the second siege of Thebes known under the title *Epigoni*; see Davies (1989) chs 3-5.

21. Aristotle, *Poetics* 1459ab.

22. Thalmann (1984) 77 aptly remarks that 'intelligible in themselves, these poems, even the immense *Iliad* and *Odyssey*, are nevertheless parts of *one* poem' [his emphasis].

23. Horace, *Ars Poetica* 146-9.

24. Logue (2001) 7.

25. The standard work (in German) is Kullmann (1960). An introduction to neo-analytical scholarship can be found in Willcock (1997).

26. Scodel (2002).

27. De Jong (1987) discusses the range of viewpoints that characterises the Homeric account. No comparable study exists for Hesiod, but if it did it its results would have to be very different.

28. *Contest* 8 (West); for discussion see pp. 30-1.

29. Graziosi (2002) 162-3.
30. Herodotus, *Histories* 2.53; for discussion see p. 30.
31. Plato, *Ion* 531c; cf. p. 32.
32. Aristotle, *Nicomachean Ethics* 1139b.
33. Aristotle, *Poetics* chs 23-4.
34. See Haubold (2002b).
35. This is implied in much recent scholarship, though it is rarely spelled out. For an attempt to integrate the gods into a discussion of Homeric society, see Hammer (2002) ch. 2.
36. Zeus turns his eyes away from the Trojan battlefield at *Il.* 13.1-9, allowing Poseidon to intervene on bahalf of the Achaeans. In book 14 Zeus is tricked by Hera. Another example of one god tricking another is discussed in Chapter 3, pp. 81-2.
37. *Theogony* 36-52.
38. For detailed discussion and older bibliography see Ford (1992) ch. 1, especially pp. 31-9.
39. Pucci (1987) 196 suggests that, singing for his listeners' pleasure, Phemius 'forgets truth'. Scodel (2002) ch. 3 discusses the disinterested stance of the Homeric bard vis-à-vis his material. At pp. 84-6 she argues that Phemius' first song is not distorted to please the suitors.
40. Trans. West (1988).
41. This assumption, which is shared by most previous scholarship, has recently been called into question: see Strauss Clay (2003) 58-65.
42. Cf. *Od.* 19.203. The line closely recalls what is said about the lying Muses at *Theogony* 27, though Pucci (1977) 9-10 rightly comments that Odysseus' Cretan tales are subject to verification whereas the song of the Muses – and, we might add, Odysseus' account of his travels at the Phaeacian court – is not.
43. See for example Segal (1994) 19-20.
44. E.g. *Il.* 9.91, *Od.* 1.149.
45. Parry (1971).
46. Finnegan (1977) discusses a wide range of performative styles; see also Foley (2002).
47. Rosen (1988) discusses the structure of the classical sonata movement.
48. Foley (1999) 6, anticipated by Nagy (1979), especially at pp. 1-6.
49. See Hainsworth (1968) 115-16.
50. At a more general level, Achilles' swiftness of foot meaningfully resonates with his 'swiftness of fate'; as Laura Slatkin has argued, he alone of Homer's characters is *ôkumoros*, 'fated to die swiftly' (Slatkin (1991) 36-7).
51. See Strauss Clay (2002) 7.
52. Crotty (1994) discusses the formal features and thematic significance of Homeric supplication scenes.
53. Carson (1999) 4.
54. Vivante (1982) 169-71.
55. Haubold (2002a) 15.
56. *Theogony* 570-90, cf. *Works and Days* 59-82. Haubold (2002a) 15-17 discusses the shift from procreation to creation in the context of the Pandora narrative.
57. E.g. *Il.* 1.397, *Od.* 1.45, *Theogony* 4, *Works and Days* 18, Hes. fr. 25.33 (M-W).
58. E.g. *Il.* 1.570, *Od.* 7.242, *Theogony* 461, Hes. fr. 43a.53 (M-W).

59. See his own discussion in Logue (2001) vii.

60. Cf. Chapter 5, pp. 126-8.

61. For more detailed discussion see Chapter 3, pp. 71-5.

62. E.g. *Il.* 4.370-4 (Agamemnon), 5.800-13 (Athena); at *Il.* 5.124-6 Athena tells Diomedes that she has filled him with the fighting spirit of his father. For further discussion, see Chapter 4, p. 113.

63. *Il.* 1.357-427.

64. One can trace the development of Achilles from a son of his mother to a son of his father in the course of the poem. Book 9 describes a crucial stage in this process; cf. Lynn-George (1988) 131-40, Wilson (2002) 83-104. See also our discussion in Chapter 5, pp. 140-1.

65. A detailed study of the semantic range of Homeric epithets can be found in Vivante (1982). While we do not share some of Vivante's assumptions about the nature of Homeric poetry, his work is valuable for its imaginative approach and the wealth of material it collects. A brief but useful account of more recent scholarship can be found in Edwards (1997).

66. Cf. *Theogony* 123, *Hymn to Hermes* 358, *Il.* 8.486 etc., *Od.* 7.253 etc., ('black' night); and *Theogony* 129, *Homeric Hymn to Pan* 12, *Il.* 13.18 ('great' mountains).

67. Typical scenes, or type scenes, were first described by Arend (1933). Lord (1960), ch. 4 integrated them into his broader vision of traditional poetry. Among the many studies that have since appeared one might mention Fenik (1968) on battle scenes, Reece (1993) on hospitality scenes, Crotty (1994) on supplication, Gainsford (2003) on recognition scenes.

68. Graziosi (2001) 65.

69. Feasting, more generally, is seen as a problem in the *Odyssey*. For example, Odysseus' comrades indulge in a forbidden feast when they are trapped on the island of the Sun (book 12). Like the suitors, they perish because they fail to contain their appetite.

70. *Il.* 1.479-87.

71. See especially *Od.* 5.262-463, but also *Od.* 9.67-75 and the many other passages where Odysseus and his comrades are driven off course by adverse winds.

72. *Works and Days* 618-94.

73. Austin (1975) makes this point very clearly.

74. A more subtle version of this line of argument has been pursued by Bakker (1997), who suggests that Homeric language reflects closely the cognitive patterns of 'day-to-day speech'.

75. Thus already Nagy (1979), Introduction.

3. Gods, Animals and Fate

1. Xenophanes, fr. 11 DK; see p. 29.

2. See Lamberton (1992), especially the contributions by Long (ch. 3), Porter (ch. 4) and Grafton (ch. 7).

3. Willcock (1970) 6 defines Athena's power as 'that which is parallel to sexual attraction for Aphrodite and killing for Ares ...'; Kirk (1974) 292 calls the intervention of Athena in *Iliad* 1 and similar scenes 'little more than *façons de parler*'; he is criticised by Griffin (1980) 147-8.

4. *Il.* 1.599.

5. *Od.* 8.343.

6. Schein (1984) 51. Taplin (1992) ch. 5.1 sees a mixture of 'the wilful and the moral, the trivial and the awesome' (p. 129).

7. *On the Sublime* 9.7.

8. The reception of the Greek gods in Renaissance Art is documented in Impelluso (2003), Section 1; see also Freedman (2003).

9. Reinhardt (1938) 25; the German phrase is 'erhabener Unernst', the translation 'sublime frivolity' is by Griffin (1980) 199.

10. Burkert (1985) part III reviews the major gods' spheres of influence.

11. Xenophanes appears to have voiced radical views about religion: for example, he posited the existence of one supreme god 'greatest among gods and men', who does not 'resemble mortals in appearance or thought' (fr. 23 DK). For a recent attempt at contextualising Xenophanes' views of the divine see Ford (2002) ch. 2.

12. Herodotus 2.53.

13. Burkert (1985) 120.

14. Otto (1954) 15.

15. It appears that for male gods the point at which they 'freeze' is less clearly defined than for female ones: Hermes, though sometimes a boy, can also father Pan, whereas Artemis is forever a maiden.

16. *Theogony* 160-6.

17. *Theogony* 453-500.

18. *Theogony* 886-900; commenting on the birth of Athena, Muellner (1996) 92-3 aptly refers to Zeus as 'the first (and only) male mother of a female son'.

19. *Theogony* 918-20 (Apollo and Artemis), 938-9 (Hermes).

20. Strauss Clay (1989) discusses the birth narratives of the *Hymn to Apollo* (ch. 1) and the *Hymn to Hermes* (ch. 2).

21. *Il.* 1.586-600.

22. *Il.* 4.257-64 (Idomeneus), 4.338-48 (Menestheus and Odysseus).

23. *Il.* 12.310-28; for further discussion see Chapter 4, pp. 104-5.

24. *Il.* 15.185-99.

25. *Il.* 15. 224-5.

26. *Theogony* 717-35; cf. 868 (Typhoeus).

27. *Theogony* 459-62 and 493-6.

28. For example, at *Theogony*, 187-200 Aphrodite is said to be born of the genitals of Heaven, whereas in the *Iliad* she is the daughter of Zeus and Dione; see, for example, *Il.* 5.370-430.

29. See Strauss Clay (2003) 171: 'The generation of the heroes form[s] part of Zeus's policy of stabilizing his sovereignty.' Cf. also our discussion in Chapter 4, pp. 98-9.

30. The wider implications of Achilles' request are explored by Slatkin (1991).

31. *Il.* 14.153-362.

32. *Il.* 15.20-2.

33. Griffin (1980) 185, Schein (1984) 50-1; *Iliad* 20.56-65 is especially close to *Theogony* 847-52.

34. *Il.* 21.389-90.

35. Scholars tend to speak of 'double motivation'. The idea goes back to Lesky (1961), parts of which are accessible in English translation in Cairns

(2001) 170-202. For further discussion and up-to-date bibliography see Cairns (2001) 12-20.

36. One may compare Apollo's discussion of Hector's fate in *Il.* 24.33-8: note, again, the emphasis on merit.

37. *Theogony* 139-46.

38. *Hymn to Hermes* 322-end.

39. *Od.* 9.106-7.

40. Dougherty (2001) 129 argues that the passage should be seen in the context of colonisation narratives.

41. E.g. *Od.* 9.187.

42. Kirk (1970) 162-71, Vidal-Naquet (1986) 21-2, reprinted in Schein (1996) 41-2. Segal (1994) 203 sees the Cyclopes as combining golden-age and silver-age characteristics.

43. *Works and Days* 109-20.

44. Segal (1994) ch. 10, esp. pp. 217-19.

45. On the relationship between Odysseus and Athena, see also p. 81.

46. It would be interesting to know more about the portrayal of the gods in the poems of the Epic Cycle. It seems that the *Telegony*, which concludes the adventures of the Trojan War, favours marriages between mortals and immortals and ends with a general granting of immortality for everybody: Telegonus, the son of Odysseus and Circe, Telemachus and Penelope. It is possible that this poem emphatically draws to a close the heroic age by making the last heroes immortal and could, in this sense, be compared to the description of the heroic age in *Works and Days* 156-73.

47. *Od.* 13.314-19.

48. *Od.* 1.21.

49. *Od.* 13.299-301. At 22.205-10, Odysseus 'thinks' that Mentor may be Athena, but still chooses to speak as if he was addressing Mentor, rather than the goddess.

50. Earlier scholarship is discussed in Burkert (1960), translated into English in Jones and Wright (1997) 249-62. For more recent discussion and bibliography see de Jong (2001) 206-9.

51. De Jong (2001) 207: 'What [immortal gods] see as no more than a game ... is deadly serious for [mortal men].'

52. When human characters other than bards and seers do have precise knowledge of the gods they feel obliged to explain how they acquired it. For example, Odysseus justifies his account of Helios' conversation with Zeus at *Odyssey* 12.374-88 by adding that he heard it from Calypso, and that Calypso in turn found out about it from Hermes (12.389-90).

53. Scodel (2002) ch. 3.

54. *Cypria* fr. 1 (Davies), discussed in Chapters 4 and 5.

55. *Scholia on Iliad* 1.5, discussed in Kirk (1985) 53.

56. There is a large volume of scholarly work on the meaning of *Iliad* 1.5. For a recent discussion and bibliography see Pulleyn (2000).

57. Zephyr (West Wind), Notos (South Wind), Euros (East Wind) and Boreas (North Wind) are *anemoi*. Although they can be invoked as gods, they cannot change direction at will.

58. *Il.* 12.237-43.

59. It is however worth recalling that Hector rejects the bird omen partly because he thinks he has already been told the will of the gods by Iris (*Il.*

12.235-6; cf. 11.200-9). Unlike the narrator, Hector does not see that the two divine messages are in fact compatible.

60. *Il.* 11.558-62.

61. *Il.* 20.403-5.

62. *Il.* 6.146-9.

63. E.g. *Od.* 7. 117-26.

64. Homeric words for 'fate' are discussed in Redfield (1994) 131-6, Janko (1992) 4-7, Yamagata (1994), ch. 7. Yamagata concludes on p. 119: 'Whether harsh or mild, *moira* and *aisa* determine the patterns of behaviour of both men and gods.'

65. Redfield (1994) 131 links fate in Homer to what we know has actually happened; Yamagata (1994) concedes that Zeus may be able to overrule fate, but only as far as the precise moment of someone's death is concerned (p. 115, with reference to Hector). Janko (1992) 5 argues, with reference to *Il.* 16.431ff., that '… the question of Zeus' power relative to fate … receives no answer'.

66. *Theogony* 950-5, Hes. fr. 25 (M-W); cf. *Homeric Hymn* 15. In the *Odyssey*, Heracles has a double afterlife: he is both in Hades and Olympus (*Od.* 11.601-3).

67. Even Heracles is envisaged as a mortal in the *Iliad*; see 22.117-19.

68. Lawson (1994), see esp. p. 127.

4. Men, Women and Society

1. Introductory discussions may be found in Redfield (1994), Yamagata (1994), Raaflaub (1997).

2. This line of interpretation goes back to Adkins (1960); for a more recent assessment of Homeric society as fundamentally competitive see e.g. van Wees (1992).

3. Brooks (1977) 455.

4. Finley (1977; first edition 1954).

5. Morris (1986); a revised version of the paper is printed in Cairns (2001).

6. Raaflaub (1997).

7. Simon (1998) 58.

8. Austin (1994) 15-16.

9. *Theogony* 570-612.

10. Hes. frr. 2 and 5 (M-W).

11. See Strauss Clay (2003) 171.

12. For *andres hêrôes* ('heroic men') see e.g. *Il.* 5.747, *Od.* 1.101.

13. It should be noted that women were worshipped in hero cult; see Kearns (1989). This is one of several ways in which epic poetry diverges from what we know about hero worship.

14. The gods do give special consideration to Menelaos as the husband of Helen, *Od.* 4.569, but not to Helen herself.

15. Slatkin (1991).

16. *Il.* 1.515-16 and 18.429-34 are most explicit, but Thetis' complaints that her son will be short-lived are also relevant.

17. Other examples of Homeric characters reflecting on what is owed them include Agamemnon (*Il.* 1.119-20), Sarpedon (12.310-21) and Menelaos (*Il.* 23.570-85). Often, the gods reflect more broadly on man's place in the world: e.g. *Il.* 16.439-57 (Hera on Sarpedon), *Il.* 22.177-81 (Athena on Hector), *Il.*

24.33-51 (Apollo on Hector and Achilles), *Il.* 24.55-70 (Hera and Zeus on Hector and Achilles).

18. Burkert (1985) 203-8, Ekroth (2002).

19. Muellner (1996).

20. Demeter's 'terrible *mênis*' is mentioned at *Homeric Hymn to Demeter* 350 and 410; one of its effects is to rob all gods of their *timai*, thus threatening a collapse of the Olympian order: lines 1-12 and 353-4. Zeus and the other gods promise *timê* at *Hymn to Demeter* 328, 443-4, 461-2; cf. line 366 (Hades to Persephone).

21. For further discussion of Achilles' speech in book 9, see Chapter 5, pp. 129-30.

22. *Od.* 5.135-6.

23. Easterling (1991).

24. *Od.* 1.337-8.

25. *Theogony* 591-602, *Works and Days* 90-5.

26. *Gilgamesh* OBV A + BM iii.2-13; the text is quoted with slight modifications from George (2003) 278; the translation is by Dalley (2000) 150.

27. *Atrahasis* I.352-end, and especially tablet III.

28. Trans. Davies (1989).

29. They are discussed in West (1997) 481-2.

30. In the *Poem of Gilgamesh*, the goddess Belet-ili complains that, as a result of the flood, her people fill the sea like fish: *Gilgamesh* SBV XI.123-4.

31. Redfield (1994) 99.

32. Redfield (1994) 104.

33. *Scholia on Iliad* 1.5-6 (Erbse) with Erbse's note.

34. It appears to be used only of heroes who are already worshipped in cult: Haubold (2000) 7 with n. 30.

35. For a full discussion of these terms, see Graziosi/Haubold (2003).

36. *Il.* 6.492-3.

37. *Od.* 1.106, 144, 2.235, 299, 16.462, 17.65, 79, 105, 18.43, 346, 20.284, 292, 21.68, 23.8.

38. E.g. *Il.* 1.263; *Od.* 3.156.

39. *Il.* 9.22, harking back to *Il.* 2.115. Some scholars have questioned the sincerity of Agamemnon's emotions; see e.g. Wilson (2002) 72. Whether sincere or not, his words certainly imply that a leader should protect his people.

40. E.g. *Il.* 16.237.

41. *Il.* 22.106.

42. See Haubold (2000) ch. 2.2.

43. Studied in Haubold (2000) ch. 1.

44. E.g. Agamemnon at *Il.* 1.22-32 and 106-20.

45. In neighbouring cultures the gods routinely adopt this role. See, for example, Good (1983).

46. Most strikingly at *Od.* 24.426-8.

47. Another parallel to Achilles' destructive behaviour can be found in the *Iliad* itself: Apollo is said to have struck down the Achaean people in the same words that are later used by Achilles to describe Zeus' plan of honouring him: *Il.* 1.454, cf. *Il.* 16.237.

48. Dike is the daughter of Zeus in *Theogony* 902. In the *Works and Days* she prevents human society from sliding into lawlessness: lines 213-24 and 256-62.

49. Zeus is said to rule as a 'king', *basileus*, over the other gods at *Theogony*

883-5 and 886. Like human kings, he distributes honours, *timai*, among his followers. However, the gods are not therefore his 'people', and Zeus does not engage in any of the protective activities that are expected from a human 'shepherd of the people'.

50. The gods of the *Theogony* live in houses, not cities: lines 40, 43, 63, 64, 75, 114, 285, 303, 386, 410, 455, 726-35 (the prison of the Titans), 744, 751-3, 758, 767, 777-9, 783, 804, 816, 933.

51. *Works and Days* 213-47.

52. *Works and Days* 109-201.

53. *Works and Days* 125.

54. *Works and Days* 130-1.

55. *Works and Days* 162.

56. *Works and Days* 189.

57. Cf. Aristotle, *Politics* 1252.

58. *Il.* 4.51-2, 21.446-9.

59. *Il.* 7.446-63.

60. *Od.* 13.128-64.

61. The Phaeacians too are of course descendants of Poseidon, but their relationship to the god is more distant.

62. *Il.* 24.27-9.

63. *Il.* 2.116-18 and 9.23-5.

64. *Od.* 22.334-5.

65. *Il.* 13.624-5; *Od.* 9.270-1, 14.283-4.

66. *Il.* 3.380-2.

67. E.g. *Il.* 1.488-92.

68. *Od.* 24.526-end.

69. E.g. *Il.* 5.304.

70. Up-to-date discussion of the Panathenaea can be found in Kotsidu (1991), Neils (1992), Parker (1996) 89-92.

71. The sources are collected and discussed in Slings (2000).

72. Cf. Haubold (2000) ch. 3.

73. *Il.* 6.305.

74. Scully (1990) 38-9.

75. Some critics may disagree; thus, Nagy (2003) argues for 'a pervasive historical connection ... between ... Homeric poetry and the festival of the Panathenaia' (p. 3). In a similar vein, Cook (1995) suggests that the *Odyssey* in particular was significantly shaped by an Athenian performance context, specifically the Panathenaea.

76. Xenophon, *Symposium* 3.5.

5. Death, Fame and Poetry

1. Some basic remarks can be found in Camps (1980) 21-9. More detailed, if somewhat dated, is Whitman (1958) ch. 8. For more advanced studies see e.g. Katz (1991) and Felson-Rubin (1994) on Penelope; Pucci (1989), Peradotto (1990) and Goldhill (1991) ch. 1 on Odysseus; Redfield (1994) on Hector and Achilles; Nagy (1979) and Zanker (1994) on Achilles; Austin (1994) on Helen.

2. The translation is adapted from Koenen (1994) 28 and 30.

3. The text adopted here is that of Merkelbach-West (1990), with added conjectures by West and Koenen (1994). Koenen discusses earlier reconstructions at pp. 28-30. For a different view, see Strauss Clay (2003) 169-72.

4. Koenen (1994) 30.

5. Hes. fr. 204.105 (M-W).

6. Described at fr. 204.124-9 (M-W).

7. West (1978) 171 points out that it is reserved for the gods unless it is further qualified.

8. The heroes are collectively called 'demigods', *hêmitheoi*, at *Il.* 12.23.

9. Trans. Davies (1989).

10. Davies (1989) ch. 6 provides a summary and discussion of the extant sources.

11. Griffin (1980) 170.

12. Schein (1984) 69.

13. See also Chapter 4, p. 105.

14. The distinction between the Homeric and the Hesiodic outlook is not entirely hard and fast: for example, at *Od.* 4.561-9 we hear that, rather than dying in Argos, Menelaos will be removed to the Elysian plain at the end of his life. This passage, together with the end of the *Telegony*, recalls Hesiodic ideas of the heroes' afterlife. See Chapter 3, n. 46.

15. See Burkert (1985) 148-9.

16. Taplin (1992) 135 discusses Diomedes as a substitute for Achilles.

17. Other explanations are possible: Nagy (1979) argues that Achilles and Apollo compete for ritual honour; Rabel (1990) shows the extent to which Apollo and Achilles are like each other.

18. Achilles' death is anticipated most explicitly at *Il.* 22.359-60; see also 19.410. The story of Achilles' death at the hands of Apollo was recounted in the *Aethiopis*; see Davies (1989) ch. 7. For further discussion, see pp. 142-3.

19. Schein (1984) 70.

20. For recent discussion see Wilson (2002) ch. 4, who cites older bibliography.

21. Wilson (2002) ch. 4 argues that the crux of Achilles' position in *Iliad* 9 is that Agamemnon is only willing to pay *apoina* (ransom), not, as custom and Achilles himself demands, *poinê* (compensation).

22. We recall that the Olympian gods have been allotted their due honours by Zeus, and that this action ensured the stability of the Olympian order: see Chapter 4, p. 99.

23. *Il.* 16.97-100.

24. Yamagata (1994) 139-44; Wilson (2002) 20-1.

25. *Theogony* 165, 210; West (1966) 226 points out that the very name 'Titans' was etymologised in antiquity as deriving from *tisis*, revenge.

26. This is not the only passage in which Achilles' behaviour appears to be subhuman rather than godlike. For a discussion of Achilles' lion similes see Clarke (1995). Richardson (1993) 281 compares *Il.* 16.33-5, where Patroclus accuses Achilles of being born of the sea and rocks.

27. Redfield (1994) 30-5 offers a concise but useful overview. For more detailed discussion see Nagy (1979) and (1990), Goldhill (1991), ch. 2.

28. Redfield (1994) 35: 'As the vehicle of the *klea andrôn*, heroic song is a kind of history; through epic the past is preserved from obliteration.'

29. *Il.* 7.81-91.

30. For the idea that this speech plays with a thematic contrast between Achillean and Odyssean traditions of song, see Nagy (1979) ch. 3.

31. See, for example, Achilles' claims at *Od.* 11.488-91, discussed on pp. 135-6.
32. Schein (1984) 70-2.
33. For the complementary relationship of *goos* and *kleos*, see Easterling (1991) and cf. Chapter 4, pp. 101-2.
34. Nagy (1979) chs 2-3.
35. Hes. fr. 204.102 (M-W); cf. *Works and Days* 171.
36. *Il.* 9.647-8 and 16.58-9.
37. E.g. Strauss Clay (1997a) 106-12.
38. E.g. Nagy (1979), Pucci (1989), Goldhill (1991), all of whom associate the *kleos* of Odysseus with his craftiness (*mêtis, doloi*).
39. A similar point has been argued in greater detail by Segal (1994) ch. 5.
40. *Od.* 9.299-305.
41. Cf. Segal (1994) chs 2-5.
42. Carson (1999) 4.
43. *Works and Days* 109-76.
44. Chiefly in the story of Prometheus: *Theogony* 535-616.
45. Haubold (2001).
46. See Chapter 4, p. 100.
47. *Il.* 1.396-406.
48. Crucial stages in this development are the speech uttered by Phoenix in *Il.* 9.430-605 and Achilles' speech to his mother in *Il.* 18.79-87.
49. MacLeod (1982) 133 compares the jar of Pandora in *Works and Days* 94.
50. Our discussion is indebted to Lynn-George (1988) chs 3-4.
51. See Chapter 3, pp. 76-7.
52. West (1966) 433 on the parallel case of the sons of Circe.
53. *Od.* 6.149-52.
54. See Chapter 3, p. 89.
55. *Il.* 24.49. For discussion see pp. 131-2.
56. *Od.* 20.292-302.
57. *Od.* 14.321-30, 470-502, 19.185-202, 220-48, 269-307.
58. E.g. Goldhill (1991) ch. 1.
59. *Od.* 14.462-506.
60. Chapter 3, pp. 88-9.
61. See pp. 141-3.
62. *Od.* 11.119-34, 23.267-84.
63. Among the more recent literature one might single out Hansen (1977), Pucci (1987), Peradotto (1990).
64. See pp. 141-2.
65. E.g. *Il.* 8.97, *Od.* 5.171; Odysseus is also called 'patient of mind', *talasiphrôn* (*Theogony* 1012, *Il.* 11.466, *Od.* 1.87); and 'enduring', *tlêmôn* (*Il.* 10.231 and 498).
66. *Od.* 9.19-20.
67. See above, n. 38.

Bibliography

Abbreviations

AJPh	American Journal of Philology
BICS	Bulletin of the Institute of Classical Studies
ClAnt	Classical Antiquity
CQ	Classical Quarterly
CW	Classical World
GRBS	Greek, Roman and Byzantine Studies
IJCT	International Journal of the Classical Tradition
JHS	Journal of Hellenic Studies
PCPS	Proceedings of the Cambridge Philological Society
PP	La Parola del Passato
QUCC	Quaderni Urbinati di Cultura Classica
Rh. Mus.	Rheinisches Museum für Philologie
TAPA	Transactions of the American Philological Association
Wien. Stud.	Wiener Studien

Adkins, A.W.H. (1960) *Merit and Responsibility: A Study in Greek Values* (Oxford University Press).

Arend, W. (1933) *Die typischen Scenen bei Homer* (Weidmann).

Arthur, M. (1982) 'Cultural strategies in Hesiod's *Theogony*: law, family, society', *Arethusa* 15, 63-82.

Austin, N. (1975) *Archery at the Dark of the Moon: Poetic Problems in Homer's Odyssey* (University of California Press).

—— (1994) *Helen and her Shameless Phantom* (Cornell University Press).

Bakker, E. (1997) *Poetry in Speech: Orality and Homeric Discourse* (Cornell University Press).

Bonfante, G. (1968) 'Il nome di Omero', *PP* 23, 360-1.

Brooks, C. (1977) 'The heroic impulse in the *Odyssey*', *CW* 70, 455-6.

Burgess, J. (2001) *The Tradition of the Trojan War in Homer and the Epic Cycle* (Johns Hopkins University Press).

Burkert, W. (1960) 'Das Lied von Ares und Aphrodite', *Rh. Mus.* 103, 130-44.

—— (1976) 'Das hunderttorige Theben und die Datierung der *Ilias*', *Wien. Stud.* 89, 5-21.

—— (1985) *Greek Religion, Archaic and Classical*, trans. J. Raffan (Basil Blackwell).

—— (1992) *The Orientalizing Revolution: Near Eastern Influence on Greek*

Culture in the Early Archaic Age, trans. M. Pinder and W. Burkert (Harvard University Press).

Butler, S. (1897) *The Authoress of the Odyssey* (Longmans, Green).

Cairns, D., ed. (2001) *Oxford Readings in Homer's Iliad* (Oxford University Press).

Camps, W. (1980) *An Introduction to Homer* (Oxford University Press).

Carson, A. (1999) *Autobiography of Red* (Random House).

Clarke, M. (1995) 'Between lions and men: images of the hero in the *Iliad*', *GRBS* 36, 137-59.

Cook, E. (1995) *The Odyssey in Athens: Myths of Cultural Origins* (Cornell University Press).

Crielaard, J.P. (1995) 'Homer, history and archaeology: some remarks on the date of the Homeric world', in J.P. Crielaard, ed., *Homeric Questions: Essays in Philology, Ancient History and Archaeology, Including the Papers of a Conference Organized by the Netherlands Institute at Athens (15 May 1993)* (Gieben), pp. 201-88.

Crotty, K. (1994) *The Poetics of Supplication: Homer's Iliad and Odyssey* (Cornell University Press).

Dalley, S. (2000) *Myths from Mesopotamia: Creation, The Flood, Gilgamesh, and Others*, 2nd edn (Oxford University Press).

Davies, M. (1989) *The Greek Epic Cycle* (Bristol Classical Press).

Dindorf, W. (1855) *Scholia Graeca in Homeri Odysseam* (Oxford University Press).

Dougherty, C. (2001) *The Raft of Odysseus: The Ethnographic Imagination of Homer's Odyssey* (Oxford University Press).

Dougherty, C., Kurke, L., eds (1993), *Cultural Poetics in Archaic Greece: Cult, Performance, Politics* (Cambridge University Press).

Easterling, P.E. (1991) 'Men's κλέος and women's γόος: female voices in the *Iliad*', *Journal of Modern Greek Studies* 9, 145-51.

Edwards, M.W. (1971) *The Language of Hesiod in its Traditional Context* (Basil Blackwell).

—— (1991) *The Iliad: A Commentary V: Books 17-20* (Cambridge University Press).

—— (1997) 'Homeric style and oral poetics', in I. Morris, B. Powell, eds, *A New Companion to Homer* (Brill), pp. 261-83.

Ekroth, G. (2002) *The Sacrificial Rituals of Greek Hero-Cults in the Archaic to the Early Hellenistic Periods* (Liège: Centre International d'Étude de la Religion Grecque Antique).

Erbse, H. (1969-88), *Scholia Graeca in Homeri Iliadem* (De Gruyter).

Felson-Rubin, N. (1994) *Regarding Penelope: From Character to Poetics* (Princeton University Press).

Fenik, B. (1968) *Typical Battle Scenes in the Iliad* (Franz Steiner).

Finley, M.I. (1975) 'Myth, memory and history', in *The Use and Abuse of History* (Chatto and Windus), pp. 11-33.

—— (1977) *The World of Odysseus*, 2nd edn (Chatto and Windus).

Finnegan, R. (1977) *Oral Poetry: Its Nature, Significance and Social Context* (Cambridge University Press).

Foley, J.M. (1999) *Homer's Traditional Art* (Pennsylvania State University Press).

—— (2002) *How to Read an Oral Poem* (University of Illinois Press).

Bibliography

Ford, A. (1992) *Homer: The Poetry of the Past* (Cornell University Press).

———— (2002) *The Origins of Criticism: Literary Culture and Poetic Theory in Classical Greece* (Princeton University Press).

Freedman, L. (2003) *The Revival of the Olympian Gods in Renaissance Art* (Cambridge University Press).

Gainsford, P. (2003) 'Formal analysis of recognition scenes in the *Odyssey*', *JHS* 123, 41-59.

George, A.R. (2003) *The Babylonian Gilgamesh Epic: Introduction, Critical Edition and Cuneiform Texts*, 2 vols (Oxford University Press).

Gill, C., Wiseman, T.P., eds (1993) *Lies and Fiction in the Ancient World* (University of Exeter Press).

Goethe, J. v. (1953) *Gedenkausgabe der Werke, Briefe und Gespräche*, ed. E. Beutler, vol. 2 (Artemis).

Goldhill, S. (1991) *The Poet's Voice: Essays on Poetics and Greek Literature* (Cambridge University Press).

Good, R.M. (1983) *The Sheep of His Pasture: A Study of the Hebrew Noun 'Am(m) and its Semitic Cognates* (Scholars Press).

Graziosi, B. (2001) 'Competition in wisdom', in F. Budelmann, P. Michelakis, eds, *Homer, Tragedy and Beyond: Essays in Honour of P.E. Easterling* (London: Society for the Promotion of Hellenic Studies), pp. 57-74.

———— (2002) *Inventing Homer: The Early Reception of Epic* (Cambridge University Press).

Graziosi, B., Haubold, J. (2003) 'Homeric masculinity: ἠνορέη and ἀγηνορίη', *JHS* 123, 60-76.

Griffin, J. (1977) 'The epic cycle and the uniqueness of Homer', *JHS* 97, 39-53.

———— (1980) *Homer on Life and Death* (Oxford University Press).

Griffith, M. (1983) 'Personality in Hesiod', *ClAnt* 2, 37-65.

Hainsworth, J.B. (1968) *The Flexibility of the Homeric Formula* (Oxford University Press).

Hammer, D. (2002) *The Iliad as Politics: The Performance of Political Thought* (University of Oklahoma Press).

Hansen, W. (1977) 'Odysseus' last journey', *QUCC* 24, 27-48.

Haubold, J. (2000) *Homer's People: Epic Poetry and Social Formation* (Cambridge University Press).

———— (2001) 'Epic with an end: an interpretation of *Homeric Hymns* 15 and 20' in F. Budelmann, P. Michelakis, eds, *Homer, Tragedy and Beyond: Essays in Honour of P.E. Easterling* (London: Society for the Promotion of Hellenic Studies), pp. 23-41.

———— (2002a) 'Greek epic: a Near Eastern genre?', *PCPS* 48, 1-19.

———— (2002b) 'Wars of *Wissenschaft*: the new quest for Troy', *IJCT* 8.4, 564-79.

Horrocks, G. (1997) 'Homer's dialect', in I. Morris, B. Powell, eds, *A New Companion to Homer* (Brill), pp. 193-217.

Impelluso, L. (2003) *Gods and Heroes in Art*, trans. T. Hartmann (Los Angeles: J. Paul Getty Museum).

Janko, R. (1982) *Homer, Hesiod and the Hymns: Diachronic Development in Epic Diction* (Cambridge University Press).

———— (1992) *The Iliad: A Commentary*, vol. 4 (Cambridge University Press).

Jones, P., Wright, G. (1997) *Homer: German Scholarship in Translation* (Oxford University Press).

Bibliography

de Jong, I. (1987) *Narrators and Focalizers: The Presentation of the Story in the Iliad* (Grüner).

——— (2001) *A Narratological Commentary on the Odyssey* (Cambridge University Press).

Katz, M. (1991) *Penelope's Renown: Meaning and Indeterminacy in the Odyssey* (Princeton University Press).

Kearns, E. (1989) *The Heroes of Attica* (London: University of London, Institute of Classical Studies).

Kirk, G.S. (1962) *The Songs of Homer* (Cambridge University Press).

——— (1970) *Myth, its Meaning and Functions* (Cambridge University Press).

——— (1974) *The Nature of Greek Myths* (Penguin).

——— (1985) *The Iliad: A Commentary I: Books 1-4* (Cambridge University Press).

Koenen, L. (1994) 'Greece, the Near East, and Egypt: cyclic destruction in Hesiod and the *Catalogue of Women*', *TAPA* 124, 1-34.

Kotsidu, H. (1991) *Die musischen Agone der Panathenäen in archaischer und klassischer Zeit: eine historisch-archäologische Untersuchung* (Tuduv).

Kullmann, W. (1960) *Die Quellen der Ilias* (Franz Steiner).

Lamberton R., ed. (1992) *Homer's Ancient Readers: The Hermeneutics of Greek Epic's Earliest Exegetes* (Princeton University Press).

——— (1997) 'Homer in antiquity', in I. Morris, B. Powell, eds, *A New Companion to Homer* (Brill), pp. 33-54.

Latacz, J. (1996) *Homer: His Art and his World*, trans. J. Holoka (University of Michigan Press).

Lawson, J. (1994) *The Concept of Fate in Ancient Mesopotamia of the First Millennium: Toward an Understanding of Šīmtu* (Harrassowitz).

Leckie, R. (1999) *The Bluffer's Guide to the Classics*, 2nd edn (Oval Books).

Lefkowitz, M. (1981) *The Lives of the Greek Poets* (Duckworth).

Lesky, A. (1961) *Göttliche und menschliche Motivation im homerischen Epos* (Carl Winter).

Lightfoot, J., ed. (2003) *On the Syrian Goddess* (Oxford University Press).

Logue, C. (2001) *War Music* (Faber & Faber).

Lord, A.B. (1953) 'Homer's originality: oral dictated texts', *TAPA* 84, 124-34.

——— (1960) *The Singer of Tales* (Harvard University Press).

——— (1991) *Epic Singers and Oral Tradition* (Cornell University Press).

Lynn-George, M. (1988) *Epos: Word, Narrative and the Iliad* (Macmillan).

MacLeod, C.W., ed. (1982) *Homer: Iliad, Book XXIV* (Cambridge University Press).

Martin, R.P. (1989) *The Language of Heroes: Speech and Performance in the Iliad* (Cornell University Press).

——— (1992) 'Hesiod's metanastic poetics', *Ramus* 21, 11-33.

Meister, K. (1921) *Die Homerische Kunstsprache* (Teubner).

Merkelbach, R., West, M.L., eds (1990) *Hesiodi Fragmenta Selecta* in F. Solmsen, ed., *Hesiodi Theogonia, Opera et Dies, Scutum*, R. Merkelbach, M. West, eds, *Fragmenta Selecta*, 3rd edn (Oxford University Press).

Metcalf, P. (2002) *They Lie, We Lie: Getting on with Anthropology* (Routledge).

Morris, I. (1986) 'The use and abuse of Homer', *ClAnt* 5, 81-138.

Morris, I., Powell, B., eds (1997) *A New Companion to Homer* (Brill).

Muellner, L. (1996) *The Anger of Achilles: Mênis in Greek Epic* (Cornell University Press).

Nagy, G. (1979) *The Best of the Achaeans: Concepts of the Hero in Archaic Greek*

Poetry (Johns Hopkins University Press).

────── (1990) *Pindar's Homer: The Lyric Possession of an Epic Past* (Johns Hopkins University Press).

────── (1996) *Homeric Questions* (University of Texas Press).

────── (2003) *Plato's Rhapsody and Homer's Music: The Poetics of the Panathenaic Festival in Classical Athens* (Harvard University Press).

Neils, J. (1992) *Goddess and Polis: The Panathenaic Festival in Ancient Athens* (Princeton University Press).

Nisetich, F. (1989) *Pindar and Homer* (Johns Hopkins University Press).

O'Sullivan, N. (1992) *Alcidamas, Aristophanes, and the Beginning of Greek Stylistic Theory* (Franz Steiner).

Otto, W.F. (1954) *The Homeric Gods*, trans. M. Hadas (Thames and Hudson).

Parker, R. (1996) *Athenian Religion: A History* (Oxford University Press).

Parry, M. (1971) *The Making of Homeric Verse: The Collected Papers of Milman Parry*, ed. A. Parry (Oxford University Press).

Peradotto, J. (1990) *Man in the Middle Voice: Name and Narration in the Odyssey* (Princeton University Press).

Pfeiffer, R. (1968) *History of Classical Scholarship* (Oxford University Press).

Powell, B. (1991) *Homer and the Origin of the Greek Alphabet* (Cambridge University Press).

────── (1997) 'Homer and writing', in I. Morris, B. Powell, eds, *A New Companion to Homer* (Brill), pp. 1-32.

Pratt, L.H. (1993) *Lying and Poetry from Homer to Pindar* (University of Michigan Press).

Pucci, P. (1977) *Hesiod and the Language of Poetry* (Johns Hopkins University Press).

────── (1987) *Odysseus Polytropos: Intertextual Readings in the Odyssey and the Iliad* (Cornell University Press).

Pulleyn, S. (2000) *Homer: Iliad 1* (Oxford University Press).

Rabel, R. (1990) 'Apollo as a model for Achilles in the *Iliad*', *AJPh* 11, 429-40.

Raaflaub, K. (1997) 'Homeric Society', in I. Morris, B. Powell, eds, *A New Companion to Homer* (Brill), pp. 624-48.

Reece, S. (1993) *The Stranger's Welcome: Oral Theory and the Aesthetics of the Homeric Hospitality Scene* (University of Michigan Press).

Redfield, J. (1994) *Nature and Culture in the Iliad: The Tragedy of Hector*, 2nd edn (Duke University Press).

Reinhardt, K. (1938) *Das Parisurteil* (Vittorio Klostermann).

Richardson, N.J. (1993) *The Iliad: A Commentary VI: Books 21-24* (Cambridge University Press).

Rosen, C. (1997) *The Classical Style*, 2nd edn (Faber & Faber).

Rosen, R. (1997) 'Homer and Hesiod', in I. Morris, B. Powell, eds, *A New Companion to Homer* (Brill), pp. 463-88.

Rowe, C.J. (1978) *The Essential Hesiod* (Bristol Classical Press).

Rutherford, R.B. (1991-3) 'From the *Iliad* to the *Odyssey*', *BICS* 38, 47-54.

Schein, S. (1984) *The Mortal Hero: An Introduction to Homer's Iliad* (University of California Press).

────── ed. (1996) *Reading the Odyssey: Selected Interpretive Essays* (Princeton University Press).

Scodel, R. (2002) *Listening to Homer: Tradition, Narrative and Audience* (University of Michigan Press).

Scully, S. (1990) *Homer and the Sacred City* (Cornell University Press).

Segal, C. (1994) *Singers, Heroes and Gods in the Odyssey* (Cornell University Press).

Simon, E. (1998) *Die Götter der Griechen*, 4th edn (Hirmer).

Slatkin, L. (1991) *The Power of Thetis: Allusion and Interpretation in the Iliad* (University of California Press).

Slings, S. (2000) 'Literature in Athens, 566-510 BC', in H. Sancisi-Weerdenburg, ed., *Peisistratos and the Tyranny: A Reappraisal of the Evidence* (Gieben), pp. 57-77.

Snell, B. et al. (1955-) *Lexikon des frühgriechischen Epos* (Vandenhoeck und Ruprecht).

Snipes, K. (1988) 'Literary interpretation in the Homeric scholia: the similes of the *Iliad*', *AJPh* 109, 197-222.

Strauss Clay, J. (1989) *The Politics of Olympus: Form and Meaning in the Major Homeric Hymns* (Princeton University Press).

——— (1997a) *The Wrath of Athena: Gods and Men in the Odyssey*, 2nd edn (Rowman and Littlefield).

——— (1997b) 'The Homeric Hymns', in I. Morris, B. Powell, eds, *A New Companion to Homer* (Brill), pp. 489-507.

——— (2002) 'Dying is hard to do', *Colby Quarterly* 38.1, 7-16.

——— (2003) *Hesiod's Cosmos* (Cambridge University Press).

Taplin, O. (1992) *Homeric Soundings: The Shaping of the Iliad* (Oxford University Press).

Thalmann, W.G. (1984) *Conventions of Form and Thought in Early Greek Epic* (Johns Hopkins University Press).

Tsagarakis, O. (1982), 'The teichoskopia cannot belong in the beginning of the Trojan War', *QUCC* 41, 61-72.

Turner, F. (1997) 'The Homeric Question', in I. Morris, B. Powell, eds, *A New Companion to Homer* (Brill), pp. 123-45.

Vidal-Naquet, P. (1986) *The Black Hunter: Forms of Thought and Forms of Society in the Greek World*, trans. A. Szegedy-Maszak (Johns Hopkins University Press).

Vivante, P. (1982) *The Epithets in Homer: A Study in Poetic Values* (Yale University Press).

van Wees, H. (1992) *Status Warriors: War, Violence and Society in Homer and History* (Gieben).

West, M.L. (1961) 'Hesiodea', *CQ* n.s. 11, 130-45.

——— ed. (1966) *Hesiod: Theogony* (Oxford University Press).

——— ed. (1978) *Hesiod: Works and Days* (Oxford University Press).

——— (1983) *The Orphic Poems* (Oxford University Press).

——— (1985) *The Hesiodic Catalogue of Women* (Oxford University Press).

——— (1995) 'The date of the *Iliad*', *Museum Helveticum* 52, 203-19.

——— (1997) *The East Face of Helicon: West Asiatic Elements in Greek Poetry and Myth* (Oxford University Press).

——— (1998) *Homeri Ilias*, vol. 1 (Teubner).

——— (1999) 'The invention of Homer', *CQ* 49, 364-82.

——— (2002) ' "Eumelos": a Corinthian epic cycle?', *JHS* 122, 109-33.

——— ed. (2003) *Homeric Hymns, Homeric Apocrypha, Lives of Homer* (Harvard University Press).

Whitman, C. (1958) *Homer and the Heroic Tradition* (Harvard University Press).

Whitmarsh, T. (2002) 'What Samuel Butler saw: Classics, authorship and cultural authority in Victorian England', *PCPS* 48, 66-86.

von Wilamowitz-Moellendorff, U. (1884) *Homerische Untersuchungen* (Weidmann).

Willcock, M. (1970) 'Some Aspects of the Gods in the *Iliad*', *BICS* 17, 1-10.

——— (1997) 'Neoanalysis', in I. Morris, B. Powell, eds, *A New Companion to Homer* (Brill), pp. 174-89.

Wilson, D. (2002) *Ransom, Revenge, and Heroic Identity in the Iliad* (Cambridge University Press).

Wolf, F.A. (1985) *Prolegomena ad Homerum*, edd. and trans. A. Grafton, G. Most and J. Zetzel (Princeton University Press).

Woolf, V. (1929) *A Room of One's Own* (Hogarth Press).

Yamagata, N. (1994) *Homeric Morality* (Brill).

Zanker, G. (1994) *The Heart of Achilles: Characterization and Personal Ethics in the Iliad* (University of Michigan Press).

Index

Accius, 29, 154 n. 59
Achilles, 18-19, 48-53, 58, 99-101,
    106, 108-9, 113, 119, 126-38, 140-
    3, 156 n. 50, 157 n. 64, 161 n. 47,
    163 nn. 16-18, n. 21, 164 n. 48
Aeschylus, 24
Agamemnon, 66, 70, 81, 101, 107-8,
    110, 129-30, 135, 160-1 n. 17,
    161 nn. 39 and 44
Alcinous, 27, 47-8, 60-1, 89
Andromache, 101, 107, 111
animals, 85-8, 131-2
Aphrodite, 66, 81-3, 113, 126, 158 nn.
    3 and 28
Apollo, 18, 51-3, 74, 126-9, 131-2, 161
    nn. 17 and 47, 163 nn. 17-18
Ares, 73, 81-3, 126, 158 n. 3
Aristophanes, 32
Aristotle, 25, 39, 43, 112
Athena, 66, 73, 76, 79, 81, 113-14,
    116-18, 157 n. 62, 157-8 n. 3, 158
    n. 18, 159 nn. 45 and 49
audiences,
    at Panathenaea, 115-18
    early Greek, 8-9, 15-34, 37-42, 50,
        66-8, 97, 100, 115-18, 154 n. 53
    implied, 23-4, 115, 136-7, 144, 147-9
    modern, 11-12, 15-34, 45, 48-50, 65-6
    Panhellenic, 153 n. 46
    relationship with heroes, 23-4, 134

bard
    relationship with Muses, 44-8, 83-4
    understanding of gods, 44-6, 82-4
biographical tradition, 22-3, 25, 28

Brooks, C., 96
Burkert, W., 67
Butler, S., 21

Calypso, 76-7, 143, 159 n. 52
Carson, A., 56, 139
Clay, J. Strauss, 38
Contest of Homer and Hesiod, 30-3,
    41-2, 154 n. 63
Cretan tales, 145-6, 156 n. 42
Cronus, 9, 36, 57, 78, 119, 131, 139
Cyclops, 29, 77-9, 138, 144, 159 n. 42

demigods, 36, 109, 111, 123-4, 129,
    143, 163 n. 8
    see also heroes
Demodocus, 23, 27, 81-3
    as autobiographical character, 23
    relationship with audience, 27
dikê, 111, 114, 162 n. 48
Diomedes, 58, 113, 126-8, 157 n. 52

Earth, 8, 31, 36, 41, 59, 74, 92, 148
Easterling, P.E., 101
epic
    and history of the cosmos, 35-43
    in comparative perspective, 7, 50
Epic Cycle, 8, 18-19, 38-9, 85, 152 n.
    8, 153 n. 43, 159 n. 46
epithets, 7-9, 18, 50-3, 57-8, 60-1,
    113, 126, 140-1, 147, 157 n. 65

fate
    in Homer, 85, 89-92, 95, 156 n. 50,
        160 n. 65

in Babylonian literature, 92
see also moira
feasting, 59, 69-70
fiction, 11-12, 42-3, 67, 74, 115, 151
    n. 7
Finley, M.I., 96
flood narratives, 103-4
Foley, J.M., 50
formula, 7-9, 18, 49-53, 55-7, 60-1,
    127, 148

gender, *see* masculinity; women
Gilgamesh, 102-3
gods, 65-93
    and bards, 80-4
    and fate, 89-92
    frivolity of, 65-75
    history of, 40-1, 45, 68
    mortal sons of, 71-80, 90-2
Goethe, J.W. v., 17
golden age, 78, 111, 139, 144, 159 n.
    42
goos, 101-2, 133
Griffin, J., 125

Heaven, 31, 36, 41-2, 57, 59, 111, 131
Hector, 53, 87-9, 101-2, 106-7, 109,
    119, 131-2, 136-7, 160 n. 59
Helen, 79, 98-9, 101, 160 n. 14
    courtship of, 36-7, 144-5
Hephaestus, 66, 69-72, 81, 83
Hera, 69-74, 90-1, 99, 112, 156 n. 36
Heraclitus, 42
Herodotus, 11-12, 25, 30, 42-3, 67-8,
    83-4, 153 n. 30
heroes, heroism, 24-5, 32, 36, 38, 41-
    2, 59-60, 85, 98-106, 109-10, 112,
    117-19, 122-5, 158 n. 29, 159 n.
    46, 160 n. 30, 163 n. 14
    see also demigods
Hesiod
    life, 28

oeuvre, 28, 31, 35-8
relationship with Homer, 27-33, 41-
    2, 68-9, 77, 123-5, 142-3, 158 n.
    28
Catalogue of Women, 19, 28, 31, 36-
    8, 41, 91, 98, 111, 123-5, 145, 155
    n. 9
Ornithomanteia, 31
Theogony, 9, 18-19, 23, 28-9, 31,
    36-8, 41, 45-7, 59, 68-9, 71-4, 77,
    91, 99, 111, 139, 143, 155 nn. 4
    and 15, 158 n. 28, 162 n. 49
Works and Days, 18-19, 28-32, 36-
    8, 45, 59-60, 68, 78-9, 111, 114,
    139, 162 n. 48
Homer
    blindness, 22-3
    life, 15-17, 21-3, 25-7
    oeuvre, 24-7, 32, 35, 38-9
    relationship with Hesiod, 27-33,
        41-2, 68-9, 77, 123-5, 142-3, 158
        n. 28
    Cypria, 24-5, 39, 85, 103, 124-5
    Homeric Hymns, 8, 25, 38, 41, 59,
        70, 77, 139, 147, 154 n. 51
    Hymn to Apollo, 25, 41, 147
    Hymn to Demeter, 101, 110
    Iliad, see Iliad
    Margites, 25
    Odyssey, see Odyssey
    Sack of Oechalia, 8, 25, 28
Homeric Question, 18-21
Homeric society, 95-119
Horace, 39
human condition, 141-2, 145-7

Iliad: (1.1-7) 84-5; (1.8-10) 39; (1.352-
    4) 100; (1.573-81) 71-2;
    (1.586-600) 69; (2.459-66) 86-7;
    (2.484-92) 44; (2.681-8) 51; (4.50-
    68) 112; (5.117-18) 113; (5.125)
    113; (5.438-42) 126-7; (5.529-33)

107-8; (6.222) 58; (6.235) 58; (6.305-6) 113-14; (6.309-10) 114; (6.506-14) 87-8; (9.406-9) 129-30; (9.410-16) 133; (9.697-700) 106; (12.10-35) 24; (12.310-28) 104-5; (13.126-33 and 339-44) 32; (14.290-1) 84; (15.14-33) 99; (15.101-12) 72-3; (15.138-41) 73; (16.237) 130-1; (16.431-49) 90-1; (16.702-11); (19.95-133) 99; (20.56-65) 73-4; (20.444-8) 127-8; (21.461-7) 74; (22.8-13) 52; (22.8-20) 128-9; (22.14) 52-3; (22.271-2) 131; (22.297-305) 136-7; (22.454-9) 107; (24.33-54) 131-2; (24.315) 86; (24.525-38) 141-3
Ithaca, 79, 89, 114-15, 144-5

kleos, 46, 96, 101-2, 119, 121, 132-8, 141-3, 146-7

lament, *see goos*
laos, 109, 117, 131
Latacz, J., 16, 23
Lawson, J., 92
leadership, 108-10, 117, 130-1
Lefkowitz, M., 22
lies, 46-8
Logue, C., 39-40, 57
Longinus, 66
Lucian, 15-6

masculinity, 98-9, 106-8
mênis, 101, 110, 140, 161 n. 20
metre, 49-50
moira, 89-92
Morris, I., 96
mortality, 58, 72, 74, 90-2, 98-103, 125-34, 140-4
Muellner, L., 101
Muses, 23, 44-8, 83-4, 156 n. 42

Nagy, G., 134-5
nature, 85-9
Nausicaa, 54-5, 144
nostos, 133-7, 146

Oceanus, 11, 42
Odysseus, 38, 47-8, 54-5, 59, 63-5, 70, 75-82, 101, 109-10, 112, 114, 122, 133-40, 143-7, 156 n. 42, 157 nn. 69 and 71, 159 nn. 46, 49 and 52
comrades of, 109, 157 n. 69
Odyssey: (1.19-21) 75; (1.68-73) 75, 77-8; (1.231-41) 137-8; (1.337-9) 45-6; (1.346-52) 46; (5.135-6) 143; (5.291-4) 82; (5.302-5) 82; (5.491-3) 82; (6.127-47) 54-5; (6.204-5) 144; (7.263) 82; (7.284-6) 82; (8.72-82) 81; (8.266-366) 81-4; (8.499-520) 81; (9.16-20) 137; (9.131-5) 78; (9.299-305) 78; (11.363-8) 47-8; (11.482-6) 135; (11.488-91) 135-6; (14.457-8) 89; (15.292) 82; (17.148-9) 82; (20.18-21) 145
oral poetry, 7-8, 17, 20, 50, 61, 148-9
Otto, W.F., 67

Panathenaea, 67, 114, 116-18, 153-4 n. 46
Parry, M., 7, 49-51, 55, 148
pathetic fallacy, 86
Patroclus, 126-8
patronymics, 57-8, 140-1, 144
Peleus, 58, 140-1
Penelope, 45-6, 78, 144-5, 159 n. 46
suitors of, 45-6, 59, 66, 81, 108, 144-5
performance, 18-19, 26-7, 40, 49-50, 61, 115-18, 154 n. 53
Phaeacians, 47, 59, 79, 112, 137, 143-4
Phemius, 45-6

Pindar, 24, 100
Plato, 32, 42, 45
polis, 110-15, 117-18
polytlas, 147
Poseidon, 65, 70-1, 75-7, 79, 81, 92, 98, 100, 112, 144

Raaflaub, K., 96
Redfield, J., 104
Reinhardt, K., 66
resonance, 48-60
rhapsodes, 26-7, 45

Sarpedon, 70, 104-5
Schein, S., 66, 125
Scodel, R., 40, 83
seasons, 88-9
similes, 24, 86-9
Simon, E., 98
Slatkin, L., 99-100

Telegonus, 38-9, 159 n. 46
Telemachus, 46, 79, 137-8
telos, 86-7, 90
Theban War, 24, 28, 38-9, 41, 58
Thetis, 58, 72, 99-100, 113, 140
timê, 96, 99-101, 106, 110, 112, 129-31, 135, 141, 145-6, 161 n. 20, 162 n. 49
tisis, 131
traditional poetry, 18-21, 26, 40, 49-60
Trojan War, 24-5, 36, 38-9, 41, 43, 45, 55, 66, 79-83, 85, 103-4, 123-5, 134, 136-7, 142-6, 159 n. 46
Tsagarakis, O., 37
type scene, 18, 53-5, 59-60

Virgil, 8, 149
Vivante, P., 56

Wolf, F.A., 17
women, 98-9, 101-4
Woolf, V., 21

Xenophanes, 29-30, 65, 67

Zeus, 9, 30-1, 36, 38, 41, 45-6, 57, 59-60, 68-77, 82, 84-92, 98-100, 105, 111-14, 119, 123-4, 130-1, 140-2, 155 n. 4, 156 n. 36, 158 nn. 28-9, 160 n. 65, 161 n. 20, 162 nn. 48-9
will of, 85-92